Study Guide

for

Durand and Barlow's

Essentials of Abnormal Psychology
Fourth Edition

David A. Santogrossi
Purdue University

Australia • Brazil • Canada • Mexico • Singapore • Spain • United Kingdom • United States

Printed in the United States of America

 2 3 4 5 6 7 09 08 07

Printer: Thomson West
ISBN-13: 978-0-495-03129-1
ISBN-10: 0-495-03129-1

Cover images: Main image: © Arno Rafael Minkkinen, "Self-portrait, Foster's Pond," 1989. Courtesy of Robert Klein Gallery. Background image: © Bruce Heinemann/Getty Images

Thomson Higher Education
10 Davis Drive
Belmont, CA 94002-3098
USA

For more information about our products, contact us at:
Thomson Learning Academic Resource Center
1-800-423-0563

For permission to use material from this text or product, submit a request online at
http://www.thomsonrights.com.
Any additional questions about permissions can be submitted by email to
thomsonrights@thomson.com.

TABLE OF CONTENTS

Preface

ABOUT THE AUTHOR:

Professor David Santogrossi has taught Abnormal Psychology through at least three versions of the Diagnostic and Statistical Manual that you will read so much about in the text. He has taught in the People's Republic of China and several times at Oxford University and in Florence, Italy. He is Associate Professor of Clinical Psychology and Associate Dean of the School of Liberal Arts at Purdue University in West Lafayette, Indiana. He has won several teaching awards from the Purdue Psychology Department and the School of Liberal Arts, as well as the career award as outstanding undergraduate instructor at Purdue University. He is a founding member of the Purdue Teaching Academy as well as the Purdue Book of Great Teachers. He is the former Director of Undergraduate Studies in Psychology at Purdue, as well as Faculty Advisor to their Psych Club and Psi Chi honorary society chapter.

Dr. Santogrossi earned his Bachelor's degree in Psychology at the University of Illinois in Urbana-Champaign and his Ph.D. in Clinical Psychology at the State University of New York at Stony Brook. His current research examines the circumstances that determine why and when people choose to seek psychological help. A Clinical Psychologist licensed for private practice and an accredited Health Service Provider, he worked one day a week for many years as a psychologist in a community mental health center and served on the human rights board for a developmental disabilities center.

Professor Santogrossi worked his way through college playing drums in a rock band. He continues to play drums and percussion in the local symphony, concert band, theater musicals, and various smaller groups, including a Dixieland group that plays in nursing homes several times a month. He played in a Psych Department student/faculty band called the Positive Reinforcers. Additional theater involvement includes being Master Carpenter for set-building crews. His other hobbies include travel, reading, word play (for example, he has a dog named Peeve), Civil War and world history, antiques, home repair, any kind of music and, of course, Psychology.

He invites your comments, criticisms, suggestions, and even alternative items for the next edition of the Study Guide. Students are usually best at detecting unclear items, so your input will be considered carefully, and appreciated. His address is:

David A. Santogrossi, Ph.D., HSPP

Associate Dean of Liberal Arts

Associate Professor of Psychological Sciences

1350 Liberal Arts and Education Building

Purdue University

West Lafayette IN 47906-1350

e-mail: dsanto@sla.purdue.edu

fax: (765) 494-3660

YOU CAN MASTER THIS MATERIAL--AND ENJOY DOING IT.

Interest in Abnormal Behavior, and Psychology in general, currently is sweeping the country. (And, as TV host David Letterman points out, the country needs a good sweeping). Courses such as this one are some of the most popular on all college campuses. We can think of more than top ten reasons to learn this material.

Some of the primary reasons to take this course may be extremely personal. Mental and behavioral disorders are so prevalent that it is likely you know someone who has experienced or will experience such a problem. This may be friend, a family member, or even yourself.

There are many more reasons to take and do well in this course. The material covered is involved in many of the controversies of today. What is the role of mental disorders in crime and violence? Are people literally "getting away with murder" by using the insanity defense? How can we solve the problems of the homeless mentally ill? Should treatment of psychological problems be paid for by taxpayers through health care programs? What are the causes of and treatments for addiction? Should perpetrators of crimes be forgiven as victims of childhood abuse? Can we predict teenage violence? If so, then what should be done?

Can sudden recollections of past events be accurate and valid? Are sexual offenders "curable," or should they be under surveillance all their lives? Why are some people starving themselves to death when food is plentiful? Can mental health influence physical health, and can physical health influence mental health? How can we discover the causes of disorders? What are the differences among the various mental health professionals? And are all the treatments they offer equally effective?

You may need to develop informed opinions about these issues, just to be an informed, educated person. Also, you'll know which expensive perfume is named for a serious psychological disorder. Or, if you're planning some heinous crime you might learn how to fake an insanity plea. At least one famous defendant did. (But the rest of the class will be on the jury.)

Mastering this material can be fun and interesting. After all, what is more fascinating than the behavior of people, and all its variations? Your instructor, your text, and this Study Guide are prepared to help you do well in this course and feel good about yourself for it. But you will need to work hard. In fact,

YOU SHOULD WORK HARDER THAN THE INSTRUCTOR

"If .....education.... means anything beyond the processing of human beings into expected roles, through credit hours, tests, and grades...it implies an ethical and intellectual contract between teacher and student.... Too often, all of us fail to teach the most important thing, which is that clear thinking, active discussion, and excellent writing are all necessary for intellectual freedom, and that these require hard work."

--Adrienne Rich

Your instructor has likely had substantial training and experience in this field. The instructor already knows the course material and probably does not really need to rehearse it one more time. The students are the ones who need to rehearse this content again and again in order to master it. You need to take an active role in the course. Actually, it would be best if you prepared the lectures, led the discussions, made up text summaries and outlines, and developed the test questions. All these would help you recall and, more importantly, understand the material. In other words,....

TO TEACH IS TO LEARN TWICE

Psychology has much to offer in the way of practical advice about studying and the learning process. Suggestions from the field will be offered throughout this Guide to help you.

One of these, cognitive reframing, involves looking at familiar situations from new thinking perspectives. One frame that can be helpful in the studying situation is the perspective of the teacher. A teacher has to distill the important points, organize them, and present them in an understandable way. If you can do these for yourself, much of the battle is won.

A way to assume this role is to prepare always as if you will need to explain the material to someone else. This frame will force you to understand and organize it in your own words. Listen to this: Researchers (one thing I love about psychology is that we don't just speculate about what might happen--we test to find out) recruited a large group of students to listen to a lecture and then be tested on its content. Half of the group, chosen at random, was told before the lecture that they would be asked to explain the material to others who could not attend. After the lecture, this group scored better on the test, even though they never actually explained the material to anyone. The mere expectation of that duty caused them to take in the information in a more effective way. This effect can work for you in your courses.

SEVERAL HEADS ARE BETTER THAN ONE

A terrific way to take advantage of this phenomenon is to study or review with other people. Find a good study partner or form a study group. Don't be shy about introducing yourself to someone. You can say I told you to, or you could just point to this page:

LET'S TEAM-WORK

Study hard on your own, but always with the expectation that you will have to explain things to your group. Get together with them often to paraphrase and rehearse the material, to get and give explanations and feedback, and to ask and answer questions. This will keep you active and involved, and will motivate you to keep up. Even if you "cram" only before your weekly study group meeting, that's almost the same as real studying. Have a good time, but mostly after you have spent substantial time on your tasks. Some groups make up quizzes to test each other, or even contrive a Jeopardy game where the answers are given and relevant questions are generated. It's all great practice for you.

GET ACTIVE. STAY ACTIVE

A principal aspect of the lecture-listeners study described above is that the effective listeners were taking an active role. Too often, listening to a lecture or even reading a text can become essentially a passive event. It is too easy to let down your interest or concentration and just coast. Instead, it is your turn to do the work. The authors and the instructor already know the material.

YOU CAN BE A MORE EFFECTIVE LISTENER

Obviously, the first task is to go to class. Of course, it helps when the instructor offers clear, organized, and interesting presentations, but that is not essential, because you need to do most of the work, even in lecture.

Get the most out of lecture by reading and studying the related text material first. And go to class expecting to explain its content to someone else. It will be easier to remain attentive and ignore distractions if you sit in the front. You'll also be less tempted to talk, write letters, or read the student newspaper if you're sitting close to the lecturer. The main thing to do is to listen, and to do it actively. Effective listening is not a passive enterprise. Keep your mind working. Relate the material to the text and associate it with other things you already know. Try to paraphrase accurately in your own words. Remember, you have to explain it clearly to someone else.

The notes you take should be brief; just a few key words to jog your memory. Your main purpose in lecture is to listen and understand. As soon as possible after the lecture, however, you should try to write out a detailed summary of the lecture. This is excellent rehearsal for you that will aid your memory. If there are ideas you did not understand, ask the lecturer, a teaching assistant, or the members of your study group. Once it is clear to you, practice explaining it back to them. When you review your notes (often), don't just reread them--that is too passive. Instead, rework them. Rephrase and rewrite the material as more excellent rehearsal.

YOU CAN READ AND STUDY MORE EFFECTIVELY

Every college bookstore carries several books offering tips to help you study. Many of them are excellent, and all can provide new ideas you can try. And they have the space to cover every aspect in more detail than we can provide here. We can here offer many suggestions based on psychological and educational research.

Typical advice that we endorse suggests that you eat nutritious food, and get plenty of exercise and rest. Seek a well-rounded social life, and work to decrease stressors that may distract you. You should approach your studying in a relaxed manner. Some advisors recommend you set a strict study schedule and stick to it.

The study setting is extremely important. You need good lighting in a distraction-free environment. Ask your friends not to interrupt you except in emergencies, and practice friendly but firm ways of asking people to call you later. Try studying in the room where you'll be tested. Conditioning research indicates this might help your recall at exam time.

You may believe you study just as well with the TV on, but if you devote even 5% of your attention to it, that is attention you could be directing to your studies. There is a reason they don't have TV sets in most workplaces. (Would you want your surgeon to have one eye on ESPN as she cuts into your body?)

You should be in a comfortable, but not too comfortable, upright position. Studying while reclining is a bad idea, as it may interfere with both your studying and your sleeping at their appropriate times (see text Chapter 10). Again, you won't find beds or reclining couches in most workplaces. Corporations know the importance of the stimulus environment in promoting concentration.

Don't just rely on your impressions to discover what works best for you. In the spirit of the psychological discipline, you should experiment with different approaches, and evaluate them with methods described in the Research Methods chapter of the text. Keep track of your work output (time spent or pages covered) each day for several days. Then introduce a new factor such as music in the background, a different study room, or TV on, and continue recording work data. Alternate the factor in and out, and the data will tell you whether it makes a difference. Be scientific.

YOU ARE NOT ALONE

Millions of people have gone through these study and learning processes before you. It makes sense for you to take advantage of their experiences and use the strategies found to be successful. You don't have to start from scratch, and it would be inefficient to do so.

Most learning experts suggest a version of the so-called SQ4R method to guide your reading. These stand for Survey, Question, Read, Recite, wRite (ok; I didn't make this up), and Review. This is a strategy that will become easier and faster for you with practice, and it will help you gain information more efficiently.

SURVEY means to scan and preview the chapter or section to be read, to familiarize yourself with its content. Examine the headings, key terms in italics and bold type, figures and tables, and initial paragraph sentences. Of course, this is the time to read the chapter summary provided in this Guide. Don't stumble blindly into the material--know where you're going in advance.

QUESTION means (guess what?) to generate questions about the content. These questions will guide and focus your reading as you search for the answers. Headings and lead sentences are easily transformed into simple queries. For example, "There are several theories of the etiology of schizophrenia" becomes "What are the theories of the etiology of schizophrenia?" "And what does 'etiology' mean anyway?" Write these questions into your notebook and leave space for the answers.

READ What many students do first should actually be the third step in your strategy. Read the material looking for answers to the questions you posed. Be on the alert for new questions and answers you may have overlooked. Highlighting or underlining is not particularly helpful, as it is relatively passive and it encourages you to put off actually studying until "later." And simply reading and rereading is NOT studying. It's better to take the active steps recommended here.

RECITE repeats the advice we offered above: you'll recall material better if you explain it to someone else. Practice reciting your answers to your roommate or study partner. Take turns--you may learn about questions you had neglected to ask.

WRITE All right, so it doesn't really start with R. Nevertheless, when you have developed succinct, understandable, and correct answers in your own words, write them down. Do this with your book closed and then check and improve your answers. Also, practice writing a summary of the material, and then compare it to the summaries at the end of the chapter and in this Guide. This process will let you know how well you're acquiring the information. Just for fun, write lectures about the material. It will require you to organize the information one more time (and will give you more appreciation of what the instructor goes through).

REVIEW Go over the material regularly at later times. You'll have your answers and summaries to help you, but don't just rely on them. That's being passive again. Instead, rework the materials. Write your own test questions, practice writing essay answers and defining key terms, and write new summaries. Discuss the material with your study group. Finally, assess your knowledge and recall by taking the sample quiz provided for each chapter in this Guide and CD-ROM. Once you have learned a concept, be sure to use it whenever possible in conversation, at least with your study group.

I'd like to add one more important R to this scenario. You have worked hard on each section of this material. Be sure to positively **REINFORCE** your good behavior to maintain motivation. You deserve it.

MOTIVATION WILL HELP KEEP YOU GOING----AND SUCCEEDING

Here is the easiest way to motivate yourself: Adopt this cognitive frame: THERE IS AN EXAM TOMORROW. If you can make yourself act as if you believe this each day, you will always keep up. Even if your typical pattern has been to study only on the night before tests ("cramming"), this belief will cause you to cram every night, which is almost the same as actual studying!! (This reminds me of the comedian who says he tries to live as if each day is his last on earth. As a result, he spends each morning making funeral arrangements.)

There are many (again, more than a mere top ten) reasons to do well in this course, and in college in general. Many are long-range or abstract reasons. Gaining knowledge for its own sake is a worthy goal. Good grades may lead to academic honors or access to good jobs or advanced education. These may result in higher pay and greater recognition in the future. You'll earn self-esteem and the respect of others.

Reframe: Think of yourself as a consumer as well as a student. You or someone close to you is paying for this course. As a good consumer, you will want to get the most education for your money. This should encourage you to excel in this course.

Reframe again: Think of yourself as a new employee still on probation for a most desirable job. You would want to impress your supervisor with the quality of your work, the quickness of your learning, and the enthusiasm of your attitude.

Reframe yet again: Think of yourself as a client or customer. You will want to hire the best, most skilled professional you can. You want the person who worked hard, learned the most, and gained extra experiences; the person who strove for excellence. You can work now to be that person. You would not want the person who did only the minimum work, enough to merely "get by," who crammed for tests and wasted a valuable educational opportunity. Nevertheless.....

YOU NEED REINFORCEMENT IMMEDIATELY

Or, at least, immediately after your hard work. These life outcomes may be too remote to influence your behavior much today. Even a good grade at the end of the semester, or the knowledge that you won't have to panic before the test in a few weeks, may not motivate you when you are tempted to postpone studying right now. Psychologists have shown that small but immediate reinforcers may be necessary to promote desirable behavior.

This principle seems simple to implement. All you need to do is identify things you like to get or do. That's easy enough: What would you be doing now if you had free time? Next, make sure that you do what you like, with one small rearrangement: Do it after you have completed a certain amount of work. Like to listen to favorite music? That's fine; just be sure to meet today's study goal first.

(Psychologist call this the Premack Principle: A highly-preferred activity can reinforce a less-preferred activity. You may know it as Grandma's Rule: You get dessert only if you eat your vegetables.)

Positive reinforcers can be different for different people or on different days. Like to watch the soaps, or Oprah, or Letterman, or the sports update? Terrific. Tape it and watch when you have earned it. Or the sooner you meet today's study goal, the sooner you can call, e-mail, or IM that special person of your favorite gender. One that works for me is to postpone getting my mail until I have met my work requirement.

Enlist your friends, roommate or family members to help you. If a phone call is your reinforcer, instruct the called friend to ask whether you have earned it. Tell these other people they should give you grief if you try to sample unearned privileges. Exchange reinforcement ideas with your study group.

Your goals could be defined in terms of the number of pages studied with the SQ4R method: "As soon as I survey, question, read, recite, write, and review ten pages from that excellent Barlow and Durand Abnormal text, I can read four pages in my spellbinding novel." Or spend 10 minutes on the Internet. Or you could set a time goal: "If I spend a solid 90 minutes SQ4Ring the Barlow and Durand chapter, I can get my fifth R, a special snack. And, of course, if I don't, I can't." An easy way to measure the time is to get a cheap analog electric clock and set it at 12 o'clock. When you begin studying, plug it in. If you daydream, or stop working for whatever reason, unplug it. Plug it in again when you resume work. At the end, the clock will show your accumulated time for the day. A watch with a stopwatch function can serve the same purpose. Record hours daily.

You can build in longer-term goals as well: "As soon as I meet my daily goal five times, no matter how many days it takes, I can rent that movie I have been eager to see. And if I quit talking to myself this way, I can have popcorn with it."

YOUR WORK PAYS OFF AT EXAMINATION TIME

Again, other books can tell you more about how to prepare for exams, but we have additional suggestions based on Psychology. The best way to be successful at test time, of course, is to know the material **cold**. If you have been "SQ4Ring" your text and lecture notes regularly and consistently, and have been working well with a study group, you can be confident that you are ready as can be. Another way to reduce mild, test anxiety is to spend time in the examination room breathing deeply and practicing relaxation. If you have severe test anxiety, be sure to seek professional help. Some colleges offer workshops or more intensive treatment for their students.

By now you probably have taken many **multiple-choice** tests. You likely know how to rule out unlikely options and choose among the likely ones. You'll have a better idea of how the testmaker's mind works if you use this Guide and you have practiced generating such questions yourself. Try it. It may be harder than you think.

Writing **definitions** is a specialized skill as well, and one that you can improve with practice. So practice. Even if your exams will not include writing definitions or essays, practicing them will help you learn the material for any type of test. The main idea behind definitions is to identify a general category for the concept being defined. Then you add details to narrow in on the specific characteristics that differentiate the concept from others in the category. For example, autism is a <u>disorder</u> (rather than a treatment or a theory, for example); autism is a <u>childhood</u> disorder; a childhood disorder characterized by . . . and so on.

If you could write a glossary for all the italicized and bold-printed terms in a chapter, you probably have nearly mastered that chapter.

For **essay questions**, part of the skill is to be thorough but succinct. The study suggestions above will prepare you for these questions, of course. Practice identifying likely essay topics, such as similar concepts that could be subjected to the familiar "compare and contrast" treatment, or major theories of causation or treatments for a particular disorder.

Following a test, be sure to identify and understand your errors, even if you have done well (and, of course, you will have). This will help you prepare better for the next test. And, who knows? You might even discover a scoring error. Discuss the test and any problems with your study group, and change your tactics as needed.

YOUR INSTRUCTOR WILL BE HAPPY TO MEET WITH YOU

Most instructors hold office hours each week. Take advantage of this time by going to meet your instructor. This is a person who has chosen a teaching career at least partially because of a liking for students, and is likely to be approachable. He or she is a person with a life and interests in addition to Psychology.

An instructor who knows you and your skills is better able to write informed reference letters on your behalf. He or she will try to help you if you are having problems in the course, especially if you are sincerely trying hard to do well. If you are seeking assistance, either about the class or career or grad school advice, be sure to do your "homework" first. For example, be sure to do basic things such as reading the syllabus.

If graduate teaching assistants are available, try to resolve any problems with them first. Do research on careers or grad school in the library. If you come in cold and expect the instructor to do all your thinking, you may not appear sincere or serious.

THE LEAST FAVORITE THINGS FOR AN INSTRUCTOR TO HEAR (students and instructors are encouraged to send additional items)

I missed last class. Did you say anything important?

What will be covered on the exam? (If it's on the syllabus.)

Do we have to know this? (Are you afraid you'll learn too much?)

Is it ok if I miss next class? I have tickets to Hawaii. (while the instructor has to stay here and work).

I can't take the test (or turn in the paper) today because I was sick yesterday. (But the test was announced, or the assignment was made, weeks ago. You should be ready before the night before.)

YOU'LL WANT TO DO YOUR BEST ON PAPERS AND PROJECTS

Many courses require that you do at least one paper or class project. Employers report written and oral communication skills are the abilities they seek most strenuously. Careful planning and hard work will yield products you can offer with pride. Again, several of the books that help you master college life can provide additional useful tips. First of all, be sure to FOLLOW INSTRUCTIONS precisely to avoid unnecessary errors. A prime complaint among employers today is that many of their workers seem unable to follow directions.

Next, START EARLY. Begin your planning and topic selection right away. You may have several weeks allotted for your project, but this may just encourage you to procrastinate. In the workplace, many projects, briefs, and reports are due "yesterday." If you're a therapist, you'll have ten minutes between clients to write up cogent notes (and to use the rest room). So get used to working without the luxury of a lot of lead time.

Procrastination is a problem for many people, but it is merely a behavior you can control. Why is it that we can procrastinate but still get it done? Because it's never too late to do a bad job. Perhaps you have seen the slogan, "If you can't find time to do it well, how are you going to find time to do it over?"

Use a SCHEDULE. You respond to deadlines--you'll have *something* finished on time--so set your own deadlines for each subtask (selecting a topic, creating an outline, doing the research, thinking, writing and rewriting, proofreading and polishing). Stick to these goals, reward the completion of each, and feel good about turning in an excellent piece of work.

Starting the writing is often the hardest step. You may believe you have it all written "in your head," but then discover you were wrong when it's too late to write a good paper. It is better for most people to just begin writing something, getting your ideas on paper without regard to form or organization. It's easier to revise something than to start from scratch. Besides, good writing is really *rewriting*. And rewriting again.

Become familiar with the library and all its resources. Do it early in the term to help you in this and many other courses. The staff and the computer equipment will be glad to assist you.

The Internet and its search engines can be a big help. But anyone can create a website, so examine the sources carefully. See page xxi for more suggestions.

Your text is a valuable starting point. It probably covers your topic and offers relevant references in the

back. These references will yield many additional references that you can use. Be sure to use the text or the *Diagnostic and Statistical Manual* to define your technical terms. A surprising number of students will get their definitions of schizophrenia, or bipolar disorder from the *dictionary* while the official source is right at hand.

On the other hand, you should use the dictionary and your spell-checker liberally in your work. The point is to offer a paper that is well-written, with perfect grammar and spelling. Remember, employers list writing and speaking skills highest on their lists of desirable abilities.

MAKE EXCELLENCE HABITUAL

Some students resent the demand for proper literacy, stating, "This is not an English course." True enough, but it is exactly where those skills you learned in English classes should show themselves. Your instructor is trying to help you. A poorly written paper is distracting to the reader and it loses credibility. Would you trust an attorney whose contracts and legal briefs were filled with errors? If I read a psych report that is poorly written, I can't help wondering whether the staffer who wrote it is well-trained.

An important step that many people neglect is to allow time to THINK. Give your ideas time to incubate, to become organized.

Ponder the material in the shower and as you drop off to sleep. Keep a notepad near your bed to jot down late-night inspirations. Watch for other material that may relate.

It is also essential that you proofread your work carefully. Why should anyone else read it if you didn't? Even your computer spell checker is not sufficient as it will miss incorrect words that are spelled correctly. You may be too close to the work to spot errors, so have a literate friend read and critique your work. And leave time to make the changes. Let some time pass and reread your own work--you'll be surprised how many improvements will leap out at you. Note that these advantages are lost if you're working at the last minute.

A common excuse for late papers these days is "My printer locked up" or "My computer crashed. " It's so common that you should expect it and prepare for it. How? By starting and finishing early, and saving your work. You can respond to such an emergency if you have time. Would your boss at work accept this excuse?

Last of all, be critical of your work. Ask, "Is this my best work?" If not -- why not? (Not enough time is no longer a valid excuse. We told you to start early). Is it good enough for that corporate employer you're trying to impress? If it is excellent work, feel good about it, reward yourself with positive self-statements and fun activities. Savor the pleasure of a strong, comfortable finish. You finished on time with a quality product.

Later, pay attention to the instructor's feedback to do even better in the future. We give feedback to help you, and become annoyed when you ignore it.

CAN GIVING A TALK EVER BE FUN?

It can be if you're well-prepared. Follow the suggestions above for preparing a paper. But in addition, be sure to rehearse and rehearse some more. Rather than memorizing your talk and risking getting stuck, it's better just to discuss your topic. Get so familiar with your topic, you'll know more about it than anyone in the room. Then share your knowledge as if you were discussing your hobby. Use notes of single words or short phrases only to remind you of the subtopics you want to cover and their sequence. Discuss the material with your study group, your friends, roommates, and family, and urge them to ask questions. You'll become comfortable with the information.

If you experience anxiety when speaking, you're not alone. Forget tips like "picture the audience naked;" it will only distract you. Excellent preparation will make you most comfortable with your talk content. And reminding yourself that you know the content better than your audience helps a lot. Seek out opportunities to talk, first in small groups where you're comfortable, later in larger groups and with people who are riskier. If your anxiety is so severe as to be debilitating, it may qualify as a social phobia (see Anxiety chapter). Perhaps you should seek programs offered by your school or professional therapy. They can help you immensely.

GROUP PROJECTS

Some instructors assign group projects to promote cooperative planning, organization, and learning. You know by now that this Guide encourages the use of group power to enhance your studying. And this simulates a circumstance you may find often in the workplace. But Social Psychologists have described and researched a phenomenon that may work against the success of a group.

Did you know that if you need emergency help, you may be *less* likely to receive it if many people are nearby than if only a few are present? You might think your chances are better with more potential helpers there, but this situation can provoke *social loafing*. Responsibility can be diffused within the group; each person may let "someone else" take care of things.

A similar pattern can develop on your group project and some, or even all members, may be inclined to loaf (including you). You need to be aware of this to prevent it. But how?

First, choose responsible co-workers, if you can. Next, organize a plan and get each member to commit, in writing if possible, to particular responsibilities and deadlines for each step. Keep in touch by phone, answering machine, or e-mail, and meet together at key points. It will be difficult for someone to fall behind, or if that happens, you will know early enough to compensate. Even if you end up doing more than your share of the work, you will learn a lot, including whom to avoid choosing next time.

TAKE ADVANTAGE OF OPPORTUNITIES

Some of the findings and conclusions described in one sentence, or one paragraph in the text, are actually the result of years of research work. In many colleges and universities, you have the opportunity to assist faculty members in their research. You might help search existing literature, work with research subjects, analyze data, and write up or present results. This opportunity allows you a different view of Psychology and learning. You can make real contributions to science, learn real skills, and begin to establish your career network, so that professors can get to know you to write informed recommendation letters to employers or graduate schools.

Many psychology departments offer talks by faculty or visiting lecturers who may discuss their research or clinical practice issues. These can help you broaden your perspective by exposing you to a wider range of opinions and experiences. Go, listen, and learn.

An additional means for broadening your education is through volunteer or paid work. You might work in a group home, on a crisis center phone line, in a developmental-disabilities center, or in a number of agencies that need your help. This experience will give life to the concepts you study in the text, and you can have a meaningful impact in important areas.

Many psychology departments have psych student organizations. They offer a chance for you to meet and become active with students who are enthusiastically involved in psychology. Many clubs provide social events, guest speakers, field trips, and information about employment and graduate education. Get involved if you are so inclined. And have fun.

AVOID THIS UNFORTUNATE ISSUE

Cheating and plagiarism are extremely serious academic problems. They both involve taking credit for work done by someone else, and are forms of theft and fraud. They are not minor offenses and are usually punished by most instructors. Cheaters are often told "you're only cheating yourself," but that is not really true. It is at least insufficient. And besides, cheaters may be perfectly content to cheat themselves.

**Cheating primarily cheats the other students who work hard to get the good grades they deserve. It is *unfair* to award the same grades to people who did not earn them.

**Cheating also cheats the people who are paying for the educational opportunity and who have a right to expect good efforts by legitimate means.

**Cheating also defrauds future employers and coworkers or graduate schools who have every right to believe that reported grades reflect true learning and skills gained.

**It also cheats instructors who want to help you expand your knowledge and skills by offering feedback on your actual performance. The existence of cheating forces instructors to be suspicious of all students.

**And it does cheat the cheater, who fails to take advantage of educational exercises and receive useful feedback.

Instead, spend the effort achieving excellence in the course. It's a good feeling.

STUDY ASSISTANCE ON THE WEB

Your college probably offers support services and workshops to help you improve your study skills and time management. Take advantage of these--most everyone can gain valuable new ideas.

Similar material can also be found on the Internet. The two outstanding resources below are extremely valuable.

http://www.sla.purdue.edu/studentserv/asc/

This award-winning site will help improve your study and test-taking skills, decrease your test anxiety, and much more.

http://owl.english.purdue.edu/

The Online Writing Lab (OWL) website receives over a million hits a year. It offers helpful guidelines to improve your writing, topic research, and presentations.

CLEAN UP YOUR COGNITIVE ECOLOGY

Which attitude is likely most beneficial to a student?

a. This coursework is impossible.

b. I'll never be able to understand this.

c. This instructor is so unreasonable.

d. This course is difficult for me; I need to work harder.

Cognitive psychologists have shown that your beliefs and expectations may have powerful effects on your behavior. How could a negative attitude help you? It will make you give up or, at least, become passive. Try to maintain an approach that is active and positive. After all, if you use these methods and work hard, you can be confident you will be successful.

ARE YOU BEING THE BEST STUDENT YOU CAN? If not, why not?

THE AUTHOR

AND FRIEND

Which of these pictured

a. is a genius? (more than one may be correct)

b. has a metal head? (more than one...)

c. was a favorite of Marilyn Monroe? (more...)

d. said, 'Imagination is more important than knowledge"?

e. said, "Knowledge is pretty important in this Psych course"?

FEATURES OF THE CHAPTER GUIDES:

LEARNING OBJECTIVES: These components were written by John Forsyth of the State University of New York at Albany. Intended to guide your studying, this list is not exhaustive. Develop your own objectives a well and work hard to learn the material.

CHAPTER SUMMARY: Become familiar with this summary as part of your survey and preparation before you read the text chapter the first time. Afterwards, continue to refer to it as you study the chapter. Cover the answers and try to fill them in mentally. Don't write them in because if the answers are there, they won't help you practice actively. Keep notes on additional chapter detail not included in this summary because this material is only a sample. Practice summarizing chapter sections yourself in your own words, and use all this material as part of your frequent reviews.

KEY WORDS: Practice defining this sample of important concepts. With your text closed, write definitions in your own words into a notebook using the suggestions offered on page 8 of this Guide. Then refer to your text to check and upgrade your definitions. Practice rephrasing the definition, being sure your words still reflect the key ideas and vocabulary necessary to the term. Then write your best definition into this Guide for later study. Keep your definitions on the right side so that later you can cover either the word or the definition to practice generating the other. Or do the it with flash cards you construct yourself. Then do the same for the larger list at the end of each text chapter.

SAMPLE QUESTIONS: As one of the later stages of your study for a chapter, you can assess your progress by taking a sample test and checking your answers. Don't make the mistake of studying just for these questions. They are merely a small sample of the thousands of questions that could appear on an exam. An excellent way to help yourself is to generate your own questions and answers. This will help you focus on important concepts, make better distinctions among similar ideas, practice writing responses, and engaging the material in general. Try them on your friends in your study group.

THINKING ALLOWED: Various activities beyond the classroom may help you actively engage course material. Try some of these with your classmates, friends, family members, or study group members. Make up new activities of your own (and send your best ideas to the author to help future students).

INTERNET RESOURCES: You can explore chapter topics in even greater depth by contacting listed Websites. Be aware that URLs change and disappear without warning, but these were available when this Guide was printed.

ACKNOWLEDGMENTS: I am extremely grateful to Mary Helen Nesbitt and word processing specialist Nancy Mowat, both of Purdue University. Their help in developing and evaluating this new edition has been invaluable, prompt, and pleasant.

This effort is dedicated to my parents, perfect models of caring and courage. -DAS

GOOD LUCK, AND ENJOY THE COURSE!!

INTERNET RESOURCES: for study and exploration in psychology:

PsychWatch psych news.http://www.psychwatch.com/

American Counseling Associationhttp://www.counseling.org/

American Psychological Associationhttp://www.apa.org/

American Psychological Societyhttp://www.psychologicalscience.org/

Careers and grad school in Psychologyhttp://www.rider.edu/users/suler/gradschl.html

http://www.gradschools.com/

International Coach Federation (personal coaches)http://www.coachfederation.org/

Library research in Psychologyhttp://www.apa.org/science/lib.html

Mental Health Nethttp://mentalhelp.net/

Mental Health InfoSourcehttp://www.mhsource.com/

Psych Humorhttp://www.psychhumor.com/

Additional, more specific sites are listed in each chapter

For most chapters or topics in the textbook you can use the text's website (see below) to find further information. You might also want to use an Internet search engine as well. Remember that not all websites you will find are equally credible. Some will turn out to be advertisements for medication, or for support groups, both of which have their uses for some people. You'll need to judge whether informational sources are supported by reputable agencies and solid research. Can you tell which theoretical approach is used in the site's presentation and interpretation? Can you determine whether statement or claims made are based on rigorous empirical research? For an excellent aid to Internet research (and college writing), including narrowing your search, evaluating sites, and using American Psychological Association (APA) formatting style, go to http://www.nutsandboltsguide.com/evidence.html for the Nuts and Bolts Guide for College Writing by Michael Harvey

The Website address for your textbook is:http://psychology.wadsworth.com/

Check here often for more study/practice questions and continually updated text material.

ABNORMAL BEHAVIOR IN HISTORICAL CONTEXT

LEARNING OBJECTIVES

1. Define abnormal behavior (psychological disorder) and describe psychological dysfunction, distress, and atypical or unexpected cultural response.

2. Describe the scientist-practitioner model.

3. Place psychopathology in its historical context by identifying historical conceptions of abnormal behavior in terms of supernatural influences.

4. Trace the major historical developments and underlying assumptions of the biological approach to understanding abnormal behavior.

5. Describe the different approaches of the psychological tradition (i.e., psychoanalysis, humanism, and behavioral) with regard to their explanations of abnormal behavior.

6. Explain the importance of science and the scientific method as applied to abnormal behavior.

7. Describe the multidimensional-integrative approach to diagnosing and evaluating abnormal behavior and explain why it is important.

8. Describe the multidimensional-integrative approach to diagnosing and evaluating abnormal behavior and explain why it is important.

CHAPTER SUMMARY

Become familiar with this summary as part of your survey and preparation before you read the text chapter the first time. Afterward, continue to refer to it as you study the chapter. Cover the answers and try to fill them in mentally. Don't write them in because if the answers are there, they won't help you practice actively. Keep notes on additional chapter detail not included in this summary because this material is only a sample. Practice summarizing chapter sections yourself in your own words, and use all this material as part of your frequent reviews.

The definition of psychological disorders, or what the public thinks of as _____ behavior includes several elements. Psychological _____ is a breakdown in cognitive, _____, or behavioral functioning, and sometimes all of these at once. For psychology professionals and most, but not all, potential clients, unhappiness or _____ is an important issue. Extreme versions of normal patterns that result in _____ in functioning, or the ability to adjust to life, are also included. Disorders involve behavior that deviates from the typical _____ of society or that violates _____ values. None of these elements alone makes up a proper definition of a disorder, but together they state: Behavioral, emotional, or cognitive _____ that are _____ in their cultural context and associated with personal _____ or substantial _____ in functioning are abnormal.

abnormal; dysfunction; emotional; distress; impairment; norms; cultural; dysfunctions; unexpected; distress; impairment

Several professions engage in the assessment, treatment, and study of psychological disorders (a field called _____), with varying degrees of education and different emphases in their work. These include psychology specialists called _____ psychologists, medical specialists called _____, and _____ social workers. Ideally, these professionals follow a _____-_____ model, in which they integrate scientific research with their treatment of clients.

psychopathology; clinical; psychiatrists; psychiatric; scientist-practitioner

A person usually comes to a clinic due to a specific problem, referred to as the _____ problem. The clinician develops a clinical description of each client, including such statistical data as _____, the number of people in the population who display the disorder; _____, the rate of new cases in a time period; _____ ratio, the percentage of those with the disorder are female or male; and _____, the typical pattern of the disorder. Three possible courses are a _____ course, which may last for a lifetime, an _____ course, in which a person repeatedly suffers from the disorder for brief periods of time, and a _____-_____ course, in which the disorder eventually improves on its own. The onset of the disorder refers to the length of time over which a disorder develops. Based on the clinical description, the clinician can develop a _____, an indication of the chance that the client will recover from the disorder. Another factor that must be considered in the study of psychological disorders is the _____, or cause of the disorder.

presenting; prevalence; incidence; sex; course; chronic; episodic; time-limited; prognosis; etiology

Throughout history, people have attempted to understand psychological disorders in many different ways. According to the _____ view, which was prevalent in the Middle Ages, mental disease was a result of the activity of spiritual forces. Thus, treatment involved _____, in which the demons causing the disorder were "cast out of" a mentally ill person. The case of King Charles VI and the New England _____ trials illustrate the supernatural approach to psychological disorders. Even then, natural explanations such as emotional _____ also were widely accepted. Explaining psychological phenomena in terms of heavenly bodies led to the term _____ as a synonym for disorders.

supernatural; exorcisms; witch; stress; mass hysteria; lunacy

A second tradition in the history of understanding psychological disorders is the_____ tradition, the idea that psychological disorders are related to brain function. This view was supported by the discovery that a disease, _____, can cause psychological disorder, by the advent of drug therapies, and by Pasteur's germ theory of disease. An early adherent to the biological tradition was Hippocrates, who assumed that psychological disorders were related to brain _____ or genetics. Galen's _____ theory maintained that personality was a result of bodily fluids, and suggested treatments included blood-letting and _____ to balance these fluids. In the 19th century, Dr.John _____, a disciple of the biological tradition, reformed mental institutions to promote bodily health. _____'s classification systems, based on symptoms, was also influenced by the biological tradition. Due to this approach to psychopathology, drug treatments including insulin _____ treatment, tranquilizers, and benzodiazepines were used and _____ shock treatments were developed to treat psychological disorders.

biological; syphilis; trauma; humoral; vomiting; Grey; Kraeplin; shock; electric

A third tradition in psychopathology, highlighting the role of environment and experience, is the _____ tradition. An early example was _____ therapy in which patients were encouraged to develop normal relationships. _____ reformed mental hospitals in France by unchaining the inmates. Tuke in England and Rush in America followed Pinel's lead. Dix, in the mental _____ movement, campaigned for the reform of mental institutions and for the right of all, including the homeless, to have adequate mental health care. This movement led to increases/decreases in hospital population and improved/reduced the quality of care.

psychological; moral; Pinel, hygiene; increases; reduced

Another example of the psychological tradition is Freud's theory of psychoanalysis, which focuses on _____ conflict among the three parts of the mind, the _____, _____, and _____. In its attempt to balance the instinctual drives of the _____ and the moral principles of the _____, the ego uses defense mechanisms, such as repression, in which troubling thoughts or memories are kept hidden in the unconscious. Freud's proposed psychosexual stages, called the_____, anal, phallic, _____, and genital stages, and his description of an _____ complex, in which young boys are claimed to be sexually attracted to their mothers, are controversial aspects of his theory. Psychoanalytic therapy may involve hypnosis, dream analysis, and free _____. Other theorists and their theories, such as Anna _____ and ego psychology, Kernberg and _____ relations, and Jung and Adler who focused on self-actualization, have used psychoanalytic theory as a starting point. The present-day form of psychoanalysis is briefer

_____ therapy. Some characteristics of psychodynamic therapy include looking for _____ in a patient's behavior and identifying the patient's _____, fantasies, and wishes. Humanistic theory, represented by Rogers' _____-_____ therapy and Maslow's hierarchy of needs, focuses on self-_____, which may be blocked by the demands of society.

unconscious; id; ego; superego; id; superego; oral; latency; Oedipal; association; Freud; object; psychodynamic; patterns; dreams; person-centered; actualization

The _____, or social learning model of Watson and Skinner is also a part of the psychological tradition, due to its focus on learning. The behavioral model focuses on conditioning, first demonstrated by _____ in his experiments with dogs. The two types of conditioning are _____ conditioning, in which an unconditioned stimulus is paired with a conditioned stimulus until the conditioned stimulus elicits a conditioned response and _____ conditioning, in which behavior is changed and maintained by its consequences. On the basis of some of these principles of conditioning, Wolpe developed systematic _____, a form of behavioral therapy to reduce fears.

behavioral; Pavlov; classical; operant; desensitization

Currently, most psychologists realize that _____, _____, cognitive, and social factors, among others, affect psychopathology, and no factor alone can explain it in entirety. This view is called the _____ approach.

biological; behavioral; integrative

KEY WORDS

Practice defining the important concepts listed below and at the end of the text chapter. Follow the definition suggestions provided in the introduction to this Guide. Be precise and accurate, and check your work with the text. Add to the definition later as you encounter more information about the term. Whenever possible, include examples. Use only the space to the right of the word so that later you can cover either the word or the definition to use one to cue the other. Define additional important terms you'll find in the chapter.

1. behavioral model

_____

_____

2. clinical psychologist

_____

_____

3. course of a disorder

_____

_____

4. etiology of a disorder

_____

_____

5. incidence

_____

_____

6. prevalence

_____

_____

7. prognosis

_____

_____

8. psychiatric nurse

_____

_____

9. psychiatric social worker

_____

_____

10. psychiatrist

_____

_____

11. psychoanalysis

_____

_____

12. psychological disorder

_____

_____

13. psychological model

_____

_____

14. psychopathology

_____

_____

15. scientist-practitioner

_____

_____

16. unconscious

_____

_____

SAMPLE QUESTIONS

As one of the later stages of your study for this chapter, you can assess your progress by taking a sample test. Don't make the mistake of studying just for these questions. They are merely a small sample of the many questions that could appear on an exam. An excellent way to help yourself is to generate your own questions and answers. This will help you focus on important concepts, make better distinctions among similar ideas, practice writing responses, and engaging the material in general. Try them on your friends in your study group.

Multiple Choice Questions

1. Which of the following is not an aspect of the definition of psychological disorders?
    a. the atypical response element, which states that a deviation from normal behavior is evidence of a psychological disorder
    b. the psychodynamic element, which suggests that abnormal behavior is the result of poor ego defense mechanisms
    c. the distress element, in which personal discomfort signals the presence of a psychological disorder
    d. the impairment in functioning element, which defines a psychological disorder based on a disruption in ability to carry out normal tasks

2. The scientist-practitioner model of psychology focuses on
    a. the psychologist's use of scientific principles to study which treatments are most effective and to decide which treatment to us
    b. the psychologist's use of statistics, such as prevalence and incidence, to diagnose clients.
    c. the exchange of information between scientists.
    d. the use of drugs in clinical practice

3. Louie was barking like a dog and walking on his hands and knees. A professional thought the cause of Louie's problem was that he had an excess of a particular neurotransmitter, and prescribed a drug for him. The professional is most likely a _____, operating under the _____ model of abnormal behavior.
    a. clinical psychologist, psychological
    b. psychiatric nurse, supernatural
    c. psychiatric social worker, behavioral
    d. psychiatrist, biological

4. The Oedipus complex, which, according to Freud, occurs during the _____ stage of psychosexual development, is characterized by_____ _____.
    a. genital; penis envy
    b. oral; penis envy
    c. phallic; castration anxiety
    d. latency; castration anxiety

5. One of the results of the discovery that the disease syphilis and the disordered behavior that results from it are both caused by the same bacterial microorganism was
    a. mental health professionals began to think that other psychological disorders might be caused by other microorganisms, and biological cures might be possible.
    b. individuals diagnosed with syphilis were referred to psychologists instead of doctors for further treatment.
    c. the mental hygiene movement was established, which attempted to provide a sterile, bacteria-free, environment for those suffering from disorders.
    d. mental health professionals adopted a genetic model, which has been supported by further scientific investigations into the causes of disorders.

6. Which of the following is an incorrect match between a drug and the problem it is used to treat?
   a. reserpine: aggression
   b. benzodiazepines: panic attacks
   c. bromides: hallucinations
   d. neuroleptics: delusions

7. Breuer discovered that
   a. hysterical symptoms were alleviated after patients discussed them under hypnosis.
   b. dogs salivate to a bell if the bell is rung prior to feeding.
   c. discussing problems while hypnotized leads to patient insight.
   d. general paresis was caused by the same bacteria that cause syphilis.

8. Which of the following is not true of classical conditioning?
   a. It involves pairing of a UCS and a CS.
   b. It was demonstrated by Pavlov with his dogs.
   c. It involves shaping procedures.
   d. The CR can be eliminated in a process called extinction.

9. The elements of person-centered therapy include
   a. hypnosis and catharsis.
   b. reinforcement and shaping.
   c. rest and relaxation.
   d. unconditional positive regard and empathy.

10. Your best friend tells you she has just gotten a job in a Veteran's Administration hospital where she will administer and interpret tests, diagnose and treat mental disorders, and continue her research on chronic disorders. All of her training in _____ has paid off.
    a. nursing.
    b. psychiatry.
    c. social work.
    d. clinical psychology.
    e. counseling.

11. Alarmingly, in some areas where the rate of new cases of AIDS had been declining, it has begun increasing again. The statistic that tells us this information is
    a. incidence.
    b. correlation.
    c. deviation.
    d. prevalence

12. Therapist Dr. X (not her real name) is working with a client who is heavily involved with body-piercing. The client enjoys it but Dr. X thinks the amount is so excessive she considers it abnormal behavior. She is employing which definition of abnormality?
    a. dysfunction
    b. culturally inappropriate or unexpected
    c. impairment
    d. distress

13. As a psychiatrist, you have a client experiencing anxiety and panic attacks. You most likely prescribe
    a. reserpine
    b. benzodiazepines.
    c. bromides.
    d. neuroleptics.

14. Early findings apparently supporting psychoanalytic therapy were based on
    a. scientific inquiry.
    b. case studies.
    c. introspection.
    d. literature reviews.

15. Defense mechanisms may be important in treatment planning because they
    a. cannot be studied scientifically.
    b. are most prevalent in people with psychological disorders.
    c. have potential significance in the study of schizophrenia
    d. may differ for different psychological disorders.

16. An individual who blocks disturbing thoughts or experiences from conscious awareness is said to be using the defense mechanism _____.
    a. sublimation
    b. rationalization
    c. projection
    d. repression

17. The purpose of psychoanalysis is
    a. to reduce the symptoms of a disorder.
    b. to examine ego defenses.
    c. to reveal unconscious conflicts.
    d. to overcome the Oedipal complex.

18. One key difference between Jung and Adler was that
    a. Jung focused on the individual reaching his or her potential while Adler emphasized the significance of the individual's contributions to a society.
    b. Adler focused on the individual reaching his or her potential, while Jung emphasized the significance of the individual's contributions to a society.
    c. Jung saw people as struggling to control their aggressive instincts, while Adler saw society as repressing peoples' desire to self-actualiz
    d. Adler saw people as struggling to control their aggressive instincts, while Jung saw society as repressing peoples' desire to self-actualiz

19. Tim owns a cat who licks her chops when she hears cellophane cat food packets being opened This is not a skill she or her wild ancestors learned in the jungle According to a classical conditioning account, the cellophane sound is
    a. a conditioned stimulus.
    b. an unconditioned stimulus.
    c. a conditioned response
    d. an unconditioned response
    e. an instrumental operant

20. What is Joseph Wolpe's most noted contribution to psychology?
    a. systematic desensitization as a means of therapy
    b. the discovery that fear can be repressed through familiarity with the feared object
    c. the definition of operant conditioning
    d. the discovery of the mechanism of the extinction process
    e. the description of the human hierarchy of needs

21. Human behavior, both normal and abnormal, is the result of biological, psychological, and social factors _____.
    a. competing
    b. operating independently
    c. interacting
    d. conflicting

Matching

1. _____ Galen
2. _____ Rogers
3. _____ Mesmer
4. _____ Grey
5. _____ Kraeplin
6. _____ Pinel
7. _____ Dix
8. _____ Erikson
9. _____ Maslow
10. _____ Wolpe
11. _____ Thorndike
12. _____ Pavlov
13. _____ Skinner

a. classification of mental disorders
b. operant conditioning
c. mental hygiene movement
d. systematic desensitization
e. father of hypnosis
f. humanistic psychology
g. moral therapy
h. Law of Effect
i. classical conditioning
j. lifetime developmental stages
k. hierarchy of needs
l. four humors
m. physical causes for psychological disorders

True or False Questions

22. Incidence refers to the number of people in the population who have a disorder; prevalence refers to the number of new cases of a disorder in a given period of time.

    TRUE or FALSE

23. During the Middle Ages, many people believed that disorders were the result of natural causes such as stress, and were treatable by providing a relaxing environment.

    TRUE or FALSE

24. Operant conditioning occurs when an unconditioned stimulus is paired with a conditioned stimulus until the conditioned stimulus alone produces the conditioned response.

    TRUE or FALSE

25. In self-psychology, objects are incorporated into the ego as a part of development.

    TRUE or FALSE

26. Freud's theory suggests that the source of psychological distress is within the individual; Jung and Adler suggest that it is a result of external or environmental barriers to self-actualization.

    TRUE or FALSE

27. A psychological disorder with an insidious onset and chronic course would probably have a favorable prognosis.

    TRUE or FALSE

28. Humanistic psychology focuses on the differences among people that make individuals unique.

    TRUE or FALSE

29. Two key concepts in behavioral therapy are insight and catharsis.

    TRUE or FALSE

30. Psychological disorders involve distress, impairment, dysfunction, and culturally unexpected behavior.

    TRUE or FALSE

Essay Questions

31. Discuss the importance of ego defense mechanisms in psychoanalytic theory.

32. Describe two different ways people with disordered behavior were treated in history. How did the understanding of the causes of psychological disorders affect the treatment offered?

33. Compare and contrast clinical psychologists, psychiatrists, psychiatric social workers, and psychiatric nurses in their training and work roles.

34. Discuss the role of science in the practice of psychology.

35. Discuss the major tenets of one of the following psychological traditions and its approach to psychopathology and treatment: Psychoanalytic, behavioral, humanistic.

36. Explain the concept of an integrative approach to psychopathology.

HOW WELL DID YOU DO?

Less than 60%	Don't take the quiz before you study the chapter. It will narrow your focus too much. You can improve your score if you increase your efforts.
60-80%	Restudy and rewrite, especially the weak areas; discuss problem areas with study partners.
Over 80%	You're on the right track; continue as you are; focus on trouble areas with study group.
Over 95%	Nice job, especially if you know the whole chapter this well. Be sure to reward your behavior, help others in your study group (they'll help you on your weak chapters), and don't forget to review.

THINKING ALLOWED

Chapter 1 Activities

Rent the video "Amadeus" and watch for the scenes (especially the very first scene) featuring Salieri in a mental institution. Or review the film "The Madness of King George." Can you tell, either from the "treatment" methods shown, or from the time period being portrayed, what was the prevailing treatment model of the time? If you'll be a mental health worker (or a patient), aren't you glad things have changed?

For a look at the somewhat more recent history of psychiatric treatment, see the video "Frances", the story of actress Frances Farmer. When they mention a treatment, for example reserpine, stop the tape and impress your friends with your knowledge about its origins. Be sure to read the disclaimer at the end of the credits so you won't condemn psychiatry and psychology forever. And then do something to cheer everyone after the excellent but depressing film.

What are the counseling stereotypes in the excellent film Good Will Hunting? Are there really key words that trigger a breakthrough? Must crying and hugging be involved? What influences besides therapy (one of which is also a cliche) may have been an aid to Will's progress?

Examine other films or TV shows (e.g., Law and Order) for similar content.

Speaking of films, it can be fun to see how psych professionals are portrayed in the media. It is clear film makers know the public is interested in the field. Brainstorm with your study group to list films that portray psych professionals:

• As cold, arrogant, and uncaring (so why did they enter the field?)

• As incompetent. Lay amateurs are always warm, caring, and more effective. (It happens to other professions as well. In movies, amateurs, even children, are better than the pros in business, law, or advertising, for example).

• As the most disordered person in the cast. Child psychologists always have the worst-behaved children. In the holiday classic "Miracle on 34th Street," the strange villain (he hates Santa Claus, of all things) is a psychometrist.

• As a sexual predator.

• As a skilled, competent caring professional.

Where are you on Maslow's hierarchy of needs? Compare with other people you know, but it may be a good idea to keep these assessments to yourself.

Account for some of your own and other's behaviors on the basis of conditioning principles. Notice how advertisers use these methods to affect your buying behaviors. For example, they may try to associate positive feelings with their products, or promise all sorts of reinforcers if you buy them. Practice identifying the conditioning components and using the correct terms. Hint: In classical conditioning, the stimulus and the response that it already provokes automatically are called unconditioned. The stimulus and response that will become associated are called conditioned, or learned. Can you identify examples of each in your life?

Perhaps you enjoy talking to yourself but are concerned what other people may think. Two tips: Put it to music--people don't mind when you sing to yourself. Or carry a cellular phone.

INTERNET RESOURCES

American Psychiatric Association

The APA's web site, contains psych-related links, information on legal cases which have affected psychiatry, continuing education for therapists and much more.

http://www.psych.org/

Today in the History of Psychology

The American Psychological Association created this web site, which allows the user to access information on the history of psychology by selecting a date on the calendar.

http://www.cwu.edu/~warren/today.html

Solutions

KEY WORDS

1. (22)	7. (7)	13. (14)
2. (5)	8. (5)	14. (5)
3. (6)	9. (5)	15. (5-6)
4. (7)	10. (5)	16. (17)
5. (6)	11. (16)	
6. (6)	12. (2)	

SAMPLE QUESTIONS

Multiple Choice Questions

1. B, 2	9. D, 22	17. C, 16
2. A, 5-6	10. D, 5	18. A, 20
3. D, 5	11. A, 6	19. A, 22-23
4. C, 19-20	12. B, 4	20. A, 23
5. A, 12-13	13. B, 14	21. C, 24
6. C, 13-14	14. B, 16-17	
7. A, 17	15. D, 18-19	
8. C, 22-23	16. D, 19	

Matching

1. l 11	6. g 14-15	11. h 24-25
2. f 21-22	7. c 15	12. i 22-23
3. e 16	8. j 21	13. b 24-25
4. m 13	9. k 21-22	
5. a 14	10. d 24	

True or False Questions

22. F, 6	25. T, 20	28. T, 21-22
23. T, 8	26. T, 20	29. F, 23-24
24. F, 24-25	27. F, 6	30. T, 2-4

Essay Questions

31. Note that ego defense mechanisms were thought to protect the ego by keeping conflicts and primitive emotions under control. Also, defense mechanisms can be adaptive or unadaptive. Explain how defense mechanisms are related to psychological disorders. (See page(s) 18-19 of the textbook.)

32. You could focus on the Middle Ages when people thought that psychological disorders were caused by physical or mental stress; treatment focused on providing a stress-free environment. Also, the belief in demon possession lead to exorcism and other "treatment" of psychological disorders. You could also discuss the moral therapy movement, mental hygiene movement, drug treatments, psychoanalysis, behavioral therapy, or humanistic therapy. Be sure to discuss the relation between the assumed cause of the disorder and the treatment. (See pages 7-25 of the textbook.)

33. Your answer should include the different educational degrees of each professional. Also, note the type of treatment each provides, what clientele each professional might treat, and in what setting each might work. (See page 5 of the textbook.)

34. Here, you should discuss the scientist-practitioner model. Your essay should include how science contributes to the understanding of the etiology and treatment of some psychological disorders. You could discuss how each of the different perspectives in psychology (psychoanalytic, behavioral, humanistic, cognitive) uses or fails to use science to support the theories. Practitioners should evaluate the effectiveness of their work, and be good consumers of the latest research, even if they don't conduct formal research themselves. (See page 5-6 of the textbook.)

35. Review the relevant text section for key points. (See pages 14-20, 21-25, and 21-22 of the textbook.)

36. The point is that biological, behavioral, cognitive and social factors all play a role in psychopathology. To assume that any single factor works in isolation misses the larger picture. (See pages 2-4 of the textbook.)

AN INTEGRATIVE APPROACH TO PSYCHOPATHOLOGY

LEARNING OBJECTIVES

1. Distinguish between multidimensional and unidimensional models of causality.

2. Identify the main influences comprising the multidimensional model.

3. Define and describe how genes interact with environmental factors to affect behavior.

4. Identify the different models proposed to describe how genes interact with environmental factors to affect behavior.

5. Identify the functions of different brain regions and their role in psychopathology.

6. Explain the role of neurotransmitters and their involvement in abnormal behavior.

7. Identify the functions of different brain regions and their role in psychopathology.

8. Compare and contrast the behavioral and cognitive theories and how they are used to explain the origins of mental illness.

9. Explain the nature and role of emotions in psychopathology.

10. Describe cultural, social, and developmental influences on abnormal behavior.

CHAPTER SUMMARY

Become familiar with this summary as part of your survey and preparation before you read the text chapter the first time. Afterward, continue to refer to it as you study the chapter. Cover the answers and try to fill them in mentally. Don't write them in because if the answers are there, they won't help you practice actively. Keep notes on additional chapter detail not included in this summary because this material is only a sample. Practice summarizing chapter sections yourself in your own words, and use all this material as part of your frequent reviews.

Linear, or _____-_____ models of causation attribute the _____ of a psychological disorder to only one factor. However, most psychologists adopt a systemic model, recognizing that a _____ of factors contributes to a disorder. _____ influences, such as conditioning and reinforcement, _____ factors, such as inherited tendencies to react to situations in certain ways, _____ influences, such as fear and anxiety, _____ influences, such as the response of others to the person suffering from a disorder, and _____ influences, such as age, all may be involved in the development of a disorder. Understanding the interaction of these influences is important when considering _____ for psychological disorders.

one-dimensional; origin (or cause or etiology); system; Behavioral; biological; emotional; social; developmental; treatment

Genetics is one of the factors that influence psychological disorders. Genes are located on _____ made up of DNA molecules; humans have ____ chromosomes, in ____ pairs. In simple cases, traits exhibited are determined by the _____ gene in a pair or by a pair of _____ genes. However, most characteristics, including behavioral and emotional ones, are _____, meaning determined by many genes. Thus, new techniques that eliminate or correct single genes are likely/unlikely to reduce vulnerability to disorders. _____ genetics refers to the study of patterns of genetic control across genes. Although genetics contributes to the development of psychological disorders, it accounts for only a part of the explanation. Eric Kandel proposed that the process of _____ may actually change the genetic structure of cells, a theory supported/unsupported by recent research.

chromosomes; 46; 23; dominant; recessive; polygenic; unlikely; Quantitative; learning; supported

According to the _____-_____ model of genetics-environment interaction, psychological disorders are the result of both a _____, or biological tendency, and a _____, or environmental situation. Thus, a person must have both to develop a disorder. Also, the smaller the vulnerability, the smaller/greater the stress must be to produce a disorder, and vice versa. A second model of interaction is the _____ gene-environment model, which suggests that the genetic _____ also includes a tendency to create situations in which one is likely to experience a stressor that would cause a _____. This theory has been applied to studies of divorce rates. Neither nature nor nurture solely determines the development of psychological disorders.

diathesis-stress; diathesis; stress; greater; reciprocal; vulnerability; disorder

Recent work has advanced the idea that researchers may have overemphasized/underemphasized the role that genetics plays in personality, temperament, and the development of abnormal behavior. In a demonstration of the importance of _____, researchers using a _____ approach found that rats with easily stressed mothers who were raised by calm mothers were more likely to be calm/stressed. This new research suggests that differences in environment may be able to outweigh the effects of genetics on _____ and the tendency to develop a psychological disorder.

overemphasized; environment; cross-fostering; calm; personality and/or temperament

Workers in the field of _____ study the function of the nervous system. The human nervous system is divided into the central nervous system, consisting of the brain and _____, and the _____ nervous system, which includes the somatic and _____ nervous systems. The central nervous system, composed of millions of neurons, receives input from the senses, processes this input, and reacts to it. Neurons branch into _____, whose receptors receive _____ impulses, and _____, which transmit chemical impulses to other nerve cells. The space between two neurons is called the _____ cleft; here the chemical substances called _____ are released by the axon of one cell and picked up by the dendrite of another cell. Excesses or _____ of neurotransmitters are implicated in some psychological disorders.

neuroscience; spinal cord; peripheral; autonomic; dendrites; chemical; axons; synaptic; neurotransmitters; deficits

The brain is composed of many structures. The brain stem, or hindbrain, is composed of the _____, pons, and _____. These regulate _____ body functions, such as _____, digestion, heartbeat, and motor coordination. The midbrain contains the _____ _____ system, responsible for arousal and tension. At the top of the brain stem, the diencephalon contains the thalamus and _____, structures involved in the regulation of emotion and _____. Another section of the brain is the forebrain, or telencephalon, which contains the _____ system, the part of the brain responsible for emotional expression. The structures of the limbic system are the hippocampus, angulate gyrus, septum, and amygdala, named for their _____. The telencephalon also contains the basal ganglia and caudate nucleus, areas that are related to motor behavior control.

medulla; cerebellum; automatic; breathing; reticular activating; hypothalamus; behavior; limbic; shapes

The _____ _____, the largest part of the forebrain, is responsible for perception, planning, reasoning, and thinking abilities. The cerebral cortex has two hemispheres: the left hemisphere appears to deal with verbal and _____ functions, while the right hemisphere is implicated in _____ and imagery. The lobes, or areas of the cerebral cortex, include the temporal lobes, associated with _____ and recognition of sights and sounds; the _____ lobe, associated with sensations of touch; the occipital lobe, associated with visual processing; and the frontal lobe, associated with reasoning and _____. Thus, the _____ lobe is of most interest in psychopathology.

cerebral cortex; cognitive; perception; memory; parietal; relating to the world around us; frontal

The peripheral nervous system, which is divided into the _____ and _____ nervous systems, works with the brain to ensure proper functioning of the body. The somatic nervous system controls the _____, while the autonomic nervous system regulates the endocrine and _____ systems, among other things. The autonomic nervous system is divided into two complementary systems, the sympathetic nervous system, which _____ arousal, and the parasympathetic nervous system, which _____ arousal. The endocrine system consists of glands that release _____. It interacts with the autonomic nervous system in pathways such as the hypothalamic-_____-adrenalcortical (HYPAC) axis, which has been implicated in several psychological disorders.

somatic; autonomic; muscles; cardiovascular; causes; inhibits; hormones; pituitary

Patterns of neurotransmitter activity in the brain are referred to as brain _____. Drugs can affect neurotransmitter activity by inhibiting neurotransmitter _____, preventing _____, or by occupying receptors, among other ways. While some psychological disorders were once thought to be associated with abnormal levels of neurotransmitters, it is more likely they result from complicated _____ between the neurotransmitters. _____, substances that increase neurotransmitter activity; _____, substances that decrease neurotransmitter activity; and inverse agonists, substances that have an effect identical to/opposite from that of a neurotransmitter, can all be used to study neurotransmitter activity.

circuits; production; reuptake; interactions; Agonists; antagonists; opposite

At least four neurotransmitters are important to psychopathology. The _____, or 5-HT, system regulates human behavior, thought processes and _____ based on information acquired by the brain. Aggression, overeating and suicide appear to be related to low/high serotonin levels. Tricyclic antidepressants act on the _____ system but serotonin reuptake _____ such as Prozac act on it more/less directly. The _____ system is related to anxiety and reduction of arousal. Its effects lead scientists to assume our bodies produce natural _____. The former view that the serotonin circuits entirely control _____ while _____ circuits entirely regulates anxiety is likely too simplistic. The _____ (or noradrenaline) hormone system is implicated in alarm responses, among other behaviors. The _____ system is related to schizophrenia and Parkinson's disease, and is implicated in out-going, exploratory behavior.

serotonin; moods; low; serotonin; inhibitors; more; GABA; benzodiazepine; depression; GABA; norepinephrine; dopamine

All these neurotransmitters operate in more/less complex ways than earlier thought. Similarly, attempts to relate brain structure and activity to psychopathology can be complex. Modern sophisticated theories recognize that neurotransmitter circuits influence ____ _____. Some studies relate brain activity to psychopathology using brain _____ methods, and some knowledge about the brain's role in psychopathology comes from personality changes that result from brain _____ or surgery. This evidence supports biological causes for psychopathology, as in the example of obsessive-compulsive disorder. However, research results are often unclear or _____.

more; one another; imaging; injury; inconsistent

Sometimes the effects of _____ can inform us about disorders. Psychosocial factors have been found to change brain _____, as in Baxter's study of the effects of treatment of obsessive-compulsive patients. Studies have shown that psychosocial interventions such as reducing stress and giving patients a sense of _____ can improve _____ system function and possibly prolong the _____ of cancer patients. Studies of yoked monkeys indicate that the effects of neurotransmitters can be different, depending on _____ factors such as experience with control. The point here is that psychosocial functions can affect _____ functions, not just the reverse.

treatment; structure; control; immune; lives; psychosocial; bodily

_____ _____, which focuses on human processes of acquiring, storing, and retrieving information, has indicated that _____ processing influences behavior. Basic conditioning facilitates cognitive learning of _____ among environmental events. Seligman, in his research with learned helplessness, noted that attribution of _____ over a situation can change the way one reacts to a stimulus, a concept that is significant in the understanding of _____ disorders. Bandura's studies of modeling, in which a person learns by _____ others, also suggest that social _____ and cognitive factor influence behavior. At the same time, biological principles seem to influence what we learn, as in the example that people are more inclined or _____ to fear snakes than to fear flowers. Blind sight and _____ _____ both support the idea that unconscious or unaware processes affect behavior. The Stroop Color test is one method used to study this processing.

Cognitive science; information; relationships; control; depression; observing; context; prepared; implicit memory

_____, as illustrated by fear and the fight or _____ response, also influence behavior. They seem to have an evolutionary function because they appear to be _____. _____ refer to emotional states that last a while, and _____ refers to the emotional tone of an action at a particular time. _____ is a known factor in heart disease, another indication that _____ can affect physical functioning. Suppressing emotions may be involved in psychological disorders, and emotions may contribute to or even _____ disorders. Emotional _____ may interfere with thinking and behavior in disorders.

Emotions; flight; adaptive; Moods; affect; Anger; emotions; define; dysregulation

Psychological disorders are also affected by social, cultural, and _____ influences. Research shows that one's social _____ are related to one's health and life span. In many cultures, induced fright disorders can even cause _____. A person's _____ can influence the form and content of a disorder, e.g., in anxiety or _____, but it does not cause the disorder.

interpersonal; relationships; death; gender; eating

Psychological disorders are occurring more/less than ever in developing countries, where mental health care is often inadequate. _____ and social factors are involved in both the causation and _____ of psychological disorders. _____ factors over the course of a life time must also be considered with psychopathology, as _____ life span developmental view suggests. The principle of _____ suggests that there can be more than one path to a particular disorder, perhaps involving the interaction of biological, social, emotional, behavioral, and other factors. This is the multidimensional _____ model emphasized in the text title. Besides studying those who develop disorders, researchers are now looking at people, such as "_____ children" who, do not develop the disorders in similar circumstances.

more; Cultural; maintenance; Developmental; Erikson's; equifinality; integrative; resilient

KEY WORDS

Practice defining the important concepts listed below and at the end of the text chapter. Follow the definition suggestions provided in the introduction to this Guide. Be precise and accurate, and check your work with the text. Add to the definition later as you encounter more information about the term. Whenever possible, include examples. Use only the space to the right of the word so that later you can cover either the word or the definition to use one to cue the other. Define additional important terms you'll find in the chapter.

1. affect

_____

_____

2. agonists

_____

_____

3. antagonists

_____

_____

4. autonomic nervous system

_____

_____

5. axon

_____

_____

6. benzodiazepine-GABA

_____

_____

7. central nervous system

_____

_____

8. diathesis-stress model

_____

_____

9. endocrine system

_____

_____

10. flight or fight response

_____

_____

11. hypothalamic-pituitary-adrenalcortical (HYPAC) axis

_____

_____

12. implicit memory

_____

_____

13. inverse agonists

_____

_____

14. learned helplessness

_____

_____

15. neurotransmitters

_____

_____

16. norepinephrine

_____

_____

17. peripheral nervous system

_____

_____

18. principle of equifinality

_____

_____

19. reciprocal gene-environment model

_____

_____

20. reuptake

_____

_____

21. serotonin

_____

_____

22. social learning

_____

_____

23. synaptic cleft

_____

_____

24. "tend-and-befriend"

_____

_____

25. vulnerability

_____

_____

SAMPLE QUESTIONS

As one of the later stages of your study for this chapter, you can assess your progress by taking a sample test. Don't make the mistake of studying just for these questions. They are merely a small sample of the many questions that could appear on an exam. An excellent way to help yourself is to generate your own questions and answers. This will help you focus on important concepts, make better distinctions among similar ideas, practice writing responses, and engaging the material in general. Try them on your friends in your study group.

Multiple Choice Questions

1. The part of the nervous system that is activated in times of stress is the _____ nervous system.
    a. parasympathetic
    b. somatic
    c. sympathetic
    d. central

2. Which of the following is an incorrect combination of neurotransmitter and what it affects?
    a. norepinephrine; emergency reactions
    b. serotonin; moderation and regulation of behavior
    c. benzodiazepine and GABA; general anxiety
    d. dopamine; depression

3. Obsessive-compulsive disorder appears to be linked to the area of the brain called the _____. The implications of this finding are that_____.
    a. orbital frontal cortex; although the disorder is related to a particular brain circuit, the causes of the disorder are not necessarily completely biological
    b. orbital frontal cortex; the disorder is probably due only to brain damage in this area
    c. occipital lobe; although the disorder is related to a particular brain circuit, the disorder causes the abnormalities in the brain
    d. occipital lobe; the disorder is most likely due to purely psychological causes

4. Research indicates that the relationship between psychological treatment and brain circuits is such that
    a. psychological treatment works regardless of the brain circuit activity.
    b. psychological treatment can alter brain circuits.
    c. brain circuit activity alone determines the response to psychological treatment.
    d. psychological treatment is not effective due to the changes in the brain caused by mental disorders.

5. According to studies with monkeys, a sense of control can influence
    a. responses to neurotransmitters.
    b. self-esteem.
    c. egotism.
    d. degree of yoking.

6. Psychological conditioning involves
    a. learning a relationship between two events.
    b. salivating to a metronome.
    c. adding body and manageability to one's hair.
    d. learning to salivate to food.

7. Seligman's main contribution to psychology was the concept of _____; Bandura's was the notion of _____.
   a. modeling, observational learning
   b. observational learning, learned helplessness
   c. learned helplessness, modeling
   d. modeling, learned helplessness

8. According to the principle of prepared learning, humans
   a. are genetically predisposed to know certain things.
   b. inherit a capacity to learn certain things that are beneficial to the survival of the species.
   c. ready to learn to read by the age of six.
   d. are unable to learn the same things that rats learn.

9. The "fight or flight" response refers to
   a. an Air Force principle for dealing with conflict.
   b. a typical response to learned helplessness.
   c. a technique used in Ellis' rational-emotive therapy.
   d. an alarm reaction in the face of adverse circumstances.

10. The limbic system, which includes the hippocampus, gyrus, septum, and amygdala, is responsible for
    a. regulation of emotional experience.
    b. the ability to learn.
    c. control of impulses.
    d. all of the above

11. The endocrine system is important because it
    a. produces the neurotransmitters that determine bodily growth.
    b. produces hormones that are implicated in some psychological problems.
    c. produces the hormones that directly cause some psychological disorders.
    d. is the main controller of the entire nervous system.

12. Judy's blood-injury-injection phobia described in the text was likely caused by
    a. a biological predisposition.
    b. behavioral influences.
    c. social influences.
    d. all of the above

13. A one-dimensional causal model
    a. uses only one perspective, such as behaviorism, to treat a disorder.
    b. attributes a disorder to a single cause.
    c. notes that many paths lead to the same disorder.
    d. looks at only one disorder at a time.

14. Most behavioral geneticists think that psychological disorders are influenced by
    a. single genes.
    b. several different genes, each of which determines the severity of the disorder.
    c. many genes, each of which exerts only a small effect.
    d. no genes in particular.

15. Which of the following is true?
    a. If either a diathesis or a stress is present, a disorder will develop.
    b. If both a diathesis and stress are present, a disorder will develop.
    c. The smaller the diathesis, the greater the stress needs to be to produce a disorder.
    d. The larger the diathesis, the greater the stress needs to be to produce a disorder.

16. Which part of the brain gives humans the capacity to think, plan, and reason?
    a. cerebellum
    b. thalamus
    c. limbic system
    d. cerebral cortex

17. This lobe is the part of the brain that is used for reasoning and relating to the world as humans.
    a. cerebral
    b. temporal
    c. limbic
    d. parietal
    e. frontal

18. Reuptake refers to
    a. a neurotransmitter being released at the synaptic cleft.
    b. a neuron reabsorbing a neurotransmitter after it is released.
    c. a neurotransmitter attaching to a receptor cell.
    d. a neurotransmitter being broken down at the synaptic cleft.

19. A circuit of this system controls alarm reactions:
    a. noradrenergic
    b. dopamine
    c. 5-HT
    d. GABA
    e. serotonin

20. Which of the following could result in learned helplessness?
    a. being in a stressful situation one cannot control
    b. being in a stressful situation and refusing to control it
    c. being in control and then encountering stressors
    d. perceiving control when none is present
    e. none of the above

21. While many fears are learned, some are more easily learned, or more prepared to be learned than others. The most likely fear-prepared stimulus below would be
    a. rocks.
    b. guns.
    c. spiders.
    d. electrical outlets.
    e. flowers.

22. Which of the following is a problem with the "snap-shot" approach to psychological disorders?
    a. It leads to poor prognosis.
    b. It fails to account for change over time.
    c. Faulty perceptions lead to improper diagnoses.
    d. It neglects certain symptoms.
    e. It temporarily blinds the patient.

23. Which of the following accurately illustrates the reciprocal gene-environment model of interaction?
    a. Due to her phobia of cats, May avoids them.
    b. Joan knows her father is an alcoholic, so she avoids alcohol.
    c. Tony has a predisposition to develop a blood-injury phobia, and he leads a cautious lifestyle.
    d. George has a vulnerability to depression, and he frequently rents sad movies on video.
    e. none of the above

24. We could change the familiar child's song from "Are You Sleeping?" to "What Is Your _____ Doing?" (But we wouldn't do that.)
    a. Sleep System
    b. Pons
    c. Medulla
    d. Reticular Activating System
    e. Serotonin Reuptake System

25. Equifinality refers to the idea that
    a. different paths may lead to the same outcome.
    b. a psychological disorder is caused by more than one factor.
    c. a disorder will have a different prognosis, depending on the individual.
    d. the same disorder can have multiple symptoms.

True or False Questions

26. Most scientists adopt a one-dimensional model of abnormal behavior, attributing each disorder to a single cause.

TRUE or FALSE

27. Heredity is not destiny. Our genetic make-up can be viewed as a set of boundaries. Although genes set the limits, environmental influences can determine how close we get to those limits.

    TRUE or FALSE

28. Recent cross-fostering studies have shown that environment and nurturing can affect behavior and personality more than previously expected.

    TRUE or FALSE

29. Research on neurotransmitters focuses on changes in neurotransmitter levels; however, neurotransmitters do not cause behavior.

    TRUE or FALSE

30. Cognitive science is the field that is concerned with human acquisition and processing of information.

    TRUE or FALSE

31. Implicit memory and blind sight are two examples of how unconscious cognitive processes may affect memory or behavior.

    TRUE or FALSE

32. Affect is an action-tendency, meaning that it is a feeling state caused by an external threat that elicits a physiological response.

    TRUE or FALSE

33. The more friends you have, the less likely you are to die.

    TRUE or FALSE

34. Brain circuits are currents of neurotransmitters throughout the body.

    TRUE or FALSE

35. Many different influences contribute to the development of psychological disorders.

    TRUE or FALSE

36. A person's gender can cause certain psychological disorders.

    TRUE or FALSE

37. Though chemically inert, placebos can cause changes in the brain.

    TRUE or FALSE

Essay Questions

38. Compare and contrast the diathesis-stress and reciprocal gene-environment models of interaction.

39. Describe the major structures of the human nervous system, noting the function of all relevant divisions.

40. Briefly describe the structure of the brain, noting the general functions of major areas.

41. Discuss the animal research that points to an interaction between environmental factors and brain activity.

42. Discuss social and interpersonal factors affecting vulnerability and resistance to psychopathology.

43. Define the concept "tend-and-befriend".

HOW WELL DID YOU DO?

Less than 60%	Did you try the sample test before really studying the chapter? You can improve if you increase your efforts and use the SQ4R method.
60-80%	Restudy and rewrite, especially the weak areas; discuss problem areas with study partners.
Over 80%	You're on the right track; continue as you are; focus on trouble areas with study group.
Over 95%	Nice job, especially if you know the whole chapter this well. Be sure to reward your behavior, help others in your study group (they'll help you on your weak chapters), and don't forget to review.

THINKING ALLOWED

Chapter 2 Activities

Select some of your own behaviors or those of your friends and try to interpret them according to several different models of behavior (cognitive, biological, etc.). Can you account for the same patterns using an integrative approach?

Monitor and take special note of the activation of your own flight or fight system for the next two weeks. What sets it off, and how do you handle it? Or are you a "stew or chew" person?

List your own personal life factors that might increase or decrease your vulnerability to psychological disorders.

In a letter to your family or a friend, describe some of the concepts you have learned in this chapter. Have there been any surprises, or any findings that apply to them? What might you do to try to improve someone else's physical or psychological well-being?

INTERNET RESOURCES

<u>Neurosciences on the Internet</u>

This site has links to other neuroscience related web pages; also contains information on the biological basis of psychiatric disorders such as Attention Deficit Disorder, Panic Anxiety Disorder, and Alzheimer's Disease.

http://www.neuroguide.com/

<u>Neuropsychology Central</u>

Links to online sources on neuropsychological assessment, treatments, software, and newsgroups just to name a few.

http://www.neuropsychologycentral.com/

Solutions

KEY WORDS

1. (62)	10. (61)	19. (41)
2. (51)	11. (50)	20. (50)
3. (51)	12. (60)	21. (51)
4. (48)	13. (51)	22. (59)
5. (45)	14. (58)	23. (45)
6. (52)	15. (45)	24. (65)
7. (44)	16. (53)	25. (40)
8. (40)	17. (48)	
9. (48)	18. (68)	

SAMPLE QUESTIONS

Multiple Choice Questions

1. C, 48	10. D, 46-48	19. A, 53
2. D, 51-53	11. B, 48-50	20. A, 58-59
3. A, 54	12. D, 34-36	21. C, 59-60
4. B, 55	13. B, 34	22. B, 67-68
5. A, 56	14. C, 39	23. D, 41
6. A, 57-58	15. C, 40-41	24. D, 46
7. C, 58-59	16. D, 46-48	25. A, 68
8. B, 59-60	17. E, 48	
9. C, 61	18. B, 50	

True or False Questions

26. F, 34
27. T, 37-38
28. T, 64-67
29. T, 50
30. T, 57
31. T, 60

32. F, 62, This is true of emotion, not affect. Be careful.
33. F, 66-67, The chance you will die is 100%. Sorry. Psychological and social factors may prolong your life, however.
34. F, 50

35. T, 34
36. F, 65
37. T, 69

Essay Questions

38. You should define both diathesis and stress and describe how both are necessary for a behavior to be exhibited. Also, note that, according to the reciprocal gene-environment model, the diathesis increases the likelihood that the stressor will be encountered. (See textbook pages 40-41.)

39. The divisions you should include are the central and peripheral systems. Note that the central system consists of the brain and spinal cord. Also, discuss the functions of the autonomic, somatic, sympathetic, and parasympathetic nervous systems. (See textbook pages 44-48).

40. For this essay, be sure to know the lobes of the brain, the hemispheres, and the functions of the brain stem, midbrain, and forebrain. Note which structures are involved in emotion, motor behavior, and other major functions. (See textbook pages 45-48.)

41. Be sure to discuss Insel's yoking experiment with monkeys and Greenough's study of "couch potato" rats. Note how the differences in environment, such as sense of control or degree of complexity, influenced responses to neurotransmitters or brain structure. (See textbook pages 46-47.)

42. Include evidence that culture, upbringing, gender may be associated with different types and degrees of psychological and physical disorders, even death. Emphasize the importance of relationships, especially in the elderly. (See textbook pages 64-67.)

43. New findings on gender specific responses to stress: females respond to stress by protecting and nurturing their young and forming alliances with larger social groups. (See textbook page 65.)

CHAPTER **3**

CLINICAL ASSESSMENT, DIAGNOSIS, AND RESEARCH METHODS

LEARNING OBJECTIVES

1. Describe the nature and function of clinical assessment and the concepts that determine the value of assessment.

2. Describe the nature and purpose of each of the principal methods of clinical assessment.

3. Explain the nature and purposes of psychiatric diagnosis and how the DSM is used to help therapists and counselors make an accurate psychiatric diagnosis.

4. Describe the basic components of research in psychopathology.

5. Explain the importance of ethical principles in the research process.

6. Compare and contrast different research designs, including the types of questions that are appropriate and inappropriate for each.

7. Explain the advantages and disadvantages of family, adoption, twin, genetic linkage, and association studies.

8. Explain how studying behavior over time and across cultures fits within the research design and the research process more generally.

CHAPTER SUMMARY

Become familiar with this summary as part of your survey and preparation before you read the text chapter the first time. Afterward, continue to refer to it as you study the chapter. Cover the answers and try to fill them in mentally. Don't write them in because if the answers are there, they won't help you practice actively. Keep notes on additional chapter detail not included in this summary because this material is only a sample. Practice summarizing chapter sections yourself in your own words, and use all this material as part of your frequent reviews.

Clinical _____ refers to an evaluation of the psychological, biological, and social factors in the issues a client _____. _____ refers to determining whether the client's behavior meets the criteria for a particular psychological disorder, as described in the _____, or DSM-IV.

assessment; presents; Diagnosis; Diagnostic and Statistical Manual of Mental Disorders, 4th Edition

Clinical assessment begins by asking the client to describe why s/he came to the office. _____ refers to the consistency of a measurement. Whether different therapists give the same diagnosis for the same symptoms refers to _____ reliability. Achieving comparable results on different occasions refers to _____-_____ reliability. _____ is defined as how well a technique measures what it claims to measure. This could include _____ validity and predictive validity. Establishing consistent administration and scoring procedures for a measure is called _____. Standardization can also involve determining norms for a set of measurements to increase the consistency of the measurements. Norms should/should not be based on a population similar to the individual being evaluated. Methods used in clinical assessment include clinical interviews, _____ _____ exams, _____ observation, psychological tests, and possibly physical examination.

Reliability; inter-rater; test-retest; Validity; concurrent or descriptive; standardization; should; mental status; behavioral

The clinical _____ is a conversation used to gather information about present and past behavior and attitudes of the client, and usually begins with a discussion of the problem that led the individual to seek treatment. The mental status exam involves systematic _____ of behavior. Some observations assess for the presences of _____, which are distorted beliefs or views of reality and can include delusions of _____, persecution, or reference. _____, which involve seeing or hearing things that are not real, may also be noted. Also assessed by the therapist would be _____ (the overriding emotion of the person), _____ (the emotional expression that accompanies an action), _____ (awareness of surroundings and being oriented to time, place and _____), and intellectual functioning. Throughout the clinical interview, the clinician should build _____ and assure the client about the confidentiality of the interview.

interview; observations; delusions; grandeur; Hallucinations; mood; affect; sensorium; identity; trust

In the past, many clinical interviews were _____, with no specified format to ensure that all relevant topics are discussed. The *Anxiety Disorders Interview Schedule for DSM-IV* (ADIS-IV) is an example of unstructured/semi-structured/structured interviews. The clinician should also make sure the client has had a recent _____ _____, to identify or rule out medical conditions or drug use that may co-exist or even _____ psychological problems.

unstructured; semi- structured; physical exam; cause

_____ assessment involves a formal assessment of behavior in specific contexts. The goal is to identify factors that influence _____ behaviors. Attention is given to behavior, its antecedents, and its _____. Formal observations use operational definitions, identifying behaviors that are observable and _____. Self-monitoring involves having one observe one's own behavior. Checklists and _____ scales may also be used. The way observations themselves affect behavior, called _____, can be a problem in behavioral assessment, and all assessment.

Behavioral; target; consequences; measurable; rating; reactivity

Formal psychological testing may involve projective tests, personality inventories, intelligence testing, and neuropsychological examinations. The *Rorschach Inkblot Test and the Thematic Apperception Test* are _____ tests, with conclusions based on responses to _____ stimuli. _____ and validity of the Rorschach were addressed by Exner, who developed a standardized version of the test called the _____ _____. Unfortunately, projective tests are widely used despite poor _____.

projective; ambiguous; Reliability; comprehensive system; validity

The pattern of responses to _____ inventories, such as the MMPI, are compared to the response pattern of others displaying psychological disorders. Many studies show that disorders can be assessed reliably and validly by the MMPI, but only if applied in _____ ways. Intelligence tests, developed by Binet, Terman, Wechsler, and others, yield IQ, or _____, scores. _____ IQ scores compare performance of people of the same age. _____ tests include the *Bender Visual-Motor Gestalt Test, the Luria-Nebraska Neuropsychological Battery*, and the Halstead-Reitan Neuropsychological Battery, which can be used to identify _____ dysfunction by observation of performance on standardized tasks.

personality; standardized; intelligence quotient; Deviation; Neuropsychological; brain

Current technologies, called _____ techniques, can produce images of the structures and functions of living brains. CAT scans use x-rays and MRIs use magnetic fields to locate abnormalities in brain _____. PET scans can reveal brain _____ such as oxygen and glucose _____ activity that might be associated with damage or psychological disorder. The newer _____-related MRI allows immediate views of brain reactions to events.

neuroimaging; structure; functioning; metabolism; event

_____ assessment involves measuring activity in the body related to psychological events. For example, brain waves, which reflect the electrical activity level of the brain, are measured with an _____. Different brain wave patterns are associated with differing levels of awareness and _____. Other psychophysiological measures include respiration, heart rate, sexual arousal, and _____ responding (aka GSR) which can help measure anxiety and stress.

Psychophysiological; EEG; sleep; electrodermal

Establishing the likely future course, or _____ for a disorder, is often based on comparisons to others with a similar disorder. Classification of disorders, called _____ in psychopathology, allows the identification of specific psychological disorders, or a _____. The categorical approach to psychopathology classification assumes that disorders are distinct and do not overlap. The _____ approach identifies a disorder as a pattern of attributes varying in severity. The _____ approach combines the categorical and dimensional approaches, by noting how well an individual case fits into the category of a disorder. A diagnostic system needs to be _____, so that any two or more psychologists will give the same diagnosis to the same individual case. Validity is also important in establishing that the diagnosis is consistent and/or _____.

prognosis; nosology; diagnosis; dimensional; prototypical; reliable; predictive

The _____-_____ format, which is retained in DSM-IV, allowed clinicians to note various factors related to the diagnosis. These features, plus additional recognition of _____ factors in DSM-IV, have increased/decreased worldwide acceptance of the DSM. DSM-IV was developed on the basis of more data about the disorders and with the recognition that _____ and environmental factors are involved in all disorders.

multi-axial; cultural; increased; biological

A continuing problem with the classification systems is that they still show blurred distinction across some categories. Also, increasing specificity and reliability may interfere with _____. Identification of some disorders may be influenced by _____, rather than scientific, factors. Through _____, an individual is identified with a particular disorder. The labeled person might then be _____ or otherwise discriminated against. Issues involved in creating new categories include risks and _____ to the individuals displaying the new disorder and the _____ of the category.

validity; historical; labeling; isolated; benefits; validity

Human behavior can be difficult to study due to its _____ and the inability to know the minds of people. Understanding research is important for those who do research and for others who need to know how to use research findings wisely. Research begins with a(n) _____, or educated guess about what to expect. The research _____ outlines how the hypothesis will be tested, based on _____ variables (the phenomena that are observed, measured, and expected to change) and _____ variables (the phenomena that are believed to influence the dependent variable). _____ validity, or whether the independent variable actually changed the dependent variable, and _____ _____, or whether the results related to situations other than the actual study, must also be considered.

complexity; hypothesis; design; dependent; independent; Internal; external validity

Hypotheses, which are supported or disproved by data, are used by psychologists to organize their study of abnormal behavior. Hypotheses should be unambiguous and _____, which refers to the ability of a hypothesis to be confirmed or disconfirmed. A _____ is a factor in a research study that prevents one from claiming that the independent variable influenced the dependent variable, and reduces internal validity. Strategies to improve internal validity include the use of _____ groups (groups that differ from the experimental group only in exposure to the independent variable), _____ (assigning people randomly to different research groups), and analogue models (representation in a controlled setting of the phenomena of interest). _____, relating to external validity, is the degree to which the results of a research study can be applied to different people in different circumstances. Internal and external validity are often <u>directly/inversely</u> related.

testable; confound; control; randomization; Generalizability; inversely

_____ refers to mathematics that is concerned with gathering, analyzing, and interpreting data from research. Statistical _____ means that the probability of getting the observed effect by chance is small. _____ _____ refers to whether a treatment is effective enough to be worthwhile and deals with the _____ (how large the difference made by the treatment is); thus, statistical significance and clinical significance <u>are/are not</u> always equivalent. Wolf has noted the importance of _____ validity, which is how effective the treatment is according to the client or the client's relatives and friends.

Statistics; significance; Clinical significance; effect size; are not; social

The belief that the participants in a study are homogeneous is the patient _____ myth. In treatment, the average results of a group of patients may not reflect the results on particular clients. The _____ _____ method focuses on the intense study of a few individuals who exhibit signs of the disorder of interest. However, this method of inquiry does not attempt to ensure internal validity, it can contain many

_____ variables, and it is subject to inaccurate interpretation due to _____. Case studies are important in the history of psychology, and were used by Freud, Wolpe, and Masters and Johnson. As we have learned more about disorders, psychologists have relied <u>more/less</u> on the case study method. Unfortunately, people are often more influenced by dramatic stories than by _____ _____.

uniformity; case study; confounding; coincidences; less; scientific research

A second method of research is the _____ method, which involves determining whether two variables are related; it does not involve manipulation of variables. Establishing a correlation <u>does/does not</u> prove causation. The _____ issue concerns the fact that we cannot know whether one variable caused the other or if the second variable led to the first. Alternatively, both correlated variables could be caused by a _____ variable. Computed as a number between +1.00 and -1.00, a correlation coefficient tells the _____ of a relationship, while the sign indicates its _____. A correlation of 0.00 indicates no relationship, a correlation of +1.00 a perfect positive relationship, and a correlation of ___ a perfect negative relationship. A positive correlation means that when one variable increases, the other does also. A negative correlation means that if one variable increases the other _____.

correlation; does not; directionality; third; strength; direction; -1.00; decreases

_____ research, which is like detective work, studies the incidence, distribution, and consequences of a problem by tracking a large number of people. _____ refers to the number of new cases in a period of time; _____ refers to the number of people with a disorder at any one time. This type of research was used to determine that one schizophrenia-like disorder was due to inadequate _____ and to discover how the AIDS virus is spread.

Epidemiological; Incidence; prevalence; nutrition

Experimental research involves the manipulation of a(n) _____ variable and the observation of the effects on the _____ variable(s). Group experimental designs compare treated groups with otherwise equivalent non-treated groups, referred to as _____ groups, to determine whether the treatment was effective. Scientists use _____ control groups, who are given inactive treatments, such as sugar pills in medication research, to account for placebo effects, which are behavior changes due to the patient's _____ that treatment will be effective. In a _____-_____ control study, both the therapist and the patient are unaware whether the patient is receiving the placebo or actual treatment. This design helps to prevent bias based on the therapist's commitment to the treatment, which is called an _____ effect. _____ treatment research allows researchers to assess how well one treatment works compared to other treatments. Two factors that need to be examined are the treatment _____, or the mechanisms that cause the behavior change, and the treatment _____, or the results of the treatment. Randomization, which is the random assignment of individuals to treatment groups, is used to prevent the problem of having groups that _____ significantly prior to treatment.

independent; dependent; control; placebo; expectation; double-blind; allegiance; Comparative; process; outcome; differ

Single-case _____ designs, such as those used by B.F. Skinner, involve the systematic study of an individual in different experimental conditions, with the use of strategies to eliminate confounds and improve _____ validity. These strategies include _____ measurement, (observing the individual in the same condition a number of times to assess the degree of change with different interventions, the variability and the _____ or direction of change), _____ design (removing and reintroducing a treatment to determine whether it caused the observed change), and _____ baselines (starting a treatment at different times or in different settings to determine its effectiveness). Multiple baseline strategies may be employed when withdrawal designs cannot be used due to permanent _____ caused by the treatment or possible adverse effects of _____ an effective treatment.

experimental; internal; repeated; trend; withdrawal, multiple; changes; removing

Behavioral geneticists attempt to determine the role of _____ in its interaction with experience to influence behavior. The human _____ project, begun in 1990, is an attempt to map all of the genes on all the 46 human chromosomes. Another way to study genetics is through _____ studies, which involve determining the rate of a disorder in the family members of an individual (proband) with that disorder. This method does/does not account for similarities that may be due to the environment. Because they involve studying the relatives of an individual with a disorder who were raised in different family settings, _____ studies are one way to rule out environmental influences. Twin studies can be even more informative because identical twins share all genetic material, and thus _____ rates can be assessed. To locate a defective gene, _____ _____ analysis compares the occurrence of a disorder in a family with related genetic _____, which are characteristics whose genetic location is known; it is assumed the gene influencing the disorder is located nearby. It is likely/unlikely that complex disorders are caused by single genes, so _____ studies compare groups of people with and without the disorder to help locate weakly associated genes.

genetics; genome; family; does not; adoption; heritability; genetic linkage; markers; unlikely; association

Understanding changes in behavior over time can yield useful information about the treatment and _____ of a disorder. _____ research involves studying risk factors for developing problems (pre-intervention research), treatment intervention to prevent problems (prevention _____ research), and structural issues such as legislation that could help prevention efforts (prevention _____ _____research). _____-_____ designs study several age groups in a population simultaneously. These designs are subject to _____ effects, which are differences between age groups due to the unique experiences of a group of people, such as exposure to anti-drug campaigns. _____ designs, which are more difficult to use, allow the researcher to study the development of a disorder over time. These involve following a group of people over time and assessing them at various ages. One problem with these designs is the _____-_____ effect, which is the problem of generalizing results to a group of people who may have had different experiences due to their age. _____ designs integrate both of these techniques by repeatedly studying several different age groups at various times.

course; Prevention; intervention; service systems; Cross-sectional; cohort; Longitudinal; cross-generational; Sequential

Understanding the differences in psychopathology across _____ is also important, and can give information about disorders. However, the study of cultural differences in psychopathology can be easy/difficult because people can/cannot be randomly assigned to cultures. Cultures may define, react to, or _____ mental disorders in different ways, and use different _____ techniques based on cultural values.

cultures; difficult; cannot; tolerate; treatment

The different methods of doing research can complement each other in a well-designed program of research, such as that done by Patterson and his colleagues in the study of childhood _____. Duplication of research results, or _____ can strengthen confidence in the results. Multi-center collaborative studies are currently required more often by grant funding agencies, to show treatment effects are not limited to one set of clients or _____. Researchers must also be sensitive to research _____, which includes the issues of withholding treatment, informed consent, full disclosure of the nature of the research, confidentiality, and protection of the participant from _____ and physical harm. True _____ _____ can be difficult to obtain if the research participant is not cognitively able to comprehend the purpose of the research or feels coerced into participation. Methods to ensure proper ethical behavior include the use of research _____ _____ and adherence to the American Psychological Association's *Ethical Principles of Psychologists*, or other such guidelines when doing research.

aggression; replication; therapists; ethics; psychological; informed consent; review boards

KEY WORDS

Practice defining the important concepts listed below and at the end of the text chapter. Follow the definition suggestions provided in the introduction to this Guide. Be precise and accurate, and check your work with the text. Add to the definition later as you encounter more information about the term. Whenever possible, include examples. Use only the space to the right of the word so that later you can cover either the word or the definition to use one to cue the other. Define additional important terms you'll find in the chapter.

1. adoption studies

    _____

    _____

2. allegiance effect

    _____

    _____

3. analog models

    _____

    _____

4. behavioral assessment

    _____

    _____

5. case study method

    _____

    _____

6. classical categorical approach

    _____

    _____

7. clinical assessment

    _____

    _____

8. clinical significance

    _____

    _____

9. cohort

_____

_____

10. confound

_____

_____

11. construct validity

_____

_____

12. content validity

_____

_____

13. control group

_____

_____

14. correlation

_____

_____

15. criterion (predictive) validity

_____

_____

16. cross-sectional design

_____

_____

17. diagnosis

_____

_____

18. dependent variable

_____

_____

19. dimensional approach

_____

_____

20. epidemiology

_____

_____

21. experiment

_____

_____

22. external validity

_____

_____

23. genotypes

_____

_____

24. hypothesis

_____

_____

25. incidence

_____

_____

26. independent variable

_____

_____

27. informed consent

_____

_____

28. internal validity

_____

_____

29. labeling

_____

_____

30. longitudinal design

_____

_____

31. mental status exam

_____

_____

32. neuroimaging

_____

_____

33. neuropsychological tests

_____

_____

34. nosology

_____

_____

35. operational definition

_____

_____

36. personality inventories

_____

_____

37. phenotypes

_____

_____

38. placebo effect

_____

_____

39. prevalence

_____

_____

40. projective tests

_____

_____

41. prototypical approach

_____

_____

42. psychophysiological assessment

_____

_____

43. randomization

_____

_____

44. reliability

_____

_____

45. standardization

_____

_____

46. twin studies

_____

_____

SAMPLE QUESTIONS

As one of the later stages of your study for this chapter, you can assess your progress by taking a sample test. Don't make the mistake of studying just for these questions. They are merely a small sample of the many questions that could appear on an exam. An excellent way to help yourself is to generate your own questions and answers. This will help you focus on important concepts, make better distinctions among similar ideas, practice writing responses, and engaging the material in general. Try them on your friends in your study group.

Multiple Choice Questions

1. The diagnostic report states "The patient was oriented to time and space, showed appropriate affect, and could do simple calculations. Short and long-term memory were intact." Someone has done
    a. a mental status exam.
    b. psychophysiological testing.
    c. projective testing.
    d. reliability evaluation.

2. You are deciding whether to purchase a new assessment measure your staff will use in your psychology clinic. The factor(s) you should consider include
    a. cost and ease of administration.
    b. its reliability.
    c. its validity.
    d. its standardization.
    e. all of the above

3. The Mental Status Exam does not directly involve
    a. observing a person's appearance.
    b. noting the presence of delusions, hallucinations, or ideas of reference.
    c. determining whether the condition is due to a medical problem.
    d. determining mood and affect.

4. One advantage of a formal observation, as compared to an informal observation, is that
   a. formal observations are easier to make.
   b. formal observations rarely require the use of naturalistic settings.
   c. formal observations are more reliable, due to the focus on behaviors that are both observable and measurable.
   d. formal observations give more information about an individual.

5. On the MMPI, results are assessed according to
   a. how the pattern of answers corresponds to that of people diagnosed with a specific disorder.
   b. how often the individual refers to specific ideas, such as aggression or sexuality.
   c. the degree of emotionality associated with results.
   d. how often an individual responds to questions that reflect aggression or some other concept.
   e. the responder's personality and appearance.

6. Binet, in an attempt to predict which children would succeed in school, developed
   a. a sentence completion test.
   b. an intelligence test, based on an intelligence quotient.
   c. an intelligence test, based on deviation IQS.
   d. achievement testing.
   e. personality inventories

7. Marguerite is tested for brain damage. Although her test results indicate that she has no brain damage, in reality, she has a brain tumor. Her test results indicate a _____, which is a problem because
   a. false positive; she will not get the treatment she needs.
   b. false positive; she may end up paying for costly treatment that is not necessary.
   c. false negative; she will not get the treatment she needs.
   d. false negative; she may end up paying for costly treatment that is not necessary.

8. The CAT scan neuroimaging technique
   a. uses X-rays to portray brain structures.
   b. uses magnetic fields to portray brain structures.
   c. follows tracer elements in the nervous system.
   d. uses magnetic fields to portray brain functions.
   e. studies brains of domestic felines.

9. This instrument measures brain wave activity, by recording the electrical activity of the brain.
   a. CAT scan
   b. MRI
   c. EEG
   d. SPECT

10. A prognosis is based primarily upon
    a. information about the course of the disorder in other individuals.
    b. whether the symptoms an individual exhibits correspond to the DSM-IV category for a particular disorder.
    c. the treatment options available to the patient.
    d. the client's desire to reform.

11. The classical and dimensional approaches to nosology differ in that
    a. the classical approach uses categories and the dimensional approach uses prototypes.
    b. the classical approach uses prototypes and the dimensional approach uses profiles.
    c. the classical approach diagnoses based on the presence of symptoms and the dimensional approach notes the degree of severity of symptoms.
    d. the classical approach places individuals in categories; the dimensional approach places symptoms in categories.

12. According to the textbook, DSM-IV is based on the
    a. classical system of nosology.
    b. dimensional system of nosology.
    c. categorical system of nosology.
    d. prototypical system of nosology.

13. Psychophysiological assessment techniques are used to
    a. determine the physiological causes of psychological disorders.
    b. measure bodily changes, such as heart rate and anxiety, that are associated with psychological processes.
    c. analyze the functioning of the brain to determine if brain damage or abnormalities contribute to psychological disorders.
    d. ensure that both the body and the mind respond appropriately to stress.

14. As a clinician, you begin your initial assessment interviews by
    a. asking broad, open-ended questions.
    b. asking specific questions related to the diagnosis.
    c. assessing neurological development.
    d. giving clients diagnostic tests.
    e. assuming a disorder is present.

15. The purpose of standardization is
    a. to make a diagnosis predictive.
    b. to increase the scores on a test.
    c. to determine whether a technique is appropriate.
    d. to make techniques consistent and comparable.
    e. to increase measurement subjectivity.

16. The purpose of structured and semi-structured interviews is
    a. to collect necessary information in a standard way to allow for comparison with similar individuals.
    b. to initiate treatment.
    c. to increase confidentiality.
    d. to help develop the therapist/client relationship.

17. You would expect a remorseless, seasoned criminal to score highly on which scale of the MMPI?
    a. paranoia
    b. psychopathic deviation
    c. psychasthenia
    d. social introversion
    e. oregano

18. A false positive result on your neuropsychological test is problematic because
    a. damage that requires treatment is more likely to be overlooked.
    b. no neurological damage may be actually present.
    c. it may call for unnecessary and expensive further testing.
    d. it may cause undue stress.
    e. all but a

19. If you wished to look for possible damage in a client's brain, which technique would be appropriate?
    a. neuropsychological testing
    b. PET scan
    c. autopsy
    d. MRI
    e. all of these

20. If using the diagnosis "depressed" allows you as a clinician to determine an effective treatment and give an accurate prognosis, the diagnosis has
    a. reliability.
    b. criterion validity.
    c. construct validity.
    d. content validity.
    e. concurrent validity.

21. Comorbidity refers to
    a. a disorder that manifests itself in several ways.
    b. the same disorder being diagnosed for two members of a family.
    c. more than one disorder diagnosed for the same individual.
    d. the severity of a particular disorder.
    e. disorders that can cause death.

22. Emily has been evaluated by three different professionals, each of whom offers a different diagnosis. She wonders whether the field has any standards because their judgments obviously lack
    a. statistical significance.
    b. clinical utility.
    c. reliability.
    d. clinical significance.
    e. statistical utility.

23. We can use a computer to score polygraph tracings to eliminate human judgment and error and, thus, increase _____. To call this system a "lie detector" is a question of _____.
    a. validity; ethics
    b. validity; standardization
    c. sensitivity; reliability
    d. reliability; validity

24. When developing an hypothesis, one important consideration is
    a. whether or not it is correct.
    b. testability.
    c. internal validity.
    d. external validity.

25. Confounds, or factors that make it difficult to interpret accurately the results of a study, directly affect
    a. reliability.
    b. external validity.
    c. internal validity.
    d. whether the results are published.

26. Shirley, a researcher, is interested in studying fathers' affection for their children. She randomly assigns a hundred men to two groups, a control group and an experimental group. She gives each man a doll to play with, and measures how affectionate they are toward the doll. The experimental group is told that the doll represents their child, but this is not mentioned to the control group. What might be a problem with Shirley's study?
    a. The internal validity may be poor, due to the use of randomization.
    b. The external validity may be poor, due to the use of a control group.
    c. The external validity may be poor, due to low generalizability.
    d. Nothing; this is a great study. Do it for your Master's thesis. Cite me.

27. Whenever Hilda smiles, the whole world smiles with her. If Hilda doesn't smile, the world doesn't smile. The correlation coefficient describing the relation between Hilda's smiles and the world's smiles is
    a. +1.00
    b. 0.00
    c. -1.00
    d. cannot be determined from this information.

CLINICAL ASSESSMENT, DIAGNOSIS, AND RESEARCH METHODS

28. The factor that distinguishes experimental research from other forms of research is
    a. the use of strategies to ensure external validity.
    b. that experimental research is done in a lab; all other research occurs in natural settings.
    c. that experimental research involves the manipulation of a dependent variable.
    d. none of the above

29. Which of the following demonstrates the placebo effect?
    a. Wanda is getting a drug to control her anxiety; therefore, her younger brother wants to get a drug.
    b. Eugene's therapist gave him an inactive medication, which she claimed would cure his insomnia. Eugene sleeps better when he takes this pill.
    c. Harvey is suffering from depression, but treatment is not available. Eventually, his depression dissipates.
    d. Hilary's therapist doesn't know how to cure her schizophrenia, but tries a variety of techniques, none of which works.

30. All of these are strategies used in single-case study designs to improve internal validity EXCEPT
    a. repeated measurement.
    b. withdrawal.
    c. control groups.
    d. multiple baselines

31. Genetic linkage analysis can be used to determine
    a. whether a disorder is caused by genetic factors.
    b. the location of the gene that causes a disorder.
    c. whether a disorder runs in a family.
    d. if linking genes can cure a disorder.

32. Sequential design refers to
    a. a type of repeated measurement.
    b. using time as an independent variable.
    c. a combination of longitudinal and cross-sectional designs.
    d. none of the above

33. The best research design to use is
    a. experimental design.
    b. correlational design.
    c. sequential design.
    d. the one that ethically and best leads to answers to the research question.

34. Which of the following is not an ethical concern related to subject participation in research studies?
    a. informed consent
    b. internal validity coercion
    c. protection from harm
    d. all are ethical issues

35. Dagwood discovered that the more intelligent a person is, the more books that person has at home. From this, Dagwood inferred that books make one more intelligent, so he rushed to the bookstore and spent hundreds of dollars on books for his home library in hopes of increasing his intelligence. Dagwood could have saved his money, because
    a. intelligence comes first, not the books.
    b. it would have been cheaper just to buy books at garage sales.
    c. based simply on a correlation between books and intelligence, it is impossible to determine directionality of causation.
    d. none of the above; excuse me while I run to the bookstore.

36. The withdrawal design should be avoided if
    a. treatment may have effects after it is ended.
    b. adverse effects may occur if treatment is suspended.
    c. treatment involves learning a technique, such as social skills.
    d. all of the above

37. Epidemiological research is useful because it
    a. directly identifies the causes of disorders.
    b. tells researchers the relationship between two variables.
    c. provides examples of cases when treatment was effective.
    d. tells the extent of a disorder in the population.

38. In an experiment with depressed patients, doctors gave some participants antidepressant pills while others received an identical pill with no active ingredients. Neither doctors nor patients knew who got what. If both groups improved substantially but equally, this is evidence
    a. the "active ingredient" has no effect.
    b. any effect of the antidepressant pill may be due to patients' expectations.
    c. any effect of the antidepressant pill may be due to the allegiance effect.
    d. all but c

39. The case study method involves
    a. generalizing the characteristics of a disorder, as evident in many similar cases.
    b. manipulation and measurement of variables.
    c. hypnosis and application of psychoanalytic theory.
    d. extensive study of one or more individuals who exhibit a particular disorder.
    e. studying a large number of people but, rather than observing them directly, merely studying their case notes.

40. A research study finds sports car drivers are more likely, per capita, to die in a car crash. The makers of a sedate family sedan take delight in referring to this fact in their ads. Why are they not justified in using this finding to claim their cars are safer?
    a. they probably did not give out sports and family cars randomly across safe and unsafe drivers.
    b. people who choose to buy sports cars may differ in their driving from those who choose to buy family cars.
    c. people who don't like to take risks may drive cautiously and buy cars they believe are safe.
    d. perhaps people who choose sports cars would be more likely to crash, no matter what they drove.
    e. all of the above

41. Your research finds a correlation between schizophrenia and income level in the population, with more people in poverty displaying the disorder. Which of the following represents the third variable issue?
    a. schizophrenic individuals may be less able to report their incomes accurately
    b. both schizophrenia and low income may be caused by the same gene
    c. schizophrenia may cause poverty, or poverty may cause schizophrenia
    d. the correlation may not be a direct one
    e. schizophrenia is only one of three causes

42. The directionality issue in correlation refers to
    a. whether two variables are correlated positively or negatively.
    b. which factor causes the other to occur.
    c. whether conclusions based on data are true or false.
    d. the strength of a correlation.
    e. whether the behaviors increase or decrease.

43. What type of research focuses on the results of an intervention?
    a. correlational
    b. treatment outcome
    c. treatment processes
    d. placebo control
    e. epidemiological

44. What is one complication in studies comparing identical twins?
    a. identical twins may influence each other more than fraternal twins do
    b. genetics may differ, even in identical twins
    c. the age of the twins is related to their similarities
    d. not all identical twins develop disorders at the same rate

45. Professor Y (not her real name) has become so convinced her treatment method is effective, she may not be objective in evaluating it. This problem is known as
    a. allegiance effect
    b. commitment effect
    c. attachment effect
    d. Parkinson's law
    e. Coles law

46. The possibility of human cloning, the production of genetically identical people, is extremely controversial. If it happens, it will allow a more thorough study of _____ components of human behavior.
    a. the genetic
    b. the environmental
    c. both the genetic and environmental
    d. neither the genetic nor environmental, because the variables are too complex

47. "My parents used to beat me all the time and I turned out OK." What is wrong with this "evidence" favoring harsh physical discipline?
    a. The case study results may not be generalizable to other people.
    b. The dependent variable, or outcome measure, is poorly defined.
    c. The judge cited may not be objective and reliable.
    d. all of the above

48. A newspaper article reports research showing that people who are single or divorced are more likely to suffer from chronic disease and to die earlier than married people. From this research we can correctly conclude
    a. unmarried people are unhappy and suffer more stress than people with partners, and these factors lead to more physical disability.
    b. if you wish to live longer, you should get married.
    c. people who suffer from chronic disease and die early are less likely to find a marriage partner.
    d. singles bars are full of deadly germs.
    e. none of the above

True or False Questions

49. Validity refers to the consistency of a measurement, and includes test-retest validity or inter-rater validity.

    TRUE or FALSE

50. Reactivity effects cause undesired behavior to increase and desired behaviors to decrease during self-monitoring.

    TRUE or FALSE

51. When assessing for a psychological disorder, a clinician should ensure that a client has had a recent physical exam, since some psychological symptoms can be due to medical conditions.

    TRUE or FALSE

52. Projective tests are based on psychoanalytic theory.

    TRUE or FALSE

53. The upcoming DSM-V will most likely include a greater emphasis on dimensional rather than categorical approaches to psychopathology.

    TRUE or FALSE

54. For personality inventories, face validity is more important than predictive validity.

    TRUE or FALSE

55. The main difference between intelligence tests and neuropsychological testing is that intelligence tests also assess for motor abilities.

    TRUE or FALSE

56. Strategies to control external validity include the use of control groups, randomization, and analog models.

    TRUE or FALSE

57. Statistical significance deals with the presence of a difference between two groups; clinical significance deals with the magnitude of the difference between two groups.

    TRUE or FALSE

58. In order to establish a causal relationship among variables, you must use a scientific research method such as an experimental research design.

    TRUE or FALSE

59. Epidemiological research is concerned with the incidence and prevalence of psychological disorders.

    TRUE or FALSE

60. Advantages of multiple baseline research over withdrawal design are that multiple baseline research does not require that treatment be stopped, and it resembles the way treatment often occurs in the real world.

    TRUE or FALSE

61. Cross-sectional designs suffer from cross-generational effects; longitudinal designs suffer from the cohort effect.

    TRUE or FALSE

62. One advantage with cross-cultural studies of behavior is that the researcher does not need to be concerned about random assignment to groups.

    TRUE or FALSE

63. Replication of research results is not necessary if the study is well-designed.

    TRUE or FALSE

64. If research shows that a drug causes hair loss in women and Mary is taking that drug, we can assume she will experience hair loss.

    TRUE or FALSE

65. Research participants must be debriefed only if they suffer psychological harm as a result of the study. TRUE or FALSE

Essay Questions

66. Describe the process of clinical assessment. How is the process like a funnel?

67. List and describe two projective tests. What are some of the advantages and disadvantages of this method of assessment?

68. Discuss the different types of neuroimaging techniques. What are the advantages and disadvantages of each?

69. Compare and contrast the classical, dimensional, and prototypical approaches to nosology.

70. Describe the multi-axial system adopted by DSM. What is the purpose of this system?

71. There are many reasons to be concerned about categorizing and labeling people and their behavior. Discuss these reasons, but also the reasons we continue to do it. There must be some advantages.

72. Describe the basic research process.

73. Describe the case study, correlational, and experimental methods. What are the advantages and disadvantages of these methods?

74. Differentiate between treatment process and treatment outcome research.

75. Compare and contrast family studies, adoption studies, and twin studies.

76. What are the major ethical issues involved in doing psychopathology research?

77. Prevention research is important in the study of abnormal behavior. Describe the major methods used.

HOW WELL DID YOU DO?

Less than 60%	Restudy the chapter (don't just reread); rework your notes completely. You can improve if you increase your efforts.
60-80%	Restudy and rewrite, especially the weak areas; discuss problem areas with study partners.
Over 80%	You're on the right track; continue as you are; focus on trouble areas with study group.
Over 95%	Nice job, especially if you know the whole chapter this well. Be sure to reward your behavior, help others in your study group (they'll help you on your weak chapters), and don't forget to review.

THINKING ALLOWED

Chapter 3 Activities

Sometimes in your role as a diagnostician you are obliged to inform your clients of negative and unpleasant findings. Imagine you are in that position. What information and approach would you use?

On the other hand, imagine and consider the implications for you if you are given a serious psychological diagnosis yourself. Can you imagine a circumstance in which someone might welcome a diagnosis?

Rate yourself on axes III, IV, and V of the DSM diagnostic protocol. Covertly try it with friends and relatives, or on TV and movie characters.

Axis III: General Medical Conditions _____

Axis IV: Psychosocial and Environmental Problems (see detailed list in text) _____

Axis V: Global Assessment of Functioning _____

For an even more ambitious challenge, practice giving total DSM-IV diagnoses (that is, all five axes) to fictional characters such as Santa Claus (yes, Virginia, he is fictional--sorry), TV and movie characters, the cast of 'Survivor' (they're not real either).

Validity is impossible without reliability. For a two-week period, compare your horoscopes from two or more sources. If they don't agree, could they all be valid? If one really were valid, how could we know which?

Which error is worse, false positive or false negative? It really depends on the situation. Think of the risks and gains of each. Can you imagine situations where one type causes more alarm, more cost, or more potential damage? The decision also depends on the available alternatives to your test, and whether further testing is available. What are the implications of each type of error in detection of pregnancy? In discovering HIV-contamination in the public blood supply? In convicting defendants? In diagnosing different psychological disorders?

A comedian has suggested that plastic surgeons should not try to guess why their patients have come in: "A facelift, right? Or at least a nose job. No? Oh, of course, liposuction. Then you must want a derriere lift. Oh, it's for a mole on your back. Sorry." Imagine how this might be good advice for a psychological diagnostician as well.

How do you suppose they got people to pose for those obscene Rorschach inkblots? They claim they're ambiguous, but we're not blind.

Find examples in the print and broadcast media where people conclude causation solely on the basis of a correlational finding. It happens all the time. Avoid this common error yourself. Try to make only uncommon errors.

You can often determine easily whether a correlational study was employed. If one of the variables cannot easily or ethically be manipulated, e.g., religious practices, intelligence, birth order, marital status (try to think of others yourself), it is likely correlational. So what are the limitations of research using these variables?

Try one of the self-motivating methods suggested in the front of this guide, or a method you develop for yourself, to improve your studying. But don't rely on impressions to determine whether it works. Use a single-subject research design, such as a withdrawal design, to evaluate the effectiveness of your program. Define and measure your study behavior for several days, then continue measurement while you try the method. (What are the next steps of this evaluation procedure?) If this method doesn't work, try revising or replacing it. How would you employ a multiple baseline design for this evaluation? (Hint: Think of your other courses.)

When you see a news account about a gene isolated as the cause of an illness or disorder, can you determine which genetic study method was employed?

- Even when the information in the text becomes outdated because of newer research, the research methods described will still be current. Evaluate the methods used in research described in the media. Are the reported conclusions justified?

The cloning of humans is a controversial issue. What would be the implications of the availability of multiple identical twins for our quest to understand the roles of genes and environment in human behavior, normal and abnormal?

INTERNET RESOURCES

Advancing DSM: Dilemmas in Psychiatric Diagnosis

A review of the DSM.

http://human-nature.com/nibbs/03/dsm.html

Two Views of the DSM-IV

Two contrasting views on the DSM-IV manual are provided by Michael T. Nietzel (pro) and Jerome C. Wakefield (con).

http://www.apa.org/journals/nietzel.html

Library Research

An APA web site, explains to the student how to find library resources on psychology by searching journals, books, newspapers, etc.

http://www.apa.org/science/lib.html

Solutions

KEY WORDS

1. (111)	17. (74)	32. (86)
2. (105)	18. (98)	33. (85)
3. (99)	19. (91)	34. (90)
4. (79)	20. (103)	35. (80)
5. (101)	21. (104)	36. (83)
6. (90)	22. (98)	37. (110)
7. (74)	23. (110)	38. (105)
8. (100)	24. (97-98)	39. (103)
9. (113)	25. (103)	40. (81)
10. (98)	26. (98)	41. (91)
11. (92)	27. (117)	42. (88)
12. (92)	28. (98)	43. (99)
13. (99)	29. (94)	44. (75)
14. (102)	30. (114)	45. (76)
15. (92)	31. (77)	46. (112)
16. (113)		

SAMPLE QUESTIONS

Multiple Choice Questions

1. A, 77
2. E, 75-76
3. C, 77
4. C, 78-79
5. A, 83-84
6. B, 84-85
7. C, 86
8. A, 86
9. C, 88-89
10. A, 89-90
11. C, 90
12. D, 90
13. B, 88-89
14. A, 75-76
15. D, 75

16. A, 77-79
17. B, 83-84
18. E, 86
19. E, 86-88, I didn't say whether the client was alive.
20. B, 92
21. C, 94
22. C, 75
23. D, 75-76
24. B, 98, Internal and external validity are important to the research design, not the development of a hypothesis.
25. C, 98-99
26. C, 98-99

27. A, 102-103
28. D, 104, Experimental research involves the manipulation of an independent variable, not a dependent variable.
29. B, 105
30. C, 106-107
31. B, 112
32. C, 114
33. D, 116-118
34. B, 117-118
35. C, 102
36. D, 107-108
37. D, 103-104
38. D, 105

39. D, 101
40. E, 102-104
41. B, 102
42. B, 102-103

43. B, 105-106
44. A, 111-112
45. A, 105, Coles law is thinly-sliced cabbage.

46. C, 112-114
47. D, 98-100
48. E, 99-100

True or False Questions

49. F, 76, This is true of reliability, not validity.
50. F, 81
51. T, 79
52. T, 81-83
53. T, 95
54. F, 76
55. F, 84-86, Neuropsychological tests, not intelligence tests, include assessment of motor skills.

56. F, 98-100, These are strategies to ensure internal, not external, validity.
57. T, 100
58. T, 104
59. T, 103-104
60. T, 107-110
61. F, 115-116, The cohort effect is associated with cross-sectional design, the cross-generational effect with longitudinal designs.

62. F, 116-118
63. F, 116-117
64. F, 99, This is an example of the patient uniformity myth.
65. F, 117-118, Debriefing is necessary whenever deception or concealment is used.

Essay Questions

66. Be able to discuss the purpose of clinical assessment and the factors that are examined in clinical assessment. Note that the assessment usually begins with broad questions, which are narrowed. You might want to mention some of the various techniques used by clinicians. (See textbook pages 75-81.)

67. Some projective tests to include are the TAT, sentence completion tests, or Rorschach inkblot tests. Note what kind of information that these tests give a clinician. Also, be sure to comment on the reliability and validity of these techniques. (See textbook pages 81-83.)

68. For this question, you will want to list several techniques (CAT, PET, the different MRIs, etc.) and briefly describe what kind of information these techniques offer. If possible, you should tell how each technique works. The types of advantages and disadvantages to discuss include cost, usefulness, and time considerations. (See textbook pages 86-88.)

69. Your answer should include a brief description of each system. Be sure to note the basis on which a diagnosis is made according to each system, as well as a discussion of the strengths and weaknesses of each. Include the assumptions on which the classical model is based (that the disorders have different underlying causes). (See textbook pages 90-91.)

70. Be sure to know what each axis reflects. Also, your answer should include the rationale for the multi-axial system. Don't forget to mention what this contributes to the diagnosis! (See textbook pages 93-94.)

71. Categories and labels are subject to misuse, but they provide a valuable format for communicating about psychopathology and organizing observations. Dangers include reifying diagnostic categories and the development of negative connotations. (See textbook page 94-96.)

72. Your answer should refer to the hypothesis, research design, dependent variables, independent variables, and the consideration of validity. (See textbook pages 97-100.)

73. Be sure to note that the case study method does not use experimental controls, and is susceptible to results that are due to coincidence. Advantages can be discussed in the context of researchers who have contributed ideas, though not proof, to psychology using this method. (See textbook page 101.)

Correlational methods involve measurement only; no variables are manipulated, and subjects usually have self-selected their behaviors or group membership. Associations between variables are computed as a correlation coefficient. Because of possible directionality and third-variable confounds, causation cannot be established, but associations themselves are valuable to find for further experimental investigation. (See textbook pages 102-104.)

Experimental methods involve systematic manipulation or control of variables. Allows determination of causal relationships among variables. Can be difficult or unethical to conduct. (See textbook pages 104-106.)

74. Be sure to note the differences between the questions generated by looking at treatment process or treatment outcome. Also, your answer should indicate that these are both components of comparative treatment research. (See textbook pages 105-106.)

75. In your answer, try to focus on the different information each method offers. Be sure to discuss the limitations of each method, and to indicate why each method might be important. (See textbook pages 111-112.)

76. Ethical issues in research include whether it is ever appropriate to withhold a potentially helpful treatment; ensuring that participants are fully informed when they agree to the research, maintaining their confidentiality rights, and ensuring they do not suffer physical or emotional harm. (See textbook pages 117-118.)

77. Prevention research involves studying risk factors for developing problems (pre-intervention research), treatment intervention to prevent problems (prevention intervention research), and structural issues such as legislation that could help prevention efforts (prevention services systems research). (See textbook page 113.)

ANXIETY DISORDERS

LEARNING OBJECTIVES

1. Describe psychological and biological similarities and differences among anxiety, fear, and a panic attack.

2. Identify the genetic and biological vulnerability factors that are known to influence the development of anxiety disorders.

3. Describe the essential features of generalized anxiety disorder, its proposed causal factors, and available treatment approaches.

4. Describe the essential features of panic disorder.

5. Identify the principal causes of specific phobias and the most typical strategies used to treat them.

6. Describe the essential features of posttraumatic stress disorder, its proposed causal factors, and available treatment approaches.

7. Describe the symptoms, defining characteristics, and integrative model of obsessive-compulsive disorder.

CHAPTER SUMMARY

By now you know what to do with chapter summaries and sample tests.

Anxiety is a _____ state, involving _____ affect and physical symptoms of stress when a person anticipates future events. Anxiety is difficult to study because it can be a subjective _____, behaviors such as fidgeting or running away, and/or _____ responses such as muscle tension. Much anxiety research is done with _____, but there is some difficulty in generalizing from animal studies of anxiety to the human mood. As demonstrated by Yerkes and Dodson, anxiety can often _____ performance as well as impair it. Anxiety helps humans anticipate and plan for the _____. Too much anxiety, however, can be harmful, and difficult to _____.

mood; negative; feeling; physiological; animals; enhance; future; eliminate

The emotion associated with an alarm reaction to immediate danger, _____, is a massive response of the _____ nervous system, and is known as the "flight or _____" reaction. Fear and anxiety are thought to be different/the same physically and physiologically. A _____ _____ is a sudden experience of fear, including physical symptoms. _____ _____ (or cued) panic attacks are associated with circumstances in which a panic attack is very likely; unexpected (_____) panic attacks occur without warning. Situationally _____ attacks occur more frequently, but not always, in particular settings.

fear; autonomic; fight; different; panic attack; Situationally bound; uncued; predisposed

While _____ predispositions affect individual's anxiety and likelihood of panic attacks, these do/do not appear to be related to any single gene. Neurobiological evidence suggests that lowered _____-benzodiazepine levels may be related to higher/lower anxiety, and that the neurotransmitter _____ is particularly involved. The _____ _____ _____ (CRF) system has significant effects on the areas of the brain related to anxiety and is related to neurotransmitter systems. Studies have implicated the _____ system of the brain in anxiety, via the behavioral _____ system (BIS), which is activated by signs of danger. The fight/flight system (FFS), a separate circuit implicated in panic, involves the brain part called the _____.

genetic; do not; GABA; higher; serotonin; corticotrophin releasing factor; limbic; inhibition; amygdala

_____ theories about anxiety include Freud's idea that anxiety was a reactivation of an earlier experience and behavioral views that it is a product of _____. An _____ model of anxiety involves a variety of factors, including the development of a sense of controllability in childhood. Most psychological accounts of panic invoke conditioning and _____ explanations. A strong fear response initially occurs under extreme stress or due to a truly dangerous situation. This response becomes associated with internal (within the body) and external (_____) cues. Social stressors, including _____ stressors, serve as triggers to anxiety, which may lead to panic attacks or headaches, perhaps depending on family _____. An _____ model notes that an individual may have a biological vulnerability to anxiety and develops a psychological vulnerability from a lack of a sense of _____ of the environment, both of which can lead to high levels of anxiety in the presence of many stressors. Panic attacks develop in much the same way, although the role of _____ may be greater, leading to learned _____. Anxiety and panic often _____ _____.

Psychological; learning; integrative; cognitive; environmental; interpersonal; heredity; integrative; controllability; learning; alarms; occur together

_____ _____ disorder (GAD), which is characterized by excessive _____ about everyday events with associated muscle tension and agitation, occurs in _____% of the population. A <u>larger/smaller</u> percentage of individuals with GAD receive treatment for it than those with panic disorder. Although GAD usually appears earlier in life than most other anxiety disorders, it is also especially prevalent in the _____, as shown by the excessive use of _____. This possibly is due to an increasing lack of _____ as individuals age and lose their _____, or suffer in other aspects of their lives. Twin studies of the etiology of GAD suggest that a genetic component plays a role in the tendency to become _____ rather than to show GAD. Also, individuals with GAD show less sympathetic arousal than those with panic disorders, although they show more _____ tenseness than normal individuals. This indicates that GAD individuals may give <u>less/more</u> attention to stress and sources of threat than do others, and much of this response is _____. One cognitive model suggests that GAD individuals use _____ as a way of avoiding sympathetic arousal and dealing with the _____ of stressful situations. Treatment for GAD formerly focused on minor tranquilizers (_____); however, recent evidence shows that these are not effective, may reduce cognitive and motor functioning, and can cause _____. _____ medications may be a better option. Effective psychological treatment for GAD may be _____ _____ in which the client confronts the normally-avoided feelings and _____ of anxiety during therapy.

Generalized anxiety; worrying; four; smaller; elderly; tranquilizers; control; health; anxious; muscle; more; automatic; worry; images; benzodiazepines; dependence; Antidepressant; cognitive-behavioral; images

_____ _____ are characterized by unexpected panic attacks and anxiety about the possibility of having another. Panic disorder with _____ involves unexpected panic attacks and _____ of situations that the person fears may not be safe in the event of a panic attack. Panic disorder <u>with/without</u> agoraphobia is similar, but does not include avoidance of such situations. Individuals may cope with panic disorder through the development of agoraphobia, which allows them to avoid potentially embarrassing situations, or with alcohol or _____ _____. They may also display _____ avoidance, which involves staying away from any activity, such as _____ that might produce _____ symptoms similar to those of a panic attack. Approximately ___ of the population meet the criteria for panic disorder at some stage in their lives. Onset normally occurs in _____ _____; panic disorder is rare in prepubescent children. Cultural differences in acceptance of panic may account for the finding that the disorder is more common in <u>males/females</u> while alcohol abuse as coping may be more common in <u>males/females</u>. Although present and similarly _____in other cultures, anxiety disorders may be expressed differently in them

Panic disorders; agoraphobia; avoidance; without; other drugs; interoceptive; exercise; physiological; 3.5%; early adulthood; females; males; prevalent

Panic disorder and agoraphobia appear to be caused by biological, psychological, and _____ factors. The causes include an _____ tendency to respond in a particular way in reaction to stress and a _____ process by which the individual learns to associate cues with anxiety. Also, a fear of _____ panic attacks must develop, possibly through internal or external cues called _____ _____. The cognitive theories of David Clark note the interaction between an _____ that a physical sensation is a symptom of anxiety, the anxiety this cognition produces, and the increased physical symptoms. Others have noted that panic disorder patients are more aware of their internal processes, or more _____ aware.

social; inherited; conditioning; future; learned alarms; interpretation; interoceptively

The finding that drugs effective for panic disorders are different from those effective for anxiety suggests that panic and anxiety involve the same/different neurotransmitters and brain locations. However, these results are not supported, since some drugs, such as high-potency _____ and _____-_____ _____ _____ (SSRIs) are effective for both panic and anxiety. Many older drugs used to treat panic disorders have disadvantages, such as side effects and _____ ___ _____. Therefore, _____ are the current treatment of choice, but they may cause _____ dysfunction as a side effect. Psychological treatments are usually based on _____ to the feared situations, and have proven to be effective in reducing agoraphobic avoidance but not necessarily "curing" it completely. Panic control treatment involves both exposing the individual to the _____ of a panic attack (not just the triggering stimuli) and _____ therapy. A large systematic study of treatment concluded that there is no advantage to combining drug and cognitive-behavior therapy. _____ _____ treatment was superior in the long term.

different; benzodiazepines; serotonin-specific reuptake inhibitors; addiction or dependence; SSRIs; sexual; exposure; symptoms; cognitive; Panic control

A _____ _____ is an irrational, interfering fear, set off by a particular object or situation which is avoided if possible. The client usually does/does not recognize the fear is excessive. _____-injection-_____ phobia differs from other anxiety responses in that heart rate and blood pressure markedly _____. _____ phobias include fears of particular places, and panic attacks do not occur outside of these situations. _____ _____ phobias are fears related to nature, and usually develop at a young age. Animal phobias are common, but are not considered a phobia unless they involve a severe _____ in functioning. _____ anxiety disorder is a childhood disorder characterized by an unrealistic fear that a parent or other significant person will be harmed or separated from the child. This fear must be differentiated from _____ phobia and, like all childhood phobias, from age-_____ fears.

specific phobia; does; Blood; injury; decrease; Situational; Natural environment; impairment; Separation; school; normal

Specific phobias <u>are/are not</u> a common psychological disorder. Of these, people with _____ phobias are most likely to seek treatment, probably because the disorder _____ with life. People with blood-injection-injury phobia, a potentially life-threatening problem, probably <u>are/are not</u> prevalent; they might be more likely to seek help if they knew _____ _____ __ _____. Cultural and gender differences exist in phobias, with <u>more/fewer</u> women and <u>more/fewer</u> Hispanic people reporting phobias than males or white Americans. Cultural and _____ factors help determine who will report phobias. Males may work hard to overcome fears or to _____ and hide them.

are; situational; interferes; are; effective treatment is available; more; more; social; endure

Conditioning experiences, such as being bitten by a dog, <u>are/are not</u> necessary for a phobia to develop. Phobias can also develop as a result of _____ _____ involving panic attacks in a particular situation, by watching another person experience extreme fear during a traumatic event, or by hearing about a particular danger, referred to as _____ _____. The development of anxiety about possibly re-experiencing an event, which can be aided by an _____ tendency to fear a particular event, is also a key component of phobias. Phobias seem to have a genetic component, with relatives of a phobic having a <u>lesser/greater</u> likelihood of having a phobia than the general population. Treatment of phobias requires _____ to the feared event or situation. Usually a therapist's guidance is needed so clients do not proceed too _____, or _____ too early, which could worsen the phobia. Clients with blood-injection-injury phobia are taught to <u>tense/relax</u> muscles in the presence of fear stimuli. Some treatments can be completed in as quickly as _____ _____.

are not; false alarms; information transmission; inherited; greater; exposure; quickly; escape; tense; one day

_____ phobia involves a fear of interacting with others, or of being humiliated, either in any situation (_____ type) or only in specific situations. Prevalence of social phobia is <u>high/low</u> and is <u>increasing/decreasing</u>. Clients are more likely to be <u>male/female</u> and <u>married/single</u> than in the general population. The most common social phobia is _____ _____. Causes of the disorder include a predisposition to fear social _____, as well as the factors already outlined for the etiology of other phobias and GAD. Effective treatment can include group role-playing, and cognitive therapy that focuses on lessening the _____ of danger in social situations. Drug treatment with tricyclic _____ and possibly _____ inhibitors, are equally effective as this cognitive-behavioral approach, but _____ is a problem when medication is stopped.

Social; generalized; high; increasing; male; single; public speaking; rejection; perception; antidepressants; MAO; relapse

_____ _____ _____ (PTSD) can occur 1 to 3 months after a person experiences a traumatic event involving fear, _____, or horror. It is characterized by re-experiencing the event through sudden memories (called _____), avoidance of reminders of the trauma, over-arousal and vigilance, and a numbing of _____ experiences. _____ _____ disorder is the DSM-IV diagnoses for posttraumatic stress syndrome that occurs less than a month following the traumatic event. Symptoms may include _____ (memory loss) for the traumatic event. PTSD development requires close _____ to the traumatic events that are experienced. Development of PTSD is also influenced by _____ and psychological vulnerabilities. PTSD has been found to be related to anxiety that runs in families. _____ vulnerabilities, such as a lack of a sense of control, are more significant if the stress is <u>lower/higher</u>, since at intense levels of stress, most people develop PTSD regardless of psychological vulnerabilities. _____ factors, such as a supportive social network, can reduce the likelihood of developing PTSD. Animal studies suggest that the brain circuit involved in PTSD is <u>similar to/different from</u> that for panic attacks, though in PTSD the initial alarm is <u>true/false</u>. Chronic activation of stress hormones may damage the _____ of individuals with PTSD, resulting in memory deficits. Treatment for PTSD focuses on gradual, imaginal _____ to the traumatic event to relieve the emotional trauma. Drugs used for _____ disorders may also be effective for PTSD.

Posttraumatic stress disorder; helplessness; flashbacks; emotional; Acute stress; amnesia; exposure; biological; Psychological; lower; Social; similar to; true; hippocampus; re-exposure; anxiety

Obsessive-compulsive disorder (OCD) involves both obsessions (intrusive recurrent _____ or impulses) and _____ (thoughts or actions used to suppress the obsessions). Other _____ disorders may occur simultaneously (_____) with OCD, and most obsessive clients report <u>single/multiple</u> obsessions. The most common compulsions are _____ and checking rituals. The types of compulsive rituals usually <u>are/are not</u> associated with particular obsessions. An example would be _____. The disorder presents <u>similarly/differently</u> in other cultures, although the exact nature of obsessions and compulsions may be influenced by cultural values. OCD may be self-perpetuating, since the individual's attempts at suppression of thoughts is <u>usually/rarely</u> successful. OCD usually starts earlier in <u>males/females</u> but in later life are more prevalent among <u>males/females</u>. Along with biological and psychological vulnerabilities, etiology includes the person must also believe that some thoughts are _____. Clients with OCD equate thoughts with the specific actions represented by those thoughts; this is called _____-_____ _____. Medical treatment for this disorder focuses on drugs that affect the _____ neurotransmitter system, but may not be very effective and discontinuation of the drug often results in _____. Psychological treatments include exposure and _____ _____, which involves preventing the individual from enacting compulsive rituals. As a last resort, neurosurgery on the _____ _____ may be used.

thoughts; compulsions; anxiety; comorbid; multiple; cleaning; are; e.g., obsession with contamination leads to excessive cleaning; similarly; rarely; males; females; unacceptable; thought-action fusion; serotonergic; relapse; ritual prevention; cingulate bundle

KEY WORDS

Practice defining the important concepts listed below. Follow the definition suggestions provided in the introduction to this Guide. Be precise and accurate, and check your work with the text. Add to the definition later as you encounter more information about the term. Whenever possible, include examples. Use only the space to the right of the word so that later you can cover either the word or the definition to use one to cue the other. Define additional important terms you'll find in the chapter.

1. agoraphobia

_____

_____

2. anxiety

_____

_____

3. compulsions

_____

_____

4. fear

_____

_____

5. generalized anxiety disorder (GAD)

_____

_____

6. fight/flight system (FFS)

_____

_____

7. obsessions

_____

_____

8. obsessive-compulsive disorder (OCD)

_____

_____

9. panic attack

_____

_____

10. panic control treatment

_____

_____

11. panic disorder

_____

_____

12. posttraumatic stress disorder (PTSD)

_____

_____

13. separation anxiety disorder

_____

_____

14. social phobia

_____

_____

15. specific phobia

_____

_____

SAMPLE QUESTIONS

As one of the later stages of your study for this chapter, you can assess your progress by taking a sample test. Don't make the mistake of studying just for these questions. They are merely a small sample of the many questions that could appear on an exam. An excellent way to help yourself is to generate your own questions and answers. This will help you focus on important concepts, make better distinctions among similar ideas, practice writing responses, and engaging the material in general. Try them on your friends in your study group.

Multiple Choice Questions

1. Anxiety is
   a. an immediate alarm reaction to stressful situations.
   b. usually a sign of an underdeveloped ego.
   c. potentially helpful in planning for the future.
   d. always a hindrance to adaptive functioning.

2. Batman is walking down a dark alley in Gotham City. Suddenly, a dark figure jumps out from behind a trash bin and points a gun at him. Batman turns and runs, faster than a speeding bullet. This is an example of
   a. alarm response.
   b. panic.
   c. anxiety.
   d. wimpy behavior.

3. Paula has frequent panic attacks, but only when she views the national news on television. However, she does not experience a panic attack every time she sees the national news. Paula's panic attacks would be classified as
   a. unexpected.
   b. situationally bound.
   c. situationally predisposed.
   d. justified.

4. Which of the following is the area of the brain most often associated with anxiety?
   a. occipital lobe
   b. orbital frontal lobe
   c. medulla
   d. limbic system

5. Research suggesting that cigarette smoking by teenagers increases the risk for developing anxiety disorders as adults indicates that:
   a. the negative effects of smoking are permanent.
   b. environmental factors can affect susceptibility to the development of anxiety disorders.
   c. adolescents have underdeveloped brain circuits.
   d. nicotine decreases anxiety levels.

6. Elliot constantly worries about his health, his finances, his job security, and the stability of his marriage. Often, his worries keep him awake at night, causing him to be so fatigued at work that he cannot perform his duties adequately. His wife is becoming frustrated with him, since he is so preoccupied with his worries that he is unable to do the dinner dishes when it is his turn. Elliot's problem might be diagnosed as
   a. panic disorder.
   b. anxiety disorder.
   c. simple phobia.
   d. obsessive-compulsive disorder.

7. Which of the following observations is NOT true of individuals with generalized anxiety disorder?
   a. They are more sensitive to threats than are other people.
   b. They show more responsiveness on physiological measures than individuals with other anxiety disorders.
   c. They exhibit more muscle tension than other people.
   d. They appear to be autonomic restrictors.

8. Which of the following is an example of interoceptive avoidance?
   a. Martha does not enter public restrooms for fear of disease.
   b. Ronald does not visit his mother-in-law because she makes him anxious.
   c. Noel does not go to church for fear of having a panic attack while there.
   d. Chelsea does not play on merry-go-rounds because the dizziness resembles the early symptoms of a panic attack.

9. The main element in psychological treatment of panic disorders is
   a. Benzodiazepines.
   b. hypnosis.
   c. exposure to the feared symptoms.
   d. teaching avoidance techniques.

10. Sportscaster John Madden's fear and avoidance of flying is an example of
    a. generalized anxiety disorder.
    b. panic disorder with agoraphobia.
    c. specific phobia.
    d. panic disorder without agoraphobia.

11. A specific phobia involving motorcycles can develop as a result of a predisposition to develop fear combined with
    a. watching another person experience a motorcycle accident.
    b. hearing your mother repeatedly warn you about the doom associated with motorcycles.
    c. experiencing a traumatic event yourself, such as a motorcycle skid.
    d. all of the above

12. The most common phobia, the fear of public speaking, is an example of
    a. specific phobia.
    b. agoraphobia.
    c. social phobia.
    d. specific, situational phobia.
    e. none of the above

13. Ritualistic, repeated actions designed to prevent intrusive thoughts are called
    a. obsessions.
    b. convulsions.
    c. compulsions.
    d. delusions.
    e. pink elephants.

14. Psychological treatment for obsessive-compulsive disorder usually involves
    a. ritual prevention.
    b. medication.
    c. exposure to feared stimuli.
    d. both a and c
    e. all of the above

15. Anxiety is difficult to study because
    a. humans may manifest it in many different ways.
    b. animal research cannot be applied to our understanding of the human anxiety experience.
    c. it is implicated in only a few types of psychopathology.
    d. it has no physiological consequences

16. External cues to panic attacks
    a. may include increases in heart rate or respiration.
    b. may be places similar to the one where the original panic attack occurred.
    c. are only places where panic attacks have occurred in the past.
    d. none of the above

17. Generalized anxiety disorder is considered the "basic" anxiety disorder because
    a. it was the first anxiety disorder to be studied using animal models.
    b. all the other anxiety disorders include intense generalized anxiety.
    c. both a and b
    d. it was the first anxiety disorder to be studied by Freud.

18. Valerie tells you that she has been receiving cognitive behavioral treatment for her generalized anxiety disorder. This treatment most likely involves
    a. bringing on the worry process during therapy sessions and confronting the anxiety-provoking images and worrisome thoughts head-on.
    b. discussing the earliest memories of anxiety-provoking events and finding snapping a rubber band on her wrist when she is anxious.
    c. the prescription of serotonin reuptake inhibitor medication.
    d. none of the above

19. Rob presented at the clinic with complaints that he is terrified to go anywhere that does not have a bathroom for fear that he will begin vomiting and not be able to stop. He has had one panic attack and reported that a week after that attack he felt no residual effects from the attack. Rob would most likely receive a DSM-IV diagnosis of
    a. panic disorder with agoraphobia.
    b. panic disorder without agoraphobia.
    c. interoceptive agoraphobia.
    d. agoraphobia without history of panic disorder.

20. Rita suffers from a panic disorder. After she begins exercising her heart rate increases. A cognitive theorist would predict that Rita would
    a. interpret the increased heart rate in a catastrophic way.
    b. experience a surge of anxiety after interpreting the heart rate increase as something dangerous.
    c. be likely to experience a panic attack if she interprets any additional physical sensations as signs of increasing danger.
    d. all of the above.

21. The following list of exercises would most likely be an example of which type of treatment 1) shop in a crowded supermarket, 2) walk five blocks away from home, 3) drive
    a. panic control treatment.
    b. cognitive behavioral treatment.
    c. gradual exposure treatment.
    d. none.

22. How do individuals with blood-injury-injection phobia differ from those with other phobias?
    a. in their avoidance behavior
    b. in their physiological reaction
    c. in their familial history of the disorder
    d. both b and c

23. You operate an anxiety-reduction clinic and know you can make predictions about your clientele. Who are most likely to seek treatment?
    a. overly reactive people with normal fears
    b. people with blood-injection-injury phobia
    c. people with GAD
    d. people with situational phobia
    e. these groups are equally likely to seek treatment

24. In the treatment you offer most of your clients with anxiety disorders, you seek to relax muscle tension and reduce blood pressure and heart rate. The exception is
    a. social phobia.
    b. specific phobia.
    c. blood-injection-injury disorder.
    d. panic disorder with agoraphobia.
    e. panic disorder without agoraphobia.

25. Acute stress disorder
    a. is really PTSD occurring directly after the trauma.
    b. can include dissociative symptoms.
    c. is a new disorder in DSM-IV.
    d. all of the above.

26. Marjorie stopped attending temple for fear that she would yell obscenities at the rabbi during service. This is an example of
    a. a compulsion.
    b. a phobia.
    c. an obsessive impulse.
    d. a ritual.
    e. none of the above

27. What is the most prevalent psychological disorder?
    a. major depression
    b. posttraumatic stress disorder
    c. schizophrenia
    d. social phobia

28. In the videotape or CD-ROM "ABNORMAL PSYCHOLOGY LIVE!", "Steve" reported that the symptoms of his panic disorder would not emerge as long as he
    a. continued to take his medication as prescribed.
    b. remained outside.
    c. was with another person.
    d. exerted a great deal of physical energy.

29. In the videotape "ABNORMAL PSYCHOLOGY: LIVE!" or your CD-ROM, "Chuck" exhibited which of the following behaviors related to his Obsessive-Compulsive Disorder?
    a. recurrent and obsessive dreams about his parents
    b. ritualistic "checking" of household items and pets
    c. avoidance of items associated with his obsession
    d. amnesia related to the exact nature of his obsessions

True or False Questions

30. Fear is a mood state which is characterized by physical symptoms of tension and negative affect in anticipation of future disasters.

    TRUE or FALSE

31. Anxiety appears to be an inherited trait, although panic does not.

    TRUE or FALSE

32. The behavioral inhibition system in the brain is implicated in anxiety and panic.

    TRUE or FALSE

33. The prevalence of generalized anxiety disorders decreases with age.

    TRUE or FALSE

34. Benzodiazepines do not seem to be any more clinically effective than placebos for generalized anxiety disorder.

    TRUE or FALSE

35. An individual who does not go to the movies because she or he is afraid of having a panic attack would be diagnosed with panic disorder with agoraphobia.

    TRUE or FALSE

36. Post-traumatic stress disorder, which occurs within the first month after exposure to a stressful event, involves flashbacks, avoidance of objects associated with the event, and symptoms of arousal.

    TRUE or FALSE

37. As a general rule, the more intense the trauma, the more likely it is that an individual will develop post-ptraumatic stress disorder..

    TRUE or FALSE

38. The rates of comorbidity among anxiety disorders are high.

    TRUE or FALSE

39. Combat and sexual assault are the most common traumas contributing to posttraumatic stress disorder.

    TRUE or FALSE

Essay Questions

40. Compare and contrast anxiety, fear, and panic.

41. Describe an integrated model for the causes of panic. Discuss some of the theories about the etiology of panic disorder.

42. Compare and contrast generalized anxiety disorder and obsessive-compulsive disorder.

43. Develop a treatment program for an individual suffering from a fear of flying.

HOW WELL DID YOU DO?

Less than 60%	Restudy the chapter (don't just reread); rework your notes completely. You can improve if you increase your efforts..
60-80%	Restudy and rewrite, especially the weak areas; discuss problem areas with study partners.
Over 80%	You're on the right track; continue as you are; focus on trouble areas with study group.
Over 95%	Nice job, especially if you know the whole chapter this well. Be sure to reward your behavior, help others in your study group (they'll help you on your weak chapters), and don't forget to review..

THINKING ALLOWED

Chapter 4 Activities

Panic clients may misinterpret, overemphasize and overreact to normal physiological activities. You can induce some of these by spinning to make yourself dizzy, or by breathing rapidly through a straw to induce hyperventilation. Can you imagine that you felt this way but could not identify the cause of these feelings? Would it be disturbing to you?

As a result of a childhood nausea experience at a carnival, the author of this Guide feels ill when he simply smells cotton candy. Why does his avoidance of the candy not qualify as a phobia? What could he do to eliminate it? [In other words, I could quit anytime I want. – DAS] How? Why doesn't he?

How might you incorporate virtual reality technology into the treatment of phobias, PTSD, and compulsive behaviors?

How might the disorders described in this chapter have application in your own life?

INTERNET RESOURCES

Generalized Anxiety Disorder

This is a page located at the "Internet Mental Health" web site; information on many psychological disorders, including anxiety disorders, can be found here.

http://www.mentalhealth.com/dis/p20-an07.html

Generalized Anxiety Disorder

Anxiety disorders, such as generalized anxiety disorder (GAD), panic disorder, and social phobia, are the most prevalent psychiatric disorder in the U.S.

http://www.aafp.org/afp/20001001/1591.html

Obsessive-Compulsive Foundation (OCF)

This web page, developed by the Obsessive-Compulsive Foundation and the Mend Association, includes information on support groups, services, and publications on this disorder.

http://www.ocfoundation.org/

"Social Anxiety Disorder: A Common Underrecognized Mental Disorder

Social phobia has shown responsiveness to specific pharmacotherapy and psychotherapy.

http://aafp.org/afp/991115ap/2311.html

Treatment of Posttraumatic Stress Disorder Expert Consensus Guidelines

The guidelines developed by a panel of experts on PTSD, address diagnosis and treatment strategies.

http://www.psychguides.com/gl-treatment_of_PTSD.html

Solutions

KEY WORDS

1. (135)
2. (124)
3. (162)
4. (125)
5. (130-135)

6. (127)
7. (162)
8. (162-166)
9. (125)
10. (142)

11. (125)
12. (155-161)
13. (146-148)
14. (125,151)
15. (144)

SAMPLE QUESTIONS

Multiple Choice Questions

1. C, 124
2. A, 125
3. C, 125
4. D, 126-127
5. B, 126-129
6. B, 130-131
7. B, 130-131
8. D, 133-135
9. C, 141-144
10. C, 144-145
11. D, 144-147

12. C, 151
13. C, 162
14. D, 165-166
15. A, 124-125
16. B, 126-127
17. B, 130-131
18. A, 133-135
19. D, 135-136
20. D, 135-137
21. C, 150
22. D, 145

23. D, 146
24. C, 145
25. D, 157
26. C, 162-163
27. D, 151-152
28. D, video
29. B, video

True or False Questions

30. F, 125, This is true of anxiety, not fear.
31. F, 124-125
32. F, 127
33. F, 126-129
34. F, 133-134

35. T, 135-136
36. F, 155-157, This describes acute stress disorder; post-traumatic stress disorder must have a duration greater than one month.
37. T, 155-160

38. T, 129
39. T, 158-160

Essay Questions

40. Your answer should include complete definitions of anxiety, fear, and panic. Be sure to discuss the different circumstances each is associated with and the symptoms of each. Also, note that anxiety is future-oriented, fear is present-oriented. (See textbook pages 124-125.)

41. Your integrated model should deal with biological and psychological tendencies to experience panic attacks, as well as particular life stressors.

Be sure to discuss genetic, neurological, and conditioning factors related to panic. The theories you should note include Clark's focus on cognitive processes, and psychodynamic theories. (See textbook pages 126-129.)

42. You should discuss the symptoms of each disorder, and note how these symptoms might be considered similar. Be sure to discuss the nature of the worry or obsession. You may wish to compare causes, treatment, and course of the disorders. (See textbook pages 130-135 and pages 162-166.)

43. The key element of your treatment program should involve exposure to the fear stimuli and the prevention of escape. Also, you might describe possible coping strategies that could be used, or drugs that may be helpful. (See textbook pages 146-150.)

SOMATOFORM AND DISSOCIATIVE DISORDERS

LEARNING OBJECTIVES:

1. Identify the defining features of somatoform disorders and distinguish the major features of hypochondriasis from illness phobia and somatization disorder.

2. Describe sensory, motor, and visceral symptoms that characterize conversion disorder.

3. Describe and distinguish among the five types of dissociative disorders.

4. Describe important etiological and treatment factors, including important known cultural influences on each disorder.

5. Discuss false memory syndrome in the context of trauma associated with dissociative disorders.

CHAPTER SUMMARY

By now you know what to do with chapter summaries and sample tests.

Somatoform disorders present as _____ disorders with no identifiable medical condition. _____ disorders are those in which individuals experience a feeling of detachment from themselves. Somatoform and dissociative disorders are linked historically, beginning with the term "_____." In _____ disorders, individuals are pathologically concerned with appearance or functioning of their bodies. In _____, patients experience severe anxiety from the perceived possibility of having a serious physical disease. They visit doctors repeatedly, convinced that they are ill, even without medical evidence. Hypochondriacs may _____ bodily symptoms as being more serious than they are and tend to seek a general _____ before being referred for mental health treatment.

physical; Dissociative; hysteria; somatoform; hypochondriasis; misinterpret; physician

Hypochondriasis shares many features with _____ disorders. However, those who fear that they might develop a disease are usually diagnosed as having an _____ _____. Hypochondriacs, on the other hand, believe that they already suffer from a serious illness. Disease _____ is thus the main feature of hypochondriasis. Hypochondriasis is fairly evenly represented across age groups and _____. Culture specific syndromes, such as Koro and dhat, are associated with ____.

anxiety; illness phobia; conviction; gender; hypochondriasis

Hypochondriasis is believed to be a disorder of cognition or _____, in which individuals experience physical sensations in a distorted way. Individuals often take a "better safe than sorry" approach with their symptoms, showing _____ concepts of health when interpreting their symptoms. There is some evidence that the disorder also may have a _____ component. Stressful life events, particularly those involving exposure to death or illness, may act as precipitating factors in the etiology of hypochondriasis. Many hypochondriacs also experienced significant family _____ during childhood. Assuming the _____ role may be reinforcing for some individuals. Treatment of hypochondriasis typically uses cognitive and behavioral techniques, and new research indicates that direct reassurance by _____ _____ _____ is beneficial.

perception; restricted; genetic; illness; sick; mental health professionals

Somatization disorder is characterized by multiple _____ complaints with no associated medical condition. Undifferentiated somatization disorder is diagnosed for individuals who report more/fewer symptoms than are required for the full diagnosis. Psychological complaints such as _____ and _____ disorders are common in individuals with somatization disorder. Across cultures, the occurrence of somatization disorder appears to be _____ _____.

somatic; fewer; anxiety; mood; relatively uniform

Somatization disorder appears to run in families, although some studies have not replicated this finding. The typical age of onset is _____. Individuals with somatization tend to be married/unmarried and from _____ socioeconomic groups. Somatization symptoms often continue into _____ _____.

adolescence; unmarried; lower; old age

Somatization disorder is associated with _____ personality disorder (ASPD). Somatization disorder is more common in males/females, but antisocial personality disorder is more common in males/females, but a _____ model helps conceptualize the connection between ASPD and somatization disorder. A neurological model of the underlying mechanisms in both somatization disorder and antisocial personality disorder proposes a behavioral inhibition system, a behavioral _____ system, and a fight-flight system. The different behavioral outcomes of the two disorders may be explained by _____ factors. Aggression and ASPD are associated with males, while _____ and somatization disorder are associated with females.

antisocial; females; males; biopsychosocial; activation; cultural; dependence

Somatization disorder is extremely easy/difficult to treat. Typical methods include reassurance, reduction of stress, and reduction of _____-_____ behaviors. The goal of reducing visits to a doctor has important implications for rising health care costs.

difficult; help-seeking

_____ disorders are characterized by physical malfunctioning with no organic pathology to account for the malfunction. Symptoms tend to affect _____-_____ systems. Common symptoms include blindness, paralysis, aphonia, mutism, and globus hystericus or "lump in the throat." Freudian theory asserts that conversion disorders are expressions of unconscious _____ that is displaced onto bodily symptoms.

Conversion; sensory-motor; anxiety

Distinguishing between conversion reactions and _____ disorders is an important challenge for clinicians; in fact, one study indicates that _____% of persons diagnosed with conversion disorder were later found to have some type of physical disorder. Individuals experiencing a conversion disorder may present "la belle _____" and have typically experienced recent stress. Furthermore, in _____ disorders, people can accomplish tasks that they would not be able to if the condition were solely medical (such as the ability to avoid objects in the case of blindness).

physical; 25; indifference; conversion

_____ is similar to conversion disorders, except that the somatic complaints appear to be "faked" or voluntary by the client. Malingerers are motivated by a specific external _____, such as a financial settlement or avoiding some negative outcome. Individuals exhibiting _____ disorders appear to voluntarily feign physical symptoms, with no apparent external gain, except the adoption of the sick role. Factitious disorder by _____ is diagnosed when an individual "makes" a family member sick for attention and pity.

Malingering; gain; factitious; proxy

The role of _____ mental processes is widely associated with conversion disorders. In the case of blindness, conversion symptoms differ from truly blind symptoms in that patients with conversion symptoms perform visual tasks better or worse than chance. Truly blind subjects do not visually discriminate stimuli, at a level different from _____.

unconscious; chance

Freud labeled four processes in the development of conversion disorder: experience of a traumatic event, repression of conflict into the _____, conversion of underlying anxiety into physical symptoms -- which results in the reduction of anxiety (_____ gain), and an increase in external attention and escape/avoidant behaviors (_____ gain). Freud's notion of primary gain has much/little support.

unconscious; primary; secondary; little

Conversion disorder often occurs with other disorders especially _____ disorder. Males frequently experience conversion disorder in times of extreme _____. Conversion disorders tend to appear in less educated, lower socioeconomic groups. The number of cases of conversion disorders has increased/decreased over time. Treatment of conversion disorders usually deals with any traumatic life events and the removal of _____ _____, although this may not be a simple task.

somatization; stress; decreased; secondary gain

Pain disorder is characterized by pain that initially may have a physical source, but _____ factors maintain the symptoms. The clinician may specify a subtype of pain disorder in which the pain results primarily from a psychological condition or from a general medical condition. It is important to note that whichever is the case, the pain is _____.

psychological; real

In _____ _____ disorder (BDD), there is an irrational preoccupation with a perceived defect in one's physical appearance. These individuals may become fixated on mirrors, and many are reluctant to seek treatment. _____ norms play a role in dictating standards for physical appearance. Individuals with BDD are often referred to as _____. Studies have shown as many as ____% of college students have issues with their bodies and _____% of them have symptoms of BDD.

body dysmorphic; Cultural; delusional; 75; 28

Little is known about the cause of body dysmorphic disorder. Psychoanalytic theory holds that the _____ of anxiety onto a specific body part helps to reduce an underlying conflict. Body dysmorphic disorder has a high comorbidity rate with _____-_____ disorder, and treatments such as _____, _____, and _____ _____ may be effective for both disorders. Individuals with body dysmorphic disorder may initiate _____ _____, but often they are not satisfied by the outcome. In fact, the severity of the disorder may increase following surgery.

displacement; obsessive-compulsive; drugs; exposure; response prevention; plastic surgery

Dissociative disorders involve experiences of unreality. They may involve _____, the temporary loss of a sense of one's own reality; and derealization, the loss of the _____ of the external world.

depersonalization; reality

_____ disorder concerns severe feelings of detachment, such that every day functioning is impaired. Symptoms may be experienced as a result of _____ or trauma. Depersonalization disorder is diagnosed frequently/rarely, and often co-occurs with _____ and _____ disorders.

Depersonalization; stress; rarely; mood; anxiety

Dissociative _____ may be generalized (unable to remember anything, including personal identity) or localized (unable to remember specific events during a specific time period). _____ amnesias are most common.

amnesia; Localized

In dissociative _____, memory loss is associated with a "flight" or an unexpected trip. Individuals experience identity confusion and may assume a new identity. The fugue states typically end shortly/abruptly, with the individual returning home, usually with _____ recollection of the events occurring during the flight.

fugue; abruptly; some

Symptoms of dissociative _____ disorder vary across cultures. Personality changes are attributed to possession by a spirit specific to the culture. If a trance state is a feature of a traditional cultural or religious practice, it <u>is/is not</u> considered abnormal. Relatively rare in Western cultures, dissociative trance disorders are <u>common/uncommon</u> in many other cultures.

trance; is not; common

In dissociative _____ disorder (DID), a person adopts one or more identities. The defining feature is that certain aspects of the person's identity become detached or dissociated. Typically, a "host identity," who seeks to hold identity fragments together, becomes the clinical patient. The patient may "switch" to _____ during treatment. Alters may represent the opposite gender or a distinctively different personality type (e.g. aggressive), or may present with other types of _____ transformations.

identity, alters; physical

People with dissociative identity disorder are highly suggestible, and treatment is facilitated with _____. Several researchers have questioned the ability of the person to "fake" multiple personalities. The physiological differences found across alters in a given person would be extremely <u>easy/difficult</u> to fake successfully. Dissociative identity disorder occurs much more frequently in <u>males/females</u>, with a ratio as high as 9:1. Estimates of the _____ of the disorder range from 1% to 6%. The course of dissociative identity disorder may be lifelong if not treated. New personalities may emerge in response to new life situations. There is <u>low/high</u> comorbidity of dissociative identity disorder with other psychological disorders.

hypnosis; difficult; females; prevalence; high

Almost all victims of dissociative identity disorder report having experienced severe _____ _____, frequently including incest and other sexual abuse. The cause of the disorder may be traced to a natural tendency to dissociate or escape abuse. Dissociative identity disorder has strong parallels with _____-_____ _____ disorder. In DID, there is <u>less/greater</u> emphasis on dissociative symptoms than in PTSD; _____ is also present in both disorders. Little is known about the etiology of dissociative disorders. There is some support for the notion that individuals with dissociative disorders may be highly _____ or "hypnotizable." There is also a high comorbidity rate between _____ activity and dissociative symptoms.

child abuse; post-traumatic stress; greater; anxiety; suggestible; seizure

Distinguishing between _____ and _____ memories of early trauma or abuse is both difficult and controversial. While there is certainly evidence that children experience abusive situations, they may not remember these events due to _____ _____. If these persons were to seek treatment, asking questions about a history of abuse is clearly necessary. However, there is research evidence that such questioning can _____ false memories of abuse. Therapists need to be extremely _____ when dealing with this issue.

real; false; dissociative amnesia; create; careful

Treatment methods vary across the different dissociative disorders. Dissociative _____ and _____ states typically remit on their own. Therapy may help in resolving stressful life situations and building coping skills. In DID, long-term psychotherapy is generally implicated, with the goal being _____ of the various identities and resolution of _____ memories. Even so, the long-term outcome for the integration of the personalities remains relatively _____.

amnesia; fugue; integration; traumatic; poor

KEY WORDS

Practice defining the important concepts listed below. Follow the definition suggestions provided in the introduction to this Guide. Be precise and accurate, and check your work with the text. Add to the definition later as you encounter more information about the term. Whenever possible, include examples. Use only the space to the right of the word so that later you can cover either the word or the definition to use one to cue the other. Define additional important terms you'll find in the chapter.

1. body dysmorphic disorder

2. conversion disorder

3. depersonalization disorder

4. dissociative disorders

5. dissociative identity disorder

_____

_____

6. factitious disorder

_____

_____

7. hypochondriaisis

_____

_____

8. malingering

_____

_____

9. somatization disorder

_____

_____

10. somatoform disorders

_____

_____

SAMPLE QUESTIONS

As one of the later stages of your study for this chapter, you can assess your progress by taking a sample test. Don't make the mistake of studying just for these questions. They are merely a small sample of the many questions that could appear on an exam. An excellent way to help yourself is to generate your own questions and answers. This will help you focus on important concepts, make better distinctions among similar ideas, practice writing responses, and engaging the material in general. Try them on your friends in your study group.

Multiple Choice Questions

1. Freud described the physical symptoms of conversion hysteria as representing
   a. a displacement of anxiety left over from the oral stage.
   b. a conversion of an unconscious conflict into a socially acceptable form.
   c. a reaction formation involving suppressed memories of a traumatic event.
   d. a conversion involving suppressed memories of a traumatic event.

2. The following symptoms are all necessary for a DSM-IV diagnosis of hypochondriasis, except
   a. significant distress in everyday functioning.
   b. misinterpretation of bodily symptoms.
   c. preoccupation with fear of acquiring a serious disease.
   d. preoccupation with fears of having a serious disease.

3. Malingering differs from factitious disorder in that
   a. in malingering, symptoms are intentionally feigned and in factitious disorder they are not.
   b. family-oriented psychotherapy is a more effective treatment for factitious disorder than for malingering.
   c. malingering may include extending the symptoms to family members by proxy.
   d. in malingering, there is an identifiable external gain.

4. Juanita, a therapist, believes that her feet are too big for her body and often complains that she will never have a normal social life because of her disability. She has begun to be absent from work, instead choosing to spend exorbitant amounts of time and money shopping for "foot-binding shoes." Her symptoms suggest
   a. body dysmorphic disorder.
   b. acute stress disorder.
   c. hypochondriasis.
   d. obsessive-compulsive disorder.

5. The term "hysteria" has historically linked
   a. conversion disorders with the schizophrenias.
   b. somatoform disorders with their subtypes.
   c. dissociative disorders and somatization disorder.
   d. somatoform and dissociative disorders.

6. Which of the following is not characteristic of dissociative disorders?
   a. individuals may be highly suggestive.
   b. treatment may include building coping skills.
   c. individuals have typically had traumatic childhood experiences.
   d. none of the above.

7. Treatment of conversion disorders
    a. follows a family systems model.
    b. deals with removing secondary gain.
    c. is supported by Freudian theory.
    d. b and c.

8. On the planet Neptar, civilians worship the sap from the ginga tree. On ceremonious holidays, the planet's executive director prepares jam from the sap and performs trance-like aerobics routines. She is probably suffering from
    a. Amok.
    b. dissociative trance disorder.
    c. schizophrenia.
    d. none of the above

9. Undifferentiated somatoform disorder
    a. is similar to somatization disorder but with fewer symptoms.
    b. was included in DSM-III but not DSM-IV.
    c. a and b.
    d. includes symptoms of somatization disorder and conversion disorder.

10. A blind person is referred to a clinician by an optometrist, who can find no physical evidence for the blindness. The clinician asks the patient to perform a series of visual tasks. Following the assessment, the clinician concludes that her patient is suffering from a conversion disorder. What observation would lead to this conclusion?
    a. The patient performed at a chance level on the task.
    b. The patient demonstrated high anxiety during the visual task and performed at the level that chance would predict.
    c. The patient performed worse than chance on the visual task until given motivation to perform correctly, at which time he performed better than chance would predict.
    d. The patient performed better than chance on the visual task until given motivation to perform correctly, at which time he performed worse than chance would predict.

11. Hypochondriasis focuses on physical sensations and illness. For example, children report the same symptoms as other family members have had. Which of the following IS NOT one of the three other influential factors of hypochondriasis?
    a. Numerous instances of disease in the family during childhood.
    b. Having suicidal thoughts or past family history of suicide.
    c. A stressful life event, such as death or illness.
    d. Realizing the benefits of being the ill person.

12. Some suicide attempts are believed to represent manipulative behavior rather than a true death wish. This type of suicide attempt
    a. is common in individuals with somatization disorder.
    b. indicates la belle indifference.
    c. both of the above
    d. none of the above

13. Somatization disorder and antisocial personality disorder are often associated with gender and may be explained by similar underlying neurological mechanisms. Which of the following statements best describes this relationship?
    a. Behavioral inhibition and activation systems (fight/flight systems) are characterized by differing behavioral outcomes in males and females due to cultural norms.
    b. Males and females both have inhibition and activation systems, but males have better developed activation systems and females have better developed inhibition systems.
    c. Women with antisocial personality disorder may have an underlying deficit in the behavioral activation system and men with somatization disorder may have an underlying deficit in the behavioral inhibition system.
    d. none of the above

14. Somatization disorder is very difficult to treat. Which of the following is not a typical treatment approach for the disorder?
    a. Reduction of help-seeking behavior.
    b. Reduction of stress.
    c. Traditional psychotherapy.
    d. Reassurance.

15. Dissociative identity disorder has been linked to post- traumatic stress disorder. People suffering from both disorders have usually experienced _____, as indicated by _____
    a. severe trauma; results of MMPI assessment.
    b. childhood abuse; correlational case studies.
    c. severe trauma; retrospective case studies.
    d. a depressive disorder; inter-rater agreement on DSM-III diagnoses.

16. Greta occasionally has sensations of detachment from her surroundings, as if she were in a dream. This feeling of unreality most often occurs when she is overtired. Greta is experiencing symptoms of
    a. conversion hysteria.
    b. a dissociative experience.
    c. neurosis.
    d. dysmorphic disorder.

17. What is the common link among somatoform disorders?
    a. In each of the disorders individuals are pathologically concerned with the appearance or functioning of their bodies.
    b. They all stem from anxiety.
    c. They are a subset of dissociative disorders.
    d. both b and c

18. A central feature of hypochondriasis is
    a. interpretation of harmful stimuli as nonthreatening.
    b. interpretation of almost any physical sensation or symptom as threatening.
    c. a distrust of medical personnel.
    d. more acute physical sensations than someone without hypochondriasis.

19. A major distinction between hypochondriasis and somatization disorder is
    a. in somatization disorder the person is concerned with the symptoms themselves, whereas in hypochondriasis the person is concerned with the meaning of the symptoms.
    b. in hypochondriasis the person is concerned with the symptoms themselves, whereas in somatization disorder the person is concerned with the meaning of the symptoms.
    c. Hypochondriasis tends to run in families, whereas somatization disorder does not.
    d. There is genetic evidence for somatization disorder, whereas for hypochondriasis there is not.

20. While both factitious disorders and malingering have feigned symptoms that are under voluntary control, they differ in that the goal of factitious disorders is _____, whereas, the goal of malingering is _____.
    a. to assume the sick role; to manipulate the system to gain a desired end.
    b. to avoid societal punishment or responsibility; to gain positive attention.
    c. Hypochondriasis tends to run in families, whereas somatization disorder does not.
    d. to present oneself in a more favorable light; to avoid societal punishment or responsibility.

21. Jenna, a recently-married young woman, described episodes of "spacing out." During these episodes, she feels as if she is observing herself from outside of her body. Her experiences seem "dream-like" and she reports feeling completely separated from what is going on around her. It is likely that Jenna is experiencing _____.
    a. stress associated with being newly married.
    b. post-traumatic episodes.
    c. detachment disorder.
    d. depersonalization disorder.

22. Patients with BDD were often also diagnosed with
    a. diabetes.
    b. depression.
    c. heart problems.
    d. all of the above

23. We are interested in prevention. Which of the following people would be most likely to develop hypochondriasis?
    a. Jacob, whose parents died from a rare but serious disease, who was then cared for by overprotective grandparents who were always worried about his "delicate condition."
    b. Marissa who has a family history of somatoform disorders.
    c. Adrian who is physically susceptible to colds and flu and catches every "bug" that is going around.
    d. Tracey who has a family history of breast cancer.

24. In a study of false memory, researchers asked 3-year-old girls who visited a physician's office whether they were touched in their genital area. The results of this study
    a. suggest that 60% of the children who were examined genitally, inaccurately reported that they were not examined.
    b. suggest that 60% of the children who were not examined genitally, inaccurately reported that they were.
    c. suggest that young children are not very accurate in reporting what happened to them.
    d. all of the above

25. Immediately following the onset of his brain damage in the videotape "ABNORMAL PSYCHOLOGY: LIVE!", Mike could not recall much of his past-including names of his closest family members. Mike has regained some of these memories; however, he still has difficulty
    a. recalling people's faces.
    b. storing emotionally-charged events.
    c. storing new memories.
    d. recalling procedural memories.

26. The cause of the Amnesic Disorder exhibited by Mike in your CD-ROM or the videotape "ABNORMAL PSYCHOLOGY: LIVE!" was
    a. brain damage resulting from Alzheimer's Disease.
    b. brain damage resulting from a heroin overdose.
    c. brain damage resulting from a racing accident.
    d. brain damage resulting from a cocaine overdose.

True or False Questions

27. The symptoms of some pain disorder may not be attributable to a medical condition.

    TRUE or FALSE

28. Somatization disorder is more common in females than in males.

    TRUE or FALSE

29. Fugue states require extensive long-term treatment before memory is restored.

    TRUE or FALSE

30. Localized amnesia is less common in dissociative disorders than is generalized amnesia.

    TRUE or FALSE

31. Somatization disorder, although rarely diagnosed in a clinical setting, is more common in the population than are eating disorders.

    TRUE or FALSE

32. Reassurance therapy is gaining support as the treatment of choice for hypochondriasis.

    TRUE or FALSE

33. In depersonalization disorder, an individual experiences a feeling of personal detachment, which predisposes disorganized behaviors and amnesia.

    TRUE or FALSE

34. There is incontrovertible evidence that memories of child abuse can be manufactured.

    TRUE or FALSE

35. Conversion disorders, like somatization disorder, are more frequently found in women and usually occur during adolescence or after.

    TRUE or FALSE

36. OCD frequently co-occurs with BDD.

    TRUE or FALSE

37. Only a small percentage of DID patients have also had other disorders, such as substance abuse, depression, borderline personality disorder, anxiety attacks, and eating disorders.

    FALSE or FALSE

Essay Questions

38. Discuss Freud's conceptualization of conversion disorder. How is his theory regarded in terms of treating the disorder today?

39. Plastic surgery appears to be a beneficial intervention for individuals who are concerned with deficits in their appearance. Discuss the impact of plastic surgery on individuals suffering from body dysmorphic disorder.

40. Dissociative identity disorder is a popular topic on television talk shows. As today's expert, tell Oprah and her audience how DID might be construed as an extreme subtype of post-traumatic stress disorder?

41. What factors make diagnosis of hypochondriasis problematic?

42. Discuss the evidence supporting the concept of false memories.

HOW WELL DID YOU DO?

Less than 60%	Don't take the quiz before you study the chapter. It will narrow your focus too much. You can improve your score if you increase your efforts.
60-80%	Restudy and rewrite, especially the weak areas; discuss problem areas with study partners.
Over 80%	You're on the right track; continue as you are; focus on trouble areas with study group.
Over 95%	Nice job, especially if you know the whole chapter this well. Be sure to reward your behavior, help others in your study group (they'll help you on your weak chapters), and don't forget to review.

THINKING ALLOWED

Chapter 5 Activities

In previous DSM editions, what category name included the terms "personality disorder" but was not a personality disorder? The answer is Multiple Personality Disorder. Why do you think the developers of DSM-IV changed the disorder name to Dissociative Identity Disorder? Is "identity" more clear or informative than "personality?" Does the term "dissociative" help you remember characteristics of the disorder?

Dissociative fugue is a favorite plot device in television series. It allows actors to display their range of skills by taking on new roles, and producers to introduce new characters without needing to pay more actors. Other dissociative disorders appear as well. Can you and your study group find such instances? Critique the accuracy of the portrayals.

INTERNET RESOURCES

Dissociative Disorders

Brief descriptions of the disorders and their treatments.

http://www.athealth.com/Consumer/disorders/Dissociative.html

Somatoform Disorders

An overview of somatization disorder, conversion disorder, pain disorder, hypochondriasis, and body dysmorphic disorder.

http://www.merck.com/pubs/mmanual/section15/chapter186/186a.html

Solutions

KEY WORDS

1. (186-187)
2. (180-181)
3. (192-193)
4. (173, 191-192)
5. (195-196)
6. (182)
7. (173)
8. (181)
9. (177-178)
10. (173)

SAMPLE QUESTIONS

Multiple Choice Questions

1. B, 173
2. C, 173-175
3. D, 181-182
4. A, 186-188
5. D, 173
6. D, 191-192
7. B, 185
8. D, 191-192
9. A, 177-180
10. C, 180-181
11. B, 173-175
12. A, 177-180
13. A, 177-180
14. C, 180
15. C, 195-196
16. B, 191-192
17. A, 173
18. B, 173-175
19. A, 177-180
20. A, 181-182
21. D, 191-192
22. D, 186-189
23. A, 173-177
24. D, 198-200
25. C, video, CD-ROM
26. C, video, CD-ROM

True or False Questions

27. F, 185-186
28. T, 178-180
29. F, 194-195
30. F, 191
31. F, 178-180
32. T, 177, This research finding is surprising, given the historical belief that people with hypochondriasis are not appeased by the reassurance of medical doctors.
33. F, 192-193
34. T, 198-200
35. T, 180-181
36. T, 187-188
37. F, 196-198

Essay Questions

38. Freud coined the term "conversion". His belief was that anxiety from unconscious conflicts needed to find a means of expression. The anxiety was converted into physical symptoms, allowing the individual to express anxiety without actually experiencing it. In your answer, outline Freud's four basic processes in the development of conversion disorder. Don't forget that Freud's notion of primary gain, as it relates to la belle indifference, is challenged. Current therapy techniques include catharsis of traumatic events, a Freudian technique, and removal of sources of secondary gain. (See textbook pages 180-181).

39. Plastic surgery has no known therapeutic benefits for people suffering from body dysmorphic disorder. Typically, the patient is not satisfied with the results and some individuals may go back repeatedly to fix the initial surgery. In many cases the severity of the disorder increases following surgery. (See textbook pages 190-192).

40. Both disorders are characterized by strong emotional reactions to traumatic events. Some people may be more biologically and psychologically vulnerable to experiencing severe anxiety in the face of trauma. Typically, individuals with DID have experienced extremely severe trauma. The construal of DID as a subtype of PTSD emphasizes the common dissociative symptoms of both disorders. (See textbook pages 195-202).

41. People with hypochondriasis usually believe their symptoms have a medical etiology. Therefore, they tend to consult general physicians, rather than psychologists or psychiatrists. Several consultations with several medical doctors may occur before a physician refers the patient to the mental health system. Reassurance from medical doctors often only motivates the patient to consult another medical doctor. (See textbook pages 173-177).

42. The idea that memories can be false is supported by several different lines of research. Studies have found that children can "recall" (as real memories) fictitious events that are told to them by someone they trust. Other research evidence suggests that even if some event does occur, children's memories can distort the event and report non-existent parts of that event. A third line of research has found that children are capable not only of creating memories, but are also capable of adding details and embellishments that may increase the believability of their report (see textbook page 200-202).

MOOD DISORDERS AND SUICIDE

LEARNING OBJECTIVES

1. Differentiate a depressive episode from a manic and hypomanic episode.

2. Describe the clinical symptoms of major depression and bipolar disorder.

3. Differentiate major depression from Dysthymic disorder and distinguish bipolar disorder from cyclothymic disorder.

4. Describe the differences in prevalence of mood disorders across the life span.

5. Describe the biological, psychological, and sociocultural contributions to the development of unipolar and bipolar mood disorders.

6. Describe medical and psychological treatments that have been successful in treating mood disorders.

7. Describe the relationship between suicide and mood disorders, including known risk factors and approaches to suicide prevention and treatment.

CHAPTER SUMMARY

By now you know what to do with chapter summaries and sample tests.

Feelings of depression are universal. Mood disorders differ from "normal" moods in _____ *intensity* and *duration*. Disorders of mood are characterized by gross deviations in mood that interfere significantly with the ability to function in daily life.

intensity; duration

Both depression and _____ are considered mood disorders. Depression in its most common and severe state is referred to as a _____ _____ _____, in which a severely depressed mood lasts for at least two weeks. _____ symptoms (feelings of worthlessness and indecisiveness) as well as changes in physical functioning (disrupted sleep patterns, appetite change, anhedonia, and decreased energy level) may be implicated. New research has found that these physical changes are _____ to the diagnosis of a major depressive episode. If left untreated, the average major depressive episode lasts ____ months.

mania; major depressive episode; Cognitive; central; 9

_____, a less common experience, is characterized by extreme elation, joy, or euphoria. Symptoms include hyperactivity, decreased sleep, grandiosity, and rapid, incoherent speech (flight of _____). The average length of an untreated manic episode is ____ months. A less severe form of mania that does not cause impaired social/occupational functioning is known as _____. The experience of only one of these mood types (usually depression) is called a _____ mood disorder. The experience of both mood types is called _____ disorder. An individual experiencing elation with simultaneous depression is said to be in a dysphoric manic or mixed manic episode.

Mania; ideas; 3-6; hypomania; unipolar; bipolar

The _____ and severity of a mood disorder differ among individuals. Depressive and manic episodes tend to remit on their own without treatment. The _____ (time) patterning of depressive and manic episodes is an important diagnostic consideration. Symptoms associated with mood disorders are variable. Either _____ too little or too much, or changes in _____ will contribute to a DSM diagnosis of Major Depression.

course; temporal; sleeping; weight

A single major depressive disorder is called a major depressive disorder, _____ episode. If an episode recurs after at least 2 months in which the individual was not depressed, a major depressive disorder, _____, is diagnosed. Recurrence is an important consideration for prediction and _____. Individuals with recurrent major depression usually (do/do not) have a family history of depression. Unipolar depression is almost always a _Chronic_ condition.

single; recurrent; treatment; do; chronic

_____ disorder includes many of the symptoms seen in major depressive disorder, but symptoms are generally milder and consistent over long periods of time. For a diagnosis, a persistently depressed mood must be present for at least _____ years. _____ depression is seen in individuals who experience dysthymic disorder and later suffer from one or more major depressive episodes. Double depression is associated with more severe psychopathology. Researchers have found that persons with double depression have low/high rates of Major Depressive Disorder recurrence.

Dysthymic; two; Double; high

The age of onset of depression is increasing/decreasing worldwide, while the incidence of depression and suicide has increased/decreased. The mean age of onset is 27 years, with a probability of recurrence of about 90%. The onset of dysthymia is typically in the early 20's, with a median duration of about _____ years. Research has found that the occurrence of dysthymic symptoms prior to age 21 is associated with higher _____, a poor _____, and a stronger likelihood of the disorder running in the _____. Studies have found a high prevalence of dysthymic disorder in _____ and 76% of these dysthymic children later develop _____ _____. However, Kovacs found almost all dysthymic children eventually _____.

decreasing; increased; five; chronicity; prognosis; family; children; depressive disorder; recover

Differentiating between a normal grieving process and major depression can be difficult. Many symptoms, such as _____, emotional numbness, and denial are shared. Generally, mental health professionals do not diagnose major depression after the death of a loved one unless the person becomes suicidal or psychotic, becomes incapacitated by the symptoms, or the symptoms last longer than _____ months. Funeral and burial ceremonies help the grieving process by providing _____ from families and friends. A victim with long-lasting grief is often encouraged to _____ the trauma, talk about the death and incorporate _____ emotions with the loss.

anxiety; two; support; re-experience; positive

Bipolar disorders have many parallels with unipolar depressive disorders. For example, there may be a single episode or a series of recurrences. _____ disorder is a milder, more chronic version of bipolar disorder. The criteria for bipolar I disorder are the same as for bipolar II except individuals experience a full _____ _____. For these manic episodes to be considered separate there must be at least _____ months symptom-free between them. During high manic episodes, patients often _____ they have a problem. They believe their behavior is perfectly reasonable and may stop taking their _____. Similar to dysthymia, in cyclothymia the alternating moods do/do not reach the severity of major depressive or manic states.

Cyclothymic; manic episode; two; deny; medication; do not

Bipolar disorders begin earlier/later than depressive disorders, with the average onset for bipolar I disorder being 18 years and bipolar II disorder being 22 years; although it is rare to develop bipolar disorder after the age of ___. Cyclothymia has an earlier onset, typically during the teenage years, and it may develop into a full-blown _____ disorder. These disorders are occasionally seen in children and adolescents.

later; 40; bipolar

Longitudinal course specifiers refer to the temporal patterning or the _____ of mood disorders. _____ cycling pattern refers to the experience of at least four manic or depressive episodes in a year in a bipolar disorder.

course; Rapid

Seasonal patterning, seen in bipolar disorders and recurrent major depressive disorders, is characterized by episodes that occur during certain times of the year. _____ _____ disorder (SAD) is associated with seasonal patterning and typically involves winter depression. One theory of SAD is that increased production of _____, which only occurs in the absence of light, may trigger depression in vulnerable individuals. Phototherapy, or systematic exposure to _____, is a new treatment technique.

Seasonal affective; melatonin; light

Mood disorders may be extremely debilitating. Frequently observed consequences include decreased productivity, job loss, and interpersonal problems. Mood disorders are represented in all ethnic groups, although blacks are more/less likely than whites and Hispanics to experience a major depressive disorder or dysthymia. Women are about half/twice as likely as men to have a mood disorder, although the genders are about equally likely to experience a bipolar disorder.

less; twice

Symptoms of depression in children may be different from those in adults and are observed in facial expressions, eating, sleeping, and _____ behavior. Depressive disorders are less common in children than in adults, but the depression rate rises dramatically in adolescents. _____ in young children is more prevalent than major depression, but the reverse is true in adolescents. Bipolar disorders appear relatively frequently/rarely in young children and more so during adolescence.

play; Dysthymia; rarely

In young children, particularly boys, depression may be associated with _____ behavior, often resulting in or combining with a diagnosis of hyperactivity or conduct disorder. Childhood and particularly adolescent mood disorders <u>need not/must</u> be taken seriously. Adolescent mood disorders tend to continue on a long-term basis or implicate more serious psychopathology. Rates of attempted suicide are very high during _____. _____ disorder is often misdiagnosed as conduct disorder or attention deficit-hyperactivity disorder. Also, _____ _____ is often misdiagnosed as hyperactivity or conduct disorder.

aggressive; must; adolescence; Bipolar; childhood depression

Recent research has also addressed mood disorders in the elderly. Mood disorders with an onset after age 60 may be particularly _____, and diagnosis is compounded with other medical illnesses or dementia. Depression in the elderly is associated with onset of physical diseases and feelings associated with the infirmities of older age. _____ disorders frequently accompany depression in the elderly. Rates of depression among the elderly are <u>declining/rising</u>. Elderly men <u>are/are not</u> as likely to be depressed as elderly women, indicating that the sex-ratio for depression changes with age.

chronic; Anxiety; rising; are

The measurement of mood disorder symptoms is problematic, particularly across cultures. For example, Western societies tend to focus on <u>individual/group</u> depression, whereas other cultures might refer to the group as a whole. The DSM and various semi-structured interviews are used as tools for systematic investigation of cross-culture psychopathology. Research using such systematic investigation has found _____ rates for the lifetime prevalence of mood disorders among different ethnic groups, although these results can vary widely in specific locations.

individual; similar

The relatively frequent occurrence of mood disorders, particularly mania, in extremely _____ individuals is curious. It is possible that vulnerability to mood disorders is somehow associated with a _____ to creativity.

creative; predisposition

Depression is highly correlated with _____. However, while virtually all depressed individuals also experience anxiety, not all anxious individuals also experience depression. Certain core symptoms of depression <u>are/are not</u> seen in anxiety (anhedonia, depressive "slowing", and more negative cognitive content). Symptoms that are central to anxiety and panic include autonomic activation, muscle tension, and apprehension. Symptoms that are not specific to either depression or anxiety are called symptoms of _____ _____. Some researchers predict that a category combining mood and _____ disorders may be appropriate following more extensive research.

anxiety; are not; negative affect; anxiety

Identifying the causes of mood disorders involves the principle of _____, where more than one cause may contribute to the resulting symptoms. An _____ theory of the etiology of mood disorders takes into consideration the interaction of biological, psychological, and social dimensions, including the strong relationship between anxiety and depression.

equifinality; integrative

Biological causes have been investigated using family studies, adoption studies, and twin studies. In family studies, first-degree relatives of an individual with a mood disorder are two to three times more/less likely to have a mood disorder. Studies of the biological and adopted family members of persons with mood disorders have found _____ results. Some studies have found a genetic component, while others have not. Twin studies have suggested that severe mood disorders may have a stronger _____ contribution than more mild mood disorders. Also, bipolar disorder may simply be a more severe variant of mood disorders rather than a fundamentally different disorder. Taken together, the research suggests that mood disorders are familial and reflect a genetic predisposition.

more; mixed; genetic

Research frequently addresses the heritability of related groups of disorders rather than singling out a specific disorder for study. These studies have revealed a close relationship among depression, anxiety and panic. Biological vulnerability for mood disorders may not be specific to that disorder but may reflect a more general vulnerability. Current scientific thinking about mood disorders revolves around the _____ of several neurotransmitter systems, rather than a single neurotransmitter. The more modern, "permissive" hypothesis suggests that high/low serotonin levels and their interaction with other systems, including the norepinephrine and dopamine systems, may account for the etiology of mood disorders. The role of dopamine specifically in manic episodes has been studied with no clear-cut conclusions.

interaction; low

The endocrine system has also been implicated in depression. Levels of _____, a "stress hormone," are elevated during stressful life events and in depressed patients. The dexamethasone suppression test (DST), used as a biological test for depression, suppresses cortisol secretion in normal patients, but does so to a much <u>lesser/greater</u> extent in depressed patients. More recent research suggests that individuals with other disorders also suppress cortisol in a manner similar to persons with depression. More recent research has focused on neurohormones, which are regulated by the _____ and impact the brain and _____ axis. There are thousands of neurohormones, and determining the relationship among them and mood disorders will be difficult.

cortisol; lesser; hypothalamus; HYPAC

Sleep and _____ rhythms may also play a role in the etiology of mood disorders. For example, depressed people experience more rapid and intense REM activity than non-depressed people. Depressed individuals have diminished _____ _____ sleep (the deepest, most restful part of sleep). Sleep <u>deprivation/excess</u> has shown temporary success in alleviating depression. Depressed people may also experience increased sensitivity to light. One popular hypothesis is that <u>high/low</u> serotonin levels affect the regulation of daily biological rhythms. Abnormal sleep profiles, disturbances in REM sleep, and poor sleep quality predict a somewhat <u>poorer/better</u> response to psychosocial treatment. New evidence based on EEG data suggests that greater _____-side activation and less _____-side activation of the anterior cerebral hemispheres is characteristic of at least some depressed persons.

circadian; slow wave; deprivation; low; poorer; right; left

Stressful life events frequently occur prior to the onset of depression, but _____ these events can be problematic. These events affect individuals differently, and current moods may _____ memories of past events. Thus it is important for the clinician to consider the individual context and meaning of life events. Nevertheless, stressful life events are predominant in patients diagnosed with depression and mania. It is possible that a stressful life event _____ _____ a vulnerability to trigger a mood disorder.

defining; distort; interacts with

The _____ _____ theory of depression suggests that people who make an attribution that they have no control over stress in their lives may become anxious and then depressed. These attributions are internal, stable, and global. A question remains as to whether attributional style is a cause or a _____ of depression. Some research suggests that a negative event early in childhood may give rise to a negative attributional style. Attributions may be important in contributing to a sense of hopelessness. A pessimistic style may predate a negative life event and contribute to later anxious or depressive episodes.

learned helplessness; correlate

Aaron Beck is considered the founder of _____ therapy. He found that depressed individuals tended to experience everyday events in a negative way, and labeled different types of "cognitive _____ " that characterize this negative thinking. Two important errors are arbitrary inference and _____. The cognitive triad of depression represents cognitive errors in terms of the individuals themselves, their immediate world, and their _____. Depressed individuals may also develop a negative schema. Much/little research supports the cognitive style of depressed individuals as described by Beck. However, establishing the existence of negative schema prior to depression onset has been more problematic than using negative schema to predict recurrence.

cognitive; errors; overgeneralization; future; Much

Marital satisfaction has a strong/weak relationship with depression. Marital stress or dissatisfaction may precede depression, or depression may contribute to marital stress. Therapists should treat disturbed marital relationships at the same time as the _____ disorder to ensure patient success and to prevent _____.

strong; mood; relapse

Like other types of disorders, major depressive disorder and dysthymia are more/less prevalent in women than in men. This may be explained by the dependent sex role that women learn, the high emphasis that women may place on intimate relationships, the tendency of women to ruminate over their personal feelings more/less than men, and the fact that women may have greater social disadvantages than men. Sex roles and stereotypes may play a role in other disorders in that the prevalence rates for disorders associated with aggression, overactivity, and substance abuse are greater/less in men than in women.

more; more; greater

Social _____ plays a powerful role in depression. Numerous studies show that people experiencing a stressful life event are less likely to become depressed if they have a strong social support network, and those who do become depressed recover more quickly with the support of others. _____ therapy deals with facilitating social support. More research is needed to identify the mechanisms by which vulnerable individuals with stressful life events experience one type of disorder instead of another.

support; Interpersonal

Several treatment approaches are used in mood disorders. Somatic treatments may include antidepressant medications, such as tricyclic antidepressants, _____ _____ (MAO) inhibitors, and selective _____ reuptake inhibitors, such as Prozac. Clinicians must consider the side effects and possibility of overdose when prescribing drugs. Newer medications to treat depression (e.g., Venlafaxine and Nefazodone) have been found to be equivalent to the older antidepressants in terms of symptom alleviation. Persons who desire an herbal approach to treating depression have tried ___ _____ _____, which early evidence suggests alters serotonin functioning in the brain. It is important to note that these drugs are not necessarily effective for children and may be associated with additional side effects. Lithium is a type of antidepressant drug that may have more serious side effects than other medications; however, one major advantage is its effectiveness in the treatment of _____.

monoamine oxidase; serotonin; St. John's Wort; mania

Electroconvulsive therapy (ECT), in which _____ _____ is administered to the brain, is used only for very severe cases of depression. Current use of ECT therapy is generally safe and reasonably effective; the reasons for its success are/are not known.

electric shock; are not

Psychosocial treatments are also widely available for individuals with mood disorders. In cognitive therapy, patients are taught to identify depressive _____ ___ _____, and, as therapy progresses, to alter underlying negative cognitive schema. The skills learned during the therapy session may then be applied to day-to-day life. _____ involves bringing patients into contact with reinforcing events in their lives.

errors in thinking; Reactivating

_____ psychotherapy involves the improvement of interpersonal problems and the skills to develop new interpersonal relationships. Four types of issues are frequently identified: dealing with interpersonal role disputes, adjusting to the loss of a relationship, acquiring ___ _____, and identifying and correcting deficits in _____ _____. These psychosocial therapies have/have not proven effectiveness in treating depression.

Interpersonal; new relationships; social skills; have

_____ of mood disorders is an important research priority. Some researchers have focused on teaching social and _____-_____ skills to children. The initial studies have reported success in this technique, but further research is needed to conduct valid evaluation studies.

Prevention; problem-solving

The combination of _____ and psychosocial treatments for depression may be superior to either approach by itself, although no strong data are currently available to support this hypothesis. Medicinal treatments have the advantage of operating more _____ than psychosocial therapy, but psychosocial therapy may have more _____-_____ benefits in the acquisition of adaptive social skills. Therefore, a _____ approach may be most suitable for some patients.

drug; quickly; long-term; combined

Treatments of mood disorders have been evaluated according to their effectiveness in preventing _____. Psychosocial treatment and continuing medication may help to prevent relapse, but more data are needed. An _____ approach suggests that biological treatments may contribute to psychological improvement and psychological treatments may contribute to biological improvement. One study found patients with recurrent depression that had already undergone drug treatment and were then treated with cognitive therapy experienced significantly <u>more/fewer</u> relapses.

relapse; integrative; fewer

Although _____ is accepted as the most effective treatment for bipolar disorder, psychosocial therapies can help manage such problems as compliance with _____ regimens and other, more practical problems. New research indicates that providing psychosocial treatment to the _____ of persons with bipolar disorder helps to prevent relapse.

lithium; medication; families

Suicide rates are extremely high and have increased dramatically in recent years. Suicide victims are predominantly Caucasian. Rates in adolescents and the elderly have dramatically increased. Males are <u>more/less</u> likely to commit suicide than females, but females are <u>more/less</u> likely to attempt suicide than males. Suicide is the third leading cause of death in _____, and there has also been an <u>increase/decrease</u> in elderly suicide rates. The country of _____ has the highest suicide rate. Suicidal _____ is an important index of suicide.

more; more; adolescents; increase; China; ideation

Durkheim identified several types of suicide. Altruistic suicide refers to a societal expectation that a dishonored individual commit suicide. _____ suicide is implicated in disintegrating social supports. Anomic suicides occur with disruptions in one's life. _____ suicides are those committed as a result of a loss of control over destiny. Freud suggested that suicide represents unconscious hostility or anger directed to the _____ rather than the real target of the anger.

Egoistic; Fatalistic; self

Psychological _____ has been used to study suicide risk factors. Increased risks are seen in those individuals who have lost a family member by suicide, although it is unclear whether this constitutes modeling of a solution or an inherited trait. Low levels of the neurotransmitter _____, associated with impulsivity, also may contribute to suicide. The overwhelming majority of suicides are associated with a psychological disorder, and usually this disorder is _____. Alcohol is frequently used during suicide attempts. Stressful life events that are perceived as shameful or humiliating are also implicated in suicide.

autopsy; serotonin; depression

_____ of suicides may be seen in adolescent peer groups, where suicide victims are elevated socially by peers. Vivid and possibly influential depictions of suicide are common in the media. The identification of individuals who are at risk for suicide is a difficult and imperfect undertaking. Mental health professionals typically ask clients about suicidal _____, humiliating events, and the presence of a _____ for the suicide. If such a plan exists, and the person has access to the materials necessary to complete the plan, then clinicians must take action. _____ _____ contracts are often tried first; however, if the person cannot agree to or comply with the terms of the contract then immediate _____ is indicated. Prevention approaches for suicide include telephone hotline and _____ _____ services.

Clusters; ideation; plan; No-suicide; hospitalization; crisis intervention

KEY WORDS

Practice defining the important concepts listed below. Follow the definition suggestions provided in the introduction to this Guide. Be precise and accurate, and check your work with the text. Add to the definition later as you encounter more information about the term. Whenever possible, include examples. Use only the space to the right of the word so that later you can cover either the word or the definition to use one to cue the other. Define additional important terms you'll find in the chapter.

1. bipolar disorders

_____

_____

2. cognitive therapy

_____

_____

3. cyclothymic disorder

_____

_____

4. dysthymic disorder

_____

_____

5. learned helplessness theory of depression

_____

_____

6. major depressive disorder

_____

_____

7. mania

_____

_____

8. mood disorders

_____

_____

9. seasonal affective disorder (SAD)

_____

_____

10. suicidal ideation

_____

_____

SAMPLE QUESTIONS

As one of the later stages of your study for this chapter, you can assess your progress by taking a sample test. Don't make the mistake of studying just for these questions. They are merely a small sample of the many questions that could appear on an exam. An excellent way to help yourself is to generate your own questions and answers. This will help you focus on important concepts, make better distinctions among similar ideas, practice writing responses, and engaging the material in general. Try them on your friends in your study group.

Multiple Choice Questions

1. Which of the following would not be present during a major depressive episode?
   a. changes in appetite and sleeping habits.
   b. anxiety.
   c. anhedonia.
   d. grandiosity.

2. Jenny has experienced long-standing feelings of depression that have never interfered with her productivity or functioning until now. During the past 10 days, she has experienced a depressed mood, feelings of emptiness, and a significant weight loss. Jenny confided in a neighbor that she is considering suicide. It is likely that Jenny is suffering from
   a. major depressive disorder, single episode.
   b. major depressive disorder, recurrent.
   c. double depression.
   d. dysthymia with depressive episode.

3. Bipolar II disorder is characterized by major depressive episodes alternating with _____, while bipolar I disorder is characterized by alternating episodes of major depression and
   _____.
   a. mania; hypomania.
   b. hypomanic episodes; mania.
   c. dysthymia; cyclothymic disorder.
   d. periods of remission; hypomania.

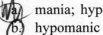

Bipolar I: Mania
Bipolar II: hypomania

4. Richard, who has not responded well to medication, experiences six or more manic and depressive cycles in a year. Diagnosed with bipolar disorder, Richard is displaying
    a. bipolar II disorder.
    b. rapid cycling pattern.
    c. seasonal patterning.
    d. inexplicable treatment response.

5. People who grieve over the death of a loved one
    a. may speed up the "process" of grief with intervention from a mental health professional.
    b. may be predisposed to depressive disorders.
    c. may exhibit undifferentiated dysthymia.
    d. rarely exhibit impacted grief reaction.

6. The statement that best describes the role of serotonin in the etiology of depression is that
    a. low levels of serotonin are solely responsible.
    b. low serotonin levels appear to have an impact, but only in relation to other neurotransmitters.
    c. elevated serotonin levels are solely responsible.
    d. fluctuating levels of serotonin are the underlying basis for depression.

7. Depressed people
    a. exhibit erratic REM patterns over the course of several nights.
    b. begin REM sleep earlier than do non-depressed people.
    c. experience intense REM activity, but may not reach the stages of deepest sleep.
    d. b and c.

8. Seligman's theory on the depressive attributional style has generated substantial research. A conclusion that can not be reached from the current conceptualization of the theory is that
    a. the first response to a stressful situation is negative feelings about one's failings.
    b. depressive attributions will occur over time and across situations if not modified.
    c. learned helplessness contributes to the maintenance of the depressive attributional style.
    d. we do not know whether learned helplessness is a cause or symptom of depression.

9. Women are more frequently diagnosed with mood and anxiety disorders than are men. A proposed explanation for this described in the text is
    a. women tend to have more dopamine than men.
    b. there is a high familial incidence of these disorders in families, suggesting that mothers "pass on" predispositions to their daughters.
    c. cultural stereotypes encourage women to develop interpersonal styles of dependency and passivity.
    d. the changing role of women in society has caused increased stress levels because of the new expectation of women to find their "place in the universe."

10. Tricyclic medications
    a. have been widely used for depression in spite of a variety of side effects.
    b. include imipramine, fluoxetine, and amitriptyline.
    c. are not beneficial for children with attention problems, but are safe for children having major depressive disorder.
    d. are given to patients demonstrating a rapid cycling pattern of depressive, manic, and hypomanic symptoms.

11. Travis suffers from acute major depressive episodes. He does not respond to therapeutic drugs and has been spotted pacing along the bridge near his home. Travis recently gave his therapist a favorite family heirloom. His psychiatrist is concerned about his suicidal ideation and is considering _____ due to the ineffectiveness of the current treatment and the severity of Travis' symptoms.
    a. electroconvulsive shock therapy
    b. frontal lobotomy
    c. insulin shock therapy
    d. hypnosis

12. IPT deals with four interpersonal issues. These include all but which of the following?
    a. issues of intimacy
    b. role disputes
    c. adjustment to loss
    d. social skills deficit correction

13. Feelings of depression
    a. are very rare and occur only in people with a genetic predisposition.
    b. occur only when triggered by a severely negative event.
    c. occur only in people between the ages of 25 and 40.
    d. are universal and experienced by everyone occasionally.

14. What is the most common experience of depression?
    a. Major depressive episode
    b. Hypomanic episode
    c. Catalepsy
    d. Atypical episode

15. The average duration of an untreated depressive episode is
    a. 2 years.
    b. 1 year.
    c. 6 months.
    d. 9 months.

16. Which of the following people are experiencing symptoms of a manic episode?
    a. Lorraine has inflated self-esteem and grandiosity.
    b. Tevon is irritable and is experiencing flight of ideas.
    c. Valerie suddenly goes on an excessive spending spree which she clearly cannot afford.
    d. all of the above

17. Dysthymic disorder shares many of the symptoms of major depressive disorder, but differs in that
    a. symptoms tend to be somewhat milder.
    b. symptoms tend to be of shorter duration.
    c. symptoms tend to be of longer duration.
    d. a and b
    e. a and c

18. Dysthymic disorder is to major depressive episode as cyclothymic disorder is to
    a. major depressive episode.
    b. dysthymic disorder.
    c. bipolar disorder.
    d. none of the above

19. Mood disorder prevention research focuses on
    a. decreasing conflict.
    b. teaching social skills to adolescents.
    c. teaching financial skills to the elderly.
    d. medications.

20. Which of the following is not a stage of interpersonal therapy?
    a. negotiation stage
    b. impasse stage
    c. resolution stage
    d. treatment stage

21. Lyle is 23 years old. His mother died two weeks ago and since then he has been so upset he has been unable to eat or sleep. He has been crying a great deal. The death was completely unexpected and Lyle has been alternating between feeling sad, to feeling very anxious, and wanting to deny that his mother is dead. Lyle appears to be experiencing
    a. rapid cycling bipolar disorder.
    b. a major depressive episode.
    c. double depression.
    d. grief.

22. Mack almost always draws conclusions from situations that emphasize the negative rather than the positive. This is an example of
    a. overgeneralization.
    b. learned helplessness.
    c. delta commentary.
    d. arbitrary inference.

23. Recently, there has been considerable interest in _____ as a herbal treatment for depression.
    a. Milk Thistle
    b. St. John's Wort (hypericum)
    c. Ginko Biloba
    d. Saw Palmetto

24. _____ is the only country that has a higher suicide rate for women than for men.
    a. China
    b. Africa
    c. The United States
    d. Taiwan

25. In the CD-RPM "ABNORMAL PSYCHOLOGY: LIVE!", on Major Depressive Disorder, "Barbara" exhibited all of the following behavior changes except
    a. intense feelings of guilt.
    b. loss of appetite and weight loss.
    c. suicidal thoughts.
    d. a sense of helplessness.

26. In the videotape or CD-ROM "ABNORMAL PSYCHOLOGY: LIVE!", the client "Mary" displayed relatively rare psychotic features associated with her Bipolar Disorder
    a. only in her manic state.
    b. only in her depressive state.
    c. in both her manic and depressive state.
    d. in neither her manic or depressive state.

True or False Questions

27. Suicide is most common in minority racial and ethnic groups having socioeconomic disadvantages.

    TRUE or FALSE

28. Psychological autopsy involves constructing premorbid profiles of suicidal victims.

    TRUE or FALSE

29. "Flight of ideas" refers to the creative tendencies of people with mood disorders, as evidenced by famous artists and leaders throughout history.

    TRUE or FALSE

30. If you fail a major psychology exam and experience lowered self esteem and "the blues," you are likely to be experiencing a depressive disorder, single episode.

    TRUE or FALSE

31. The most frequently occurring mood disorder in relatives of people suffering from bipolar disorder is unipolar depression.

    TRUE or FALSE

32. The notion of a relationship between depression and anxiety has support from biological researchers.

    TRUE or FALSE

33. Prevention of mood disorders in childhood usually deals with modifying the depressive attributional style before it becomes habitual.

 TRUE or FALSE

34. Dysthymic disorder differs from a major depressive episode because its severity, chronicity and number of symptoms are milder and fewer but do not last as long.

TRUE or FALSE

35. A greater prevalence of current personality disorders has been found in patients with early onset dysthymia than in patients with major depressive disorder.

TRUE or FALSE

36. Patients with major depressive disorder are more likely to attempt suicide than patients with dysthymia.

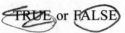 TRUE or FALSE

37. Babies as young as three months old can be depressed.

TRUE or FALSE

38. Cases of children as young as 2-5 years old attempting suicide have been reported.

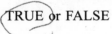 TRUE or FALSE

Essay Questions

39. Discuss the various treatment techniques available for your depressed clients.

40. Explain the specifiers that clinicians may use in "fine-tuning" a DSM-IV diagnosis

41. Discuss the risk factors that are associated with suicide attempts.

42. Explain the neurological basis for mood disorders. Is drug therapy sufficient?

HOW WELL DID YOU DO?

Less than 60%	Restudy the chapter (don't just reread); rework your notes completely. You can improve if you increase your efforts.
60-80%	Restudy and rewrite, especially the weak areas; discuss problem areas with study partners.
Over 80%	You're on the right track; continue as you are; focus on trouble areas with study group.
Over 95%	Nice job, especially if you know the whole chapter this well. Be sure to reward your behavior, help others in your study group (they'll help you on your weak chapters), and don't forget to review.

THINKING ALLOWED
Chapter 6 Activities

In a private notebook, keep track of your own moods for a week. Can you quantify them? And can you identify the reasons for changes in moods? Any surprises? Do you think this project affects your moods because you are more aware of them?

You have found the perfect person to be your lifetime partner. After your relationship has blossomed for over a year, you suddenly discover this person has a history of major depressive disorder and continues to take medication for it. What is your reaction and how does it change your relationship, if at all?

Some researchers have analyzed song lyrics for reflections of mood states. Traditional Country and Western songs have provided many examples of the irrational cognitive beliefs that may perpetuate depression (e.g., life is not worth living without you). Listen carefully from now on and do your own analysis. Do you think these songs cause or merely reflect such beliefs?

INTERNET RESOURCES

Clinical Depression Screening Test

General Hospital, an "ongoing art and information project of the artist team Margaret Crane/Jon Winet, which looks at mental health and society" developed this online depression examination.

http://sandbox.xerox.com/pair/cw/testing.html

Cyclothymia

Internet Mental Health provides this informative web page; information on other disorders are provided as well.

http://www.mentalhealth.com/dis/p20-md03.html

Depression in Children and Adolescents

This fact sheet, prepared by NIMH, summarizes some of the latest scientific findings on child and adolescent depression and lists resources.

http://www.athealth.com/Consumer/disorders/ChildDepression.html

Eight Factors Found Critical in Assessing Suicide Risk

http://www.apa.org/monitor/feb00/suicide.html

Management of Bipolar Disorder

Discusses the clinical presentation of this disorder, and treatment with effective mood stabilizers and a comprehensive management program.

http://www.aafp.org/afp/20000915/1343.html

Solutions

KEY WORDS

1. (217-218)
2. (244)
3. (218)
4. (212)
5. (233-234)
6. (212)
7. (210)
8. (210)
9. (220)
10. (252)

SAMPLE QUESTIONS

Multiple Choice Questions

1. D, 210-211
2. C, 212-213
3. B, 216-218
4. B, 218-220
5. D, 215-216
6. B, 229-231
7. D, 230-231
8. A, 233-234, Remember that Seligman stressed that feelings of anxiety precede the negative feelings associated with depressive attributional styles.
9. C, 235-238
10. A, 240-243
11. A, 243-244
12. A, 245-246
13. D, 210-211
14. A, 210-211
15. D, 210-211
16. D, 210-211
17. E, 212
18. C, 216-218
19. B, 246
20. D, 245-246
21. D, 215-216
22. D, 234-235
23. B, 240-243
24. A, 250-252
25. B, video, CD-ROM
26. C, video, CD-ROM

True or False Questions

27. F, 250-252
28. T, 253
29. F, 210-211
30. F, 212
31. T, 217-219
32. T, 229
33. F, 246, Prevention of depression typically deals with instilling social skills in children.
34. F, 212
35. T, 212
36. F, 212
37. T, 222-224
38. T, 250-252

Essay Questions

39. In your answer, be sure to discuss drug therapy, interpersonal therapy, cognitive therapy, maintenance treatment, and others. Note the advantages and disadvantages of each (See textbook pages 240-250).

40. Outline the 3 types of specifiers, including the longitudinal and temporal components. Be sure to emphasize that individual specifiers may not be possible in all mood disorders. (See textbook pages 219-221).

41. Psychosocial and biological factors have been implicated in suicide and suicide attempts, and the presence of a psychological disorder is also a strong risk factor. Note the possibility that suicide may be a contagious phenomenon. (See textbook pages 253-255).

42. You will probably want to include the various hypotheses dealing with specific neurotransmitter systems. Remember that no single neurotransmitter can account for depression; the interactions in the brain are complex and not fully understood. Think about drug treatment as it pertains to the many and serious social problems that accompany mood disorders. Is some form of "talk therapy" necessary? For which disorders does it appear to be most relevant? (See textbook pages 228-231).

PHYSICAL DISORDERS AND HEALTH PSYCHOLOGY

LEARNING OBJECTIVES

1. Distinguish between behavioral medicine and health psychology.

2. Identify the relationships among immune system function, stress, and physical disorders.

3. Describe the relationships between stress and cardiovascular disease, AIDS, and career.

4. Define acute and chronic pain and their potential causes.

5. Describe the use of biofeedback and progressive muscle relaxation as treatments for stress-related disorders.

6. Identify some procedures and strategies used in stress management and in prevention and intervention programs.

CHAPTER SUMMARY

By now you know what to do with chapter summaries and sample tests.

Psychological and social, as well as biological, factors contribute to physical illness and death. _____ medicine involves using an understanding of behavioral science to prevent, diagnose, and treat medical problems. _____ psychology, a subfield of behavioral medicine, involves the study of psychological factors that promote and maintain health and the application of this knowledge to the health care system.

Behavioral; Health

Psychological factors influence health either by affecting processes that lead to _____ or through _____ that put a person at risk for disease. These two processes may also interact to affect one's health. For example, stress has a direct effect on the _____ system, which may limit the body's ability to combat diseases such as AIDS and cancer. In addition, people often _____ in ways that increase the probability of contracting one of these diseases (e.g., engaging in unprotected sex, smoking, etc.).

In fact, 50% of deaths from the 10 leading causes of death in the U.S. can be traced to _____ common to certain _____.

disease; lifestyles; immune; behave; behaviors; lifestyles

Selye noted that _____ resulted in increased physical symptoms. The stages the body goes through in response to sustained stress, called general adaptation syndrome by Selye, include an alarm response (the immediate presence of danger), a resistance stage (the coping mechanisms necessary to deal with the stress), and _____ (the body suffers permanent damage). Studies of stress have focused on the _____ axis and endocrine neuromodulators, or _____, which are secreted directly into the blood stream. _____ _____ _____ (CRF) stimulates the pituitary gland, which in turn stimulates the _____ gland. This gland then secretes cortisol, one of the _____ _____. The feedback loop significant in stress involves the hippocampus' reaction to stress hormones, which turns off the HYPAC activity. Increased levels of these hormones can lead to hippocampal damage, and possibly dementia.

stress; exhaustion; HYPAC; neuropeptides; Corticotropin releasing factor; adrenal; stress hormones

Stress involves an interaction of biological, psychological, and social factors. Sapolsky's studies of baboons indicated that the levels of _____ and the increase in cortisol levels in the presence of an emergency are related to the social position of the baboon. Also, subordinate baboons had indications of immune system depression. Sapolsky suggested that _____ and _____ are the factors influencing stress hormone levels.

cortisol; predictability; controllability

Vaillant's study of Harvard men shows that those with psychological disorders are more likely to suffer from _____ illness, and that stress, depression, and anxiety are related. The physiology of excitement, stress, anxiety, and depression are similar; the difference among these is based on individuals' feelings, particularly of _____-_____, which Bandura defined as one's perception of one's ability to cope with situations. Exposure to cold _____ is necessary to develop a cold, but the level of _____ is also very influential. There is also direct evidence that _____ lowers immune system functioning, especially in the _____.

chronic; self-efficacy; viruses; stress; depression; elderly

These are related to a suppression of the _____ system, which normally functions to remove foreign cells and viruses from the body. The two branches of the immune system are the _____, which involves the blood and bodily fluids, and the _____, which protects the cells. White blood cells, or leukocytes, are the main agents of the immune system, and may be _____, which surround and destroy antigens, or _____ ___ _____, which are produced in bone marrow and aid in the development of antibodies. _____ combine with antigens and neutralize them, after which memory B cells are created to speed the reaction to the antigen in the next encounter. Type T lymphocytes, or ___ _____ destroy antigens at the cellular level. T4 cells, or helper T cells, help initiate T cell activity. _____ disease refers to when an excess of T4 cells exists and they begin attacking the body's tissues instead of antigens. The HIV virus attacks the helper T cells. A final type of cell is the natural killer cell, operating on the cellular level of the immune system, which attacks viruses in cells and tumors. _____, or PNI, refers to the study of the psychological factors influencing neurological responses in the immune system.

immune; humoral; cellular; macrophages; Type B lymphocytes; Antibodies; T cells; Autoimmune; Psychoneuroimmunology

In the year 2000, the total number of people living with HIV was estimated at over ____ million. After the body becomes infected with HIV, symptoms, referred to as _____-_____ _____ (ARC), may occur after a variable course of time, with the diagnosis of AIDS made when a serious _____ appears, usually within 7 to 10 years from infection. Some people with strong immune systems, especially the cellular branch, do not become infected even after exposure. _____ _____ has been found to improve mood and immune system functioning, even in those with AIDS. These results suggest that stress-reducing techniques may influence _____ _____ functioning in AIDS patients and others, although the complete impact of psychosocial factors on AIDS is not yet known. Psychosocial interventions to slow deterioration of the immune system would be especially important for _____ and _____ because of the numerous stressors in their environment and because they have fewer options for _____.

34; AIDS-related complex; disease; Stress reduction; immune system; women; minorities; coping

Psychoncology is the study of psychosocial influences that affect the course and development of _____. Spiegel discovered that women with breast cancer survived longer when given psychological therapy, a result that may be due to _____ _____ provided by group therapy, to compliance with medical treatment based on group influences, or to increased immune system functioning. There is evidence that better health habits, close medical monitoring, and low levels of _____ reduce the development of cancer. Also, psychological treatments focusing on _____ can reduce the aversive side effects of chemotherapy, thus increasing treatment compliance. Using psychological techniques to help children has also been shown to aid in treatment for disease.

cancer; social support; stress; relaxation

The heart, blood vessels, and control mechanisms compose the _____ system. _____, or cerebral vascular accidents, are blockages or ruptures of blood vessels leading to or in the _____, which can create temporary or permanent brain damage. _____, or high blood pressure (over 160/95), is a risk factor for heart disease, stroke, and kidney disease. Essential hypertension can not be linked to a particular physical cause. Blood pressure when the heart is pumping is _____ blood pressure; when it is resting, is _____ blood pressure. Hypertension occurs in about 20% of adults, and is more/less prevalent in African-Americans than whites. Genetic influences contribute to hypertension. Neurobiological factors related to hypertension include autonomic nervous system activity in response to stress and mechanisms in the kidneys that regulate levels of _____. Psychological factors such as anger and _____ are also associated with hypertension.

cardiovascular; Strokes; brain; Hypertension; systolic; diastolic; more; sodium; hostility

Coronary heart disease (CHD) involves the blockage of blood vessels supplying the myocardium, or _____ _____. Angina pectoris is partial obstruction of these arteries; atherosclerosis is the build up of plaque that causes an obstruction in _____; _____ is the narrowing of arteries due to plaque; myocardial infarction (_____ _____) is when heart tissue dies due to the blockage of an artery with plaque. _____ factors for CHD include smoking, obesity, hypertension, high cholesterol diets, and lack of exercise. Frasure-Smith's studies of men who had an acute myocardial infarction indicate that _____ _____ lessens the likelihood of future heart attacks and death. The _____ _____ behavior pattern, which involves competitiveness, impatience, energy, and anger, was identified by Friedman and Rosenman. The Type B pattern is more relaxed. Studies indicate that Type A people are more likely to suffer CHD, although this is influenced by socioeconomic factors. _____ seems to be the factor in Type A personality that puts one at risk for CHD, although anxiety and depression may also play a role.

heart muscle; arteries; ischemia; heart attack; Risk; stress reduction; Type A; Anger

Acute pain follows injuries and disappears after healing; _____ pain does not decrease over time. Chronic pain, experienced by over 65 million Americans, appears to be psychologically and socially based, and severity of pain does/does not seem to be related to one's reaction to it. A sense of _____ over the pain helps reduce it. Phantom limb pain refers to pain in a limb that has been _____. Social factors, such as the way others react to one's pain, also influence pain and pain _____. Social support may reduce pain, as noted by Jamison and Virts' study of chronic pain sufferers. The _____ _____ theory of pain suggests that the dorsal horns of the spinal column act as a gate and determine whether sensations of pain are intense enough to be transmitted. Small fibers open the gate and large fibers close it. The brain sends messages, which may be based on _____ states that determine the intensity of stimuli needed to open the gate.

chronic; does not; control; amputated; behavior; gate control; emotional

Endogenous _____, such as endorphins and enkephalins, are the body's way to combat pain. Bandura found that individuals with high _____-_____ produced more of these substances when in pain than did individuals with lower self-efficacy. Gender differences indicate that _____ may have more powerful endogenous opioids, and that both genders have separate additional mechanisms to deal with pain.

opioids; self-efficacy; males

Neurasthenia, or lack of nerve strength, was the name given to the epidemic of the last century involving energy loss, fatigue, aches and pain. _____ _____ _____ (CFS), a similar phenomenon of this century, was first linked to the Epstein-Barr virus, immune system dysfunction, and toxins, but no evidence supports these theories. Abbey and Garfinkel suggest that this is a _____ reaction to stress, and the possible effectiveness of psychosocial treatments does/does not lend support to this theory.

Chronic fatigue syndrome; nonspecific; does

Liebeskind's experiments with rats suggest that stress interacts with _____ to affect immune system functioning, indicating the possible importance of pain killers for diseases in humans. _____, in which patients are made aware of physiological responses, can be used to help people control their bodily processes. Andrasik and Holroyd used biofeedback on headache sufferers and discovered that the illusion of controlling the headache led to improvement in the headache. _____ and meditation are also used to treat physical disorders. Progressive muscle relaxation, developed by Edwin Jacobsen, involves reducing tension in specific muscle groups. Transcendental meditation focuses attention on a specific syllable, while breathing regularly and slowly. Benson's relaxation response involves reducing _____ by focusing on a single thought or word.

pain; Biofeedback; Relaxation; distractions

Comprehensive stress and pain reduction programs include teaching relaxation and coping techniques to create a sense of control and reduce negative emotions. One program involves monitoring stress, relaxation, _____ therapy (which is used to develop realistic attitudes about stressful events), and development of _____ strategies. Coping techniques may involve _____ _____, which is standing up for oneself, and _____-_____ techniques, which may focus on prioritizing. These treatments can be highly effective. However, they do not seem to be as effective for those people who rely on medications, such as analgesics.

cognitive; coping; assertiveness training; time-management

Psychology can help _____ some physical problems. _____ has negative effects on physical health, such as interfering with whether a person will follow treatment regimens and whether a person will notice and report symptoms. Initial denial, though, may reduce _____ and be advantageous. High risk behaviors are poor eating habits, lack of exercise, and smoking. Injury control refers to prevention of _____, and involves education about and practice with possible sources of injury, such as fires. Other prevention methods are biofeedback and the _____ response.

prevent; Denial; stress; accidents; relaxation

Prevention of AIDS is critical because no cure exists. Adoption of safe sex practices is enhanced by cognitive-behavioral _____-_____ training and social support to encourage _____-_____ and perceived control. AIDS prevention for women, who are contracting the disease four times more quickly than men, may be different than for men, since women who become infected with AIDS often engage in high risk behavior, such as prostitution, due to socioeconomic problems. _____ interventions include the anti-smoking campaign initiated in China's schools and the use of counselors and _____ presentations to reduce coronary heart disease risk factors.

self-management; self-efficacy; Community; media

KEY WORDS

Practice defining the important concepts listed below. Follow the definition suggestions provided in the introduction to this Guide. Be precise and accurate, and check your work with the text. Add to the definition later as you encounter more information about the term. Whenever possible, include examples. Use only the space to the right of the word so that later you can cover either the word or the definition to use one to cue the other. Define additional important terms you'll find in the chapter.

1. AIDS-related complex (ARC)

   _____

   _____

2. behavioral medicine

   _____

   _____

3. endogenous opioids

   _____

   _____

4. essential hypertension

_____

_____

5. health psychology

_____

_____

6. immune system

_____

_____

7. psychoneuroimmunology (PNI)

_____

_____

8. self-efficacy

_____

_____

9. stress

_____

_____

10. Type A behavior pattern

_____

_____

11. Type B behavior pattern

_____

_____

SAMPLE QUESTIONS

As one of the later stages of your study for this chapter, you can assess your progress by taking a sample test. Don't make the mistake of studying just for these questions. They are merely a small sample of the many questions that could appear on an exam. An excellent way to help yourself is to generate your own questions and answers. This will help you focus on important concepts, make better distinctions among similar ideas, practice writing responses, and engaging the material in general. Try them on your friends in your study group.

Multiple Choice Questions

1. While conducting his relaxation procedure, Jim silently repeats a sound to minimize distracting thoughts. The name for this procedure is
    a. progressive muscle relaxation.
    b. autogenic relaxation training.
    c. relaxation response.
    d. biofeedback.

2. Susan has a systolic blood pressure of 145 and a diastolic blood pressure of 95. Susan's blood pressure would be
    a. considered high by World Health Organization standards.
    b. cause for concern, even though her blood pressure is not categorically high.
    c. considered normal.
    d. deemed too low, and therefore unhealthy.

    140/95= High
    140/90 'concern

3. It was initially assumed that emotional disorders seemed to make us more susceptible to developing physiological disorders. Current evidence has
    a. supported this initial assumption.
    b. been inconclusive.
    c. suggested that depression lowers immune system functioning.
    d. suggested that depression raises immune system functioning.

4. Biofeedback is
    a. a process of stress reduction requiring subjects to tense muscles in order to facilitate better relaxation.
    b. used by farm animals to store and recycle unused food for later consumption.
    c. a process through which patients monitor their own physiological functions.
    d. the process through which neurotransmitters are released into synaptic clefts.

5. What field of study is concerned with the application of knowledge taken from behavioral science to the prevention, diagnosis, and treatment of medical problems?
    a. health psychology
    b. psychosocial medicine
    c. behavioral psychology
    d. none of the above

    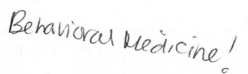
    Behavioral Medicine!

6. Which of the following is not considered a part of health psychology?
    a. promoting and maintaining good health
    b. performance enhancement during athletic competition
    c. improving healthcare systems and delivery
    d. forming health policies

7. Studies of links between Type A behavior patterns and coronary heart disease (CHD) have revealed which of the following?
    a. a positive relationship between Type A behavior and CHD
    b. no relationship between Type A behavior and CHD
    c. a negative relationship between Type A behavior and CHD
    d. all of the above

8. While jogging last week, Ignacio was hit by a car. He felt pain in his left hip and was taken to the hospital. Now, he is displaying pain behavior. Which of the following is not characteristic of pain behavior?
    a. continuous complaining about pain to others
    b. an active interest in resuming work and leisure activities
    c. a change in posture and walking style
    d. facial expressions communicating pain

9. A person infected with HIV
    a. is diagnosed with AIDS after the infection is discovered.
    b. is diagnosed with AIDS upon the development of AIDS-related complex.
    c. is diagnosed with AIDS only after the development of one of several serious diseases e.g., wasting syndrome.
    d. the diagnosis of AIDS is made at the discretion of individual physicians.

10. What are the potential effects of increased levels of stress hormones in stress response?
    a. Among the aged, deficits in problem-solving skills and dementia may develop.
    b. The ability of the hippocampus to "turn off" the body's stress response may be compromised.
    c. The high level of stress hormones will cause the stress response to stop.
    d. both a and b

11. Studies involving group therapy and cancer suggest that
    a. social support within groups has had little effect in increasing the life span of terminally ill cancer patients in the groups.
    b. patients in group therapy may be more compliant to medical treatment.
    c. social support within the group may result in the development of a high sense of self-efficacy.
    d. both b and c are true.

12. George Vaillant's study of over 200 Harvard men suggests that
    a. stress-related factors that lead to psychological disorders may also contribute to the development of later physical disorders.
    b. stress-related factors that lead to psychological disorders are not related to the development of later physical disorders.
    c. stress, depression, and anxiety are related.
    d. both a and c

13. What theory of pain accommodates both psychological and physical factors?
    a. gate control theory of pain
    b. 281-282
    c. psychophysiological pain theory
    d. behavioral medicine theory
    e. none of the above

14. Many diseases that are biological in nature
    a. are affected by psychological factors.
    b. are affected by behavioral choices.
    c. are affected by stress.
    d. all of the above

15. Current data suggest that, with physical disorders and mental disorders,
    a. biological factors clearly differentiate physical disorders.
    b. psychological and social factors clearly differentiate mental disorders.
    c. psychological, biological, and social factors all are implicated in the cause and maintenance of each type of disorder.
    d. none of the above

16. Every year during finals week in December, Judy came down with a severe cold. It was the only cold she got each year. Which is the most likely explanation for this pattern of colds?
    a. Cold viruses are present only in December.
    b. The stress of final exams left Judy more susceptible to colds.
    c. Judy's roommate caught a cold every December and gave it to Judy.
    d. There is no rational explanation. It is just a random pattern of colds.

17. The main branches of the immune system are
    a. the B cells and the leukocytes.
    b. the humoral and the macrophages.
    c. the humoral and the cellular.
    d. the bacteria, viruses, and parasites.
    e. the cellular and the digital.

18. Psychoneuroimmunology is
    a. the study of psychological influences on the neurological responding implicated in the immune response.
    b. the study of the effects of immune-suppressing drugs on psychological functioning and behavior.
    c. feelings of stress arising from relationships with other people.
    d. an immune disorder associated with decreased activity of macrophages.

19. Vaillant studied 200 Harvard University sophomores over a 30-year period. He found that those who developed psychological disorders or who were highly stressed
    a. were also chronically ill.
    b. died at a significantly higher rate.
    c. were less likely to finish their degrees.
    d. a and b
    e. were tired of being sophomores for so long.

20. Increased levels of cortisol in response to chronic stress
    a. may lead to brain damage.
    b. may increase susceptibility to infectious disease.
    c. may compromise hippocampal activity.
    d. all of the above

21. The shift to focusing on psychological factors in illness is referred to as a revolution in public health because
    a. there was a great deal of debate in medical circles as to whether psychological factors played a role in physical illness.
    b. previously the focus was much more on infectious disease.
    c. it figured prominently into the debate over health care reform.
    d. it has health policy implications.

22. The term "psychosomatic medicine" is no longer in favor because
    a. it implies that the other disorders that are studied (those without a more obvious physical component) do not have a strong biological component.
    b. it is hard to spell.
    c. it implies a strong psychological component for somatic illnesses.
    d. "neurasthenia" is the preferred term.

23. As an example of gender differences in pain, women are more likely to experience _____, whereas men are more likely to experience _____.
    a. migraine headache; arthritis
    b. backache; cardiac pain
    c. migraine headache; labor pain
    d. arthritis; backache

24. Programs to prevent injuries in children
   a. are typically not effective since most injuries are due to fate.
   b. are almost nonexistent in most communities.
   c. are less effective than repeated warnings.
   d. have not been evaluated for their effectiveness.

25. Reports from war veterans wounded in combat that they did not feel pain at the time of injury are evidence that
   a. there is a significant psychological component to the experience of pain.
   b. war veterans are reluctant to report feeling pain for fear that they won't appear brave.
   c. they probably were not injured very badly.
   d. both b and c

True or False Questions

26. If a person senses a lack of control or a lack of perception of an ability to cope with stress, he or she would have a high level of self-efficacy.

   TRUE or FALSE

27. Studies involving denial as a method of coping with chronic illness have shown only negative effects.

   TRUE or FALSE

28. Research suggests that unemployment among previously employed men increases the risk of death within the following five years.

   TRUE or FALSE

29. Endogenous opioids are substances that are injected into the body to help stop pain.

   TRUE or FALSE

30. Some studies suggest that the success of biofeedback is due to the fact that it increases self-efficacy.

   TRUE or FALSE

31. Pat has high blood pressure, which has been traced to previously diagnosed kidney disease. Pat has essential hypertension.

   TRUE or FALSE

32. General Adaption Syndrome (GAS) is the process that Hans Selye theorized the body experiences in response to sustained stress.

   TRUE or FALSE

33. Few common diseases can be prevented, delayed, or controlled through implementing life-style changes.

   TRUE or FALSE

34. Researchers have isolated stress due to economic uncertainty as the principal cause of decreasing life expectancy in Eastern Europe.

    TRUE or FALSE

35. Psychology comes to your aid in developing excuses: exam periods are stressors shown to produce an increase in infections.

    TRUE or FALSE

36. Changing high-risk behavior is the only effective prevention strategy for AIDS.

    TRUE or FALSE

Essay Questions

37. Describe the physiology of the stress response.

38. Describe the different types of relaxation procedures that have been used to treat physical disorders and pain. How are these methods used in conjunction with other treatment approaches?

39. Discuss the influence that psychological and social factors have on the treatment of AIDS and cancer.

40. Discuss the gender differences in pain. Specifically, what different types of pain are common among men? Among women? What are the similarities and differences between male and female systems, and what are the implications of gender differences in the reduction of pain?

HOW WELL DID YOU DO?

Less than 60%	Restudy the chapter (don't just reread); rework your notes completely. You can improve if you increase your efforts.
60-80%	Restudy and rewrite, especially the weak areas; discuss problem areas with study partners.
Over 80%	You're on the right track; continue as you are; focus on trouble areas with study group.
Over 95%	Nice job, especially if you know the whole chapter this well. Be sure to reward your behavior, help others in your study group (they'll help you on your weak chapters), and don't forget to review.

THINKING ALLOWED

Chapter 7 Activities

We hope it doesn't happen to you, but if you should become ill while taking this course, monitor and record your thoughts and moods during your time of physical illness. Can these be quantified? Can you detect patterns? Do you think stress affected the onset? Recovery?

Keep records of your physiological status, as well as your thoughts and moods, during times of stress. What are the risks for you if the stress persists?

Now is the time to change your behaviors that are damaging to your health. Use suggestions gleaned from this and other chapters in the text. Where will you start?

INTERNET RESOURCES

Health Screening in Older Women

This article discusses the important aspect of health promotion and disease prevention in health screening in women over 65 years of age.

http://www.aafp.org/afp/990401ap/1835.html

Positive Emotions in Early Life and Longevity: Findings from the Nun Study

A new finding suggests a link between writing about positive experiences and living a longer life.

http://www.apa.org/journals/psp/psp805804.html

Solutions

KEY WORDS

1. (271)
2. (264)
3. (282)
4. (275)

5. (264)
6. (268)
7. (270)
8. (268)

9. (265)
10. (277)
11. (277)

SAMPLE QUESTIONS

Multiple Choice Questions

1. C, 286
2. B, 275-278
3. C, 267-268
4. C, 285-286
5. D, 263-264
6. B, 264-265
7. D, 276-278
8. B, 277-278
9. C, 271-272

10. D, 267-268
11. D, 272-274
12. D, 267-268
13. A
14. D, 264-266
15. C, 264-266
16. B, 267-268
17. C, 268-269
18. A, 270

19. E, 267-268
20. D, 267-268
21. B, 267-269
22. A, 263
23. D, 269-270
24. B, 289-290
25. A, 284-285

True or False Questions

26. F, 267-268
27. F, 288-289
28. T, 264-265
29. F, 282

30. T, 267-268
31. F, 275-276
32. T, 265
33. F, 264-265

34. T, 265-266
35. T, 267-268
36. T, 271-272

Essay Questions

37. Your answer should begin with information from Chapter 2 concerning the sympathetic nervous system and the fight/flight response. This system also activates the endocrine system via the HYPAC axis. Corticotropin Releasing Factor is secreted by the hypothalamus, which activates the pituitary gland -- which in turn activates the adrenal gland, releasing cortisol. (See textbook pages 265-268.)

38. Progressive muscle relaxation teaches patients to become aware of tension of their bodies and to relax specific muscle groups to relieve this tension. Transcendental meditation (TM) involves focus on a specific part of the body or a single thought through the use of a repeating sound or mantra. Relaxation response, similar to TM, involves silent repetition of a sound to minimize distractions and close the mind to other thoughts. Relaxation procedures have been used independently and as components in comprehensive stress- and pain-reduction programs. (See textbook pages 286-288.)

39. Stress-reduction programs have been shown to increase immune system function. There is optimism that psychological intervention might increase immune system activity and help prevent the deterioration of the immune system. Studies have shown social support, e.g., that developed through group therapy, may increase life expectancy and increase compliance to medical treatment in cancer patients. This generally leads to improvement in physical and mental health. (See textbook pages 271-274.)

40. Men and women seem to experience different types of pain. Men experience more cardiac pain and backache while women suffer more frequently than men from migraine headaches and arthritis. Both male and female systems seem to be based on endogenous opioids, although the system in men may be more powerful. Males and females may have additional pain systems that are separate. These separate pain systems indicate that males and females may benefit from different kinds and combinations of psychosocial and medical treatments when dealing with pain. (See textbook pages 277-278.)

EATING AND SLEEP DISORDERS

LEARNING OBJECTIVES

1. Describe the defining features and clinical manifestations of bulimia nervosa.

2. Describe the clinical manifestations and medical complications associated with anorexia nervosa.

3. Compare the symptoms and psychological features of binge-eating disorder and bulimia.

4. Describe the possible social, psychological, and neurobiological causes of eating disorders.

5. Compare the use of medications with psychological therapies for the treatment of eating disorders.

6. Explain the causes and prevalence of obesity.

7. Describe current treatment options for obesity.

8. Identify the critical diagnostic features of each of the major sleep disorders.

9. Describe the nature of REM and non-REM periods of sleep and how they relate to the parasomnias.

10. Define circadian rhythms and explain their relation to the sleep-wake cycle.

11. Describe the medical and psychological treatments used for the treatment of sleep disorders.

12. Describe the uses and limitations of medical treatments for chronic sleep problems.

13. Match the nature of sleep problems (e.g., intrusive thoughts) with the specific treatment recommendation.

CHAPTER SUMMARY

By now you know what to do with chapter summaries and sample tests.

_____ disorders are becoming an epidemic in the Western world, with the number of new cases increasing dramatically since the 1950s. _____ _____, which involves a drop in body weight, and _____ _____, which involves binge eating and purging, are the two most common eating disorders, both centered around a desire to be thin. _____ refers to attempts, such as inducing vomiting or using laxatives, to relieve the body of food. People with these disorders have a higher death rate than the normal population. The mortality rate from _____ _____ is highest for any psychological disorder. Eating disorders are culture-specific, occurring mainly in young, white females from upper socioeconomic status in Western civilizations. Thus, the main contributors to the etiology of the disorders are _____ factors. However, patterns in _____ are beginning to mimic Western rates.

Eating; Anorexia nervosa; bulimia nervosa; Purging; eating disorders; sociocultural; Asia

Bulimia nervosa is characterized by uncontrolled _____, defined as eating more food than most people would eat under the same circumstances. Bulimics may also try to _____ for the amount of food eaten by purging, which can involve induced _____ or use of laxatives. Others compensate by exercise or fasting. Thus, bulimia is classified in DSM-IV as either _____ type or _____-_____ type, with purging types exhibiting more frequent binges and higher lifetime prevalence of depression and panic disorders. According to DSM-IV, bulimia involves binge-eating at least twice a week for three months. DSM-IV criteria for bulimia also note that body _____ plays a large role in self-evaluation. The medical consequences of bulimia include salivary gland enlargement, erosion of dental _____, calloused hands and fingers, and _____ imbalances that can result in kidney failure and/or heart problems. Psychological problems such as _____ and/or _____ _____ often co-occur with bulimia nervosa.

binges; compensate; vomiting; purging; non-purging; shape; enamel; electrolyte; anxiety; mood disorders

_____ _____ differs from bulimia in that anorexics actually lose weight, becoming dangerously underweight. Anorexia is/is not as common as bulimia. Anorexia centers around the fear of obesity and desire to be thin, and often involves excessive exercise, caloric restriction, and possibly purging behaviors. DSM-IV describes two types of anorexia: _____ type, which does not involving purging; and the binge-eating/purging type, which uses purging in attempts to lose weight. Binge/purge types of anorexics exhibit more impulsive behavior than do restricting types, and are less/more likely to have been obese. Anorexics also have distortions in body image, viewing themselves as obese in spite of reality. Medical conditions associated with anorexia are cessation of menstruation, sensitivity to _____, brittle hair and nails, and growth of downy hair on limbs and cheeks. Again, anxiety and mood disorders are often comorbid in persons with anorexia nervosa, with _____-_____ _____ being common.

Anorexia nervosa; is not; restricting; more; cold; obsessive-compulsive disorder

_____-_____ disorder involves binge eating without _____ behaviors, and many people with this disorder are in weight-control programs. Although this disorder is listed in the DSM-IV as a potentially new disorder, evidence suggests that it is fairly common (with prevalence rates of approximately ___% in obese samples).

Binge-eating; compensatory; 30

Age of onset for bulimia is usually between 16 and 19 years of age, and the disorder is most common in white, upper-middle class men/women. Surveys suggest that 6-8% of college women and 9% of high school girls meet criteria for bulimia. The lifetime prevalence of the disorder is higher for younger/older women than it is for younger/older women. Age of onset of anorexia is typically around 13 years of age, although anorexia is not as common as bulimia.

women; younger; older

Anorexia and bulimia occur at the same/different rates in minority populations. The rate of eating disorders among African-American and Asian-American females is higher/lower than among Caucasian females; however, a comparison of the rates between Caucasian and Hispanic females indicates relative _____. The rate is even higher among _____ _____. In China, the focus of the disorder is not obesity but may be related to skin conditions, reflecting the cultural ideal of beauty. The disorders are also subject to _____ influences, with onset during adolescence suggesting a relationship to _____ development. However, the disorder has been found in young children and older adults.

different; lower; equivalence; Native Americans; developmental; physical

Sociocultural factors related to the etiology of anorexia and bulimia includes equating _____ _____ with physical attractiveness as defined by cultural ideals. Studies of Playboy magazine centerfolds and Miss America contestants reveal that women in these are thinner and have a different body shape than in previous years. This depiction of slenderness seems to be particularly focused on women in that overweight males are ____ to ____ times more likely to appear on television as are overweight women. Research has established a strong/weak relationship between media exposure and the presence of eating disorder symptoms. Achieving this look may be impossible for many women. The emphasis on thinness has increased/decreased steadily over the centuries. Younger girls typically diet more/less than older girls. Fallon and Rozin found that women rated their current body size as lighter/heavier than their most attractive body size, which was heavier than their ideal body size. Ironically, the women's ratings of ideal body size were/were not as heavy as men's ratings of women's most attractive body size. Women preferred the male body without the added _____. Others note that adolescent girls who _____ are eight times more likely to develop an eating disorder than those who do not. Another important factor in dieting and body image in adolescent girls is their clique of _____ (or peers). In another study, the body image in males who believed they looked too small is referred to as _____ anorexia nervosa. Another body image influence for males is in the _____ culture. In groups that pressure girls to remain thin, such as ballet dancing, eating disorders are less/more prevalent. Families of girls with eating disorders tend to be _____-_____, with mothers who are not as satisfied with their family as other mothers are. Eating disorders can affect families severely.

self worth; 2; 5; strong; increased; less; heavier; were not; muscles; diet; friends; reverse; gay; more; high-achieving

Biological theories of anorexia and bulimia tend to focus on the maintenance of eating disorders. Genetic factors are involved in eating disorders, as evidenced by twin studies, although _____ characteristics that lead to eating disorders, instead of the disorders themselves, may be inherited. The hypothalamus regulates eating and weight, and research on _____ suggests that they affect eating as well. Low levels of _____ have been linked to both impulsive behavior in general and binge-eating behavior in particular. Biological models of eating disorders have difficulty distinguishing the causes from the _____ of eating disorders.

personality; neurotransmitters; serotonin; results

Women with eating disorders tend to have lower _____ and higher social anxiety. They often perceive themselves as _____, feeling their impressions on others are false. Rosen and Leitenberg noted that bulimics have anxiety about eating, and that purging may be a way of _____ _____.

confidence; frauds; relieving anxiety

_____ medications are used in drug treatment of bulimia, and have been found to reduce binging and purging, although long-term effects are not evident. Current cognitive behavioral treatment involves education about the effects of binging and purging, scheduling small/normal-size/large and _____ meals, altering dysfunctional _____ about eating and body image, and development of _____ strategies. This treatment method has been found to reduce purging by 79%, with evidence of long term results. Interpersonal therapy, which does not focus on eating habits or weight, is also effective with bulimia. Similar treatment strategies have shown promising results for _____-_____. Treatment for anorexia first involves helping the client _____ _____ to reduce medical complications. Then, treatment is similar to cognitive behavioral treatment for bulimia, and often includes the family. Combining drugs with psychosocial treatments improves/hinders/does not affect overall outcomes. Self-help procedures have been effective/ineffective as treatment for binge eating disorder. Long term results of treatments for anorexia have higher/lower rates of full recovery than for bulimia.

Antidepressant; small; frequent; thoughts; coping; binge-eaters; gain weight; improves; effective; lower

As is the case with other psychological disorders, _____ may be the best method to reduce the prevalence of eating disorders. One approach involves screening 11-12 year old girls for the most predictive factor, _____ _____ _____ _____, and providing corrective information. This program can be provided on the _____. _____, an eating disorder found mainly in infants and children, is characterized by regurgitating and reswallowing food, and can interfere with proper nutrition. Suggested causes of the disorder include a biological predisposition to gastroesophageal _____, depression and environmental stress. Behavioral treatment, such as applying lemon juice to the mouth at the beginning of rumination, is often successful. Rumination can be found in bulimics. _____ is an eating disorder that involves eating non-nutritive substances, such as paint, wood, plaster, hair, or cloth, that is not culturally approved. Pica is most common in individuals with severe _____ disabilities. Mineral deficiencies, neglect, abuse, and reinforcement may be involved in the development of pica, but the disorder does not have an accepted treatment. One failure to thrive syndrome, or _____ disorder, is failing to eat enough for sufficient weight gain. This is often due to trouble in the family or with a caregiver. Treatment involves _____ _____ and improving _____ functioning.

prevention; concern about being overweight; Internet; Rumination; reflux; Pica; intellectual; feeding; regulating eating; family

Even though obesity is not considered an eating disorder in the DSM, it constitutes a very serious _____ risk for millions of Americans. Not only does obesity have physical implications, it may also affect _____ and psychological functioning. Affecting 20% of the American population in 2000, obesity has accounted for over _____ deaths in the United States alone. Recently, obesity has become the single most _____ health problem in the United States, surpassing the costs of smoking and alcohol abuse. _____ seems to be a contributing factor in rates of obesity worldwide. In the United States, rates of obesity are higher/lower among African-American and Hispanic American women than for Caucasian women. Urban settings have lower/higher rates of obesity than do rural settings. Cases of obesity are due to two forms of maladaptive eating patterns. The first form is binge eating and the second is _____ _____ _____. Binge eating accounts for between ____ and _____ of obese people. This group of obese people is typically treated through _____ _____ _____. Night eating syndrome affects between ____ and _____of obese individuals seeking weight loss treatment and as many as 27% of those with extreme obesity seeking _____ surgery. Individuals with night eating syndrome consume at least a quarter/third/half of their daily intake after their evening meal and get out of bed at night to consume a _____calorie snack. These individuals do/do not binge or purge and are/are not fully aware of their eating habits late at night.

health; social; 300,000; expensive; Ethnicity; higher; higher; night eating syndrome; 7%; 19%; weight loss programs; 7%; 15%; bariatric; third; high; do not; are

The spread of _____ is linked to the obesity epidemic. The consumption of _____ _____ _____ and _____ lifestyles are the largest contributors. This _____ environment interacts with peoples' genetics, _____ and _____ to cause an ever-increasing amount of obesity in the United States.

modernization; high fat foods; inactive; toxic environment; physiologies; personalities

Treatment options have been less successful on an _____ basis with a greater long-term impact on _____ and _____ than on adults. Treatment plans typically involve a series of _____ for obese individuals. The first step usually includes self-directed weight loss programs, like those found in _____ _____ _____. Short term _____ can be witnessed from these programs, but few long-lasting benefits are seen. The second step is _____ _____-_____ _____, such as Weight Watchers, and Jenny Craig. These programs receive a much better/worse success rate than do individual programs with 19% to 37% of people weighing within _____ pounds of their goal weight at least five _____ after treatment. The third and most successful step includes professionally directed _____ _____ _____. Group _____ sessions and _____ therapies help those individuals who are more dangerously obese, but are still not permanently effective. The last step for individuals who are extremely obese is a _____ approach. _____ surgery has become a popular approach in more recent years and holds reasonably _____ success rates. Gastric bypass is another option for limiting _____ _____ and the _____ of calories. For the treatment of obese children, _____ _____ programs are most effective.

individual; children; adolescents; steps; popular diet books; effects; commercial self-help programs; better; five; years; behavior modification programs; maintenance; drug; surgical; Bariatric; high; food intake; absorption; behavior modification

Sleep is a vital activity for mental, psychological, and social functioning. Chronic lack of sleep has been widely studied. Sleep problems are rare/common in many psychiatric disorders, as either precursors or symptoms of pathology. A study found keeping people from sleeping elicits bizarre behavior that seems _____. The limbic system of the brain is related to REM (_____ _____ _____) sleep. Irregular REM patterns have been observed in _____ patients, and these patterns have remitted with cognitive-behavior therapy. Furthermore, _____ depressed people of sleep may aid in remission of depressive symptoms.

common; psychotic; rapid eye movement; depressed; depriving

The DSM-IV divides sleep disorders into _____ (difficulty in getting enough sleep) and _____ (abnormal behavioral or physiological events that occur during sleep). Assessment of sleep disorders requires an analysis of sleep habits. A _____ (PSG) evaluation involves comprehensive analysis of an individual's sleep in a laboratory. Current technology allows the measurement of brain wave activity during sleep (by an _____ or EEG), eye moments (by an electrooculograph or EOG), _____ movements (by an electromyograph or EMG), and _____ activity (by an electrocardiogram or EKG). Other helpful data collected during the assessment process include the individual's total sleep time, sleep _____, and percentage of time spent sleeping. _____ allows the collection of all of these data outside of the laboratory or clinic. A watch-sized device, the _____, measures the length and quality of sleep by recording _____ _____.

dyssomnias; parasomnias; polysomnographic; electroencephalograph; muscle; heart; efficiency; Polysomnography; Actigraph; arm movements

Insomnia involves several symptoms. Individuals who are not sleeping adequately may begin having brief periods of _____. _____ insomnia is diagnosed for individuals for whom the chief complaint is a sleep problem, rather than another medical or psychiatric problem. Patients may have difficulty both falling asleep and _____ sleep. Chronic fatigue during the daytime also characterizes the disorder. Insomnia is a frequently reported disorder (almost _____ of the general population reports some symptoms), with women reporting episodes half/twice/three times as often as men. Other disorders that may be associated with insomnia include depression, substance abuse, anxiety disorders, and dementia. In addition, reported episodes of insomnia change with age. _____ and _____ adults report more frequent insomnia than do adolescents and young adults.

microsleeps; Primary; maintaining; 1/3; twice; Children; older

Insomnia may be caused partly by physical _____, respiratory problems, or body temperatures and rhythms. Drug use and environmental conditions like a change in light, noise, or temperature may also be involved. _____ and cognitions about our sleep needs can contribute to insomnia. _____ _____ research with children concludes that sleep can be negatively affected by cultural norms. Biological and non-biological factors reciprocally contribute to the _____ of most sleep problems, and are _____ related to each other. Predisposing conditions can make some people more vulnerable than others. Sleep stress may be brought out by poor sleep _____ habits. The use of over-the-counter sleeping pills or the altering of sleep patterns can exacerbate sleep difficulties.

pain; Stress; Cross-cultural etiology; reciprocally; hygiene

Primary _____ involves excessive sleepiness and sleeping too much. A related problem is sleep _____, or breathing difficulties while sleeping. A variety of biological factors have been implicated in hypersomnia. Narcolepsy is characterized by chronic sleepiness during waking hours. _____, or a sudden loss of muscle tone, is common in these individuals. It is presumed that people experiencing cataplexy progress to _____ sleep almost directly from being awake. Narcoleptics also report sleep paralysis and hypnagogic _____. Such sleep disturbances may account for reports of UFO sightings. Using _____ models, researchers have begun to investigate possible biological explanations for narcolepsy.

hypersomnia; apnea; Cataplexy; REM; hallucinations; animal

The DSM-IV also lists breathing-related sleep disorders, characterized by numerous brief arousals during sleep. People may experience _____ or, in more extreme form, sleep apnea. Sleep _____, or episodes of falling asleep during daytime hours may occur. Typically people are/are not aware that their sleep difficulties are due to breathing problems. Three types of apnea are noted. In _____ sleep apnea a person's airflow stops but respiratory activity continues. In _____ sleep apnea, respiratory activity stops for a period of time. _____ sleep apnea presents as a combination of obstructive and central sleep apnea.

hypoventilation; attacks; are not; obstructive; central; Mixed

_____ _____ disorder is characterized by sleep difficulties brought on by the body's inability to adjust to current patterns of day and night (as in daylight savings time). The _____ _____ in the hypothalamus detects light over the course of the day and signals the brain to "reset" its _____ clock. The light-dark cycle is called Zeitgebar.

Circadian rhythm; suprachiasmatic nucleus; biological

Individuals who have nontraditional work schedules may be predisposed to circadian rhythm sleep disorder, _____ _____ type. _____ _____ type is caused by rapidly crossing multiple time zones. People who tend to stay up late and sleep late in the morning may have _____ _____ _____ type. Advanced sleep phase type of circadian rhythm disorder is characterized by going to sleep and rising at a time that is earlier/later than average. Not included in the DSM-IV is the non-24-hour sleep-wake syndrome.

shift work; Jet lag; delayed sleep phase; earlier

The hormone _____ is probably involved in setting the biological clock. It is stimulated by _____ and turned off in daylight. Studies of blind subjects suggest that melatonin may be used as a _____ for some sleep disorders.

melatonin; darkness; treatment

Insomnia is typically treated with a medical approach. Frequently prescribed drugs include the benzodiazepines and _____. These drugs may become _____ or create other side effects such as sleepiness. _____ insomnia may occur after the cessation of drug treatment. Both pharmacotherapy and behavior therapy are effective in the short term, but _____ _____ shows superiority over the long term. Hypersomnia and narcolepsy have been treated with stimulants such as Ritalin or _____. Antidepressant drugs may aid in reducing cataplexy. Treatment for breathing-related sleep disorders may involve behavioral changes, including weight loss, which is <u>often/rarely</u> successful. Mechanical devices to aid breathing may also be used, as well as respiration stimulant drugs such as medroxyprogesterone or the tricyclic _____.

flurazepam; addictive; Rebound; behavior therapy; amphetamine; rarely; antidepressants

Circadian rhythm sleep disorders may first be treated with short-term use of sleeping pills, although this practice is not highly recommended. Other methods include chronotherapy or _____ _____, in which individuals adjust their sleep patterns by staying up in later and later increments. Systematic exposure to _____ _____ may "trick" the brain into resetting the biological clock.

phase delays; bright light

Psychological treatments of sleep disorders may include progressive relaxation or cognitive techniques when sleep problems are associated with _____. Sleep problems can be prevented by lifestyle changes, called _____ _____, such as reserving the bed and bedroom for only sleep and sexual activities. Limiting exercise and _____ before bedtime is another method. For young children, specific bedtime routines are developed to be followed consistently by parents. <u>Little/much</u> outcome research is currently available for these psychological techniques.

anxiety; sleep hygiene; caffeine; Little

_____ are abnormal intrusive events that occur during sleep or in the period between being asleep and being awake. They may occur during REM or NREM sleep. Examples of parasomnias are sleepwalking, _____, and sleep paralysis. Sleep terrors, occurring during NREM sleep, resemble nightmares. _____ _____ is diagnosed when nightmares significantly impair an individual's daily functioning. Little is known about the cause of nightmares, except that they generally occur during _____ sleep.

Parasomnias; nightmares; Nightmare disorder; REM

_____ _____ are a form of parasomnia that is often mistaken for a nightmare. They are often initiated by a piercing _____, sweating, and rapid heartbeat. Terrors occur during _____ sleep and are/are not remembered by the person. Sufferers are most likely to be _____, and most grow out of the disorder without treatment. If treatment is indicated, medication may be given, although its usefulness has not been tested adequately. A simple, effective treatment seems to be _____ _____, which involves awakening the child 30 minutes before episodes typically occur.

Sleep terrors; scream; NREM; are not; children; scheduled awakening

_____ (or somnambulism) occurs during NREM sleep. Typically sleepwalking is experienced by children and tends to remit after the teenage years. In adults, sleepwalking is associated with _____ _____ _____. Related to somnambulism is _____ _____ syndrome, where persons get out of bed and eat -- although they are still asleep and will not recall the event upon awakening.

Sleepwalking; other psychological disorders; nocturnal eating

KEY WORDS

Practice defining the important concepts listed below. Follow the definition suggestions provided in the introduction to this Guide. Be precise and accurate, and check your work with the text. Add to the definition later as you encounter more information about the term. Whenever possible, include examples. Use only the space to the right of the word so that later you can cover either the word or the definition to use one to cue the other. Define additional important terms you'll find in the chapter.

1. anorexia nervosa

    _____

    _____

2. binge

    _____

    _____

3. binge eating disorder

    _____

    _____

4. bulimia nervosa

_____

_____

5. cataplexy

_____

_____

6. circadian rhythm sleep disorders

_____

_____

7. dyssomnias

_____

_____

8. narcolepsy

_____

_____

9. nightmares

_____

_____

10. obesity

_____

_____

11. parasomnias

_____

_____

12. polysomnograph

_____

_____

13. purging techniques

_____

_____

14. rapid eye movement (REM) sleep

_____

_____

15. rebound insomnia

_____

_____

16. scheduled awakening

_____

_____

17. sleep apnea

_____

_____

18. sleep efficiency

_____

_____

19. sleep terrors

_____

_____

SAMPLE QUESTIONS

As one of the later stages of your study for this chapter, you can assess your progress by taking a sample test. Don't make the mistake of studying just for these questions. They are merely a small sample of the many questions that could appear on an exam. An excellent way to help yourself is to generate your own questions and answers. This will help you focus on important concepts, make better distinctions among similar ideas, practice writing responses, and engaging the material in general. Try them on your friends in your study group.

Multiple Choice Questions

1. The psychological disorder category with the highest mortality rate is
   a. depression.
   b. panic disorders.
   c. eating disorders.
   d. sleep disorders.

2. The multidimensional view of sleep disorders makes the assumption that biological and nonbiological factors will be present in most sleep problems and that these factors will be
   a. directly related.
   b. indirectly related.
   c. reciprocally related.
   d. not related.

3. Which of the following is not a typical characteristic of those who develop anorexia nervosa or bulimia nervosa?
   a. female
   b. upper socioeconomic status
   c. low intelligence
   d. competitive environments

4. What appears to be the main cause of anorexia and bulimia?
   a. perfectionistic mothers
   b. sociocultural factors
   c. genetic predisposition
   d. malnutrition

5. While cheering for his son, Jim suddenly collapses to the floor and gets up after a few moments. What characteristic of narcolepsy may Jim have experienced?
   a. Cataplexy
   b. sleep paralysis
   c. hypnagogic hallucinations
   d. none of the above

6. Which of the following is not necessary for a diagnosis of bulimia?
   a. binge eating
   b. sense of a lack of control of eating during binges
   c. purging
   d. all are necessary symptoms

7. _____ are disturbances in arousal and sleep stage transition while _____ are disturbances in the amount, timing, or quality of sleep.
   a. dyssomnias; parasomnias
   b. parasomnias; hypersomnia
   c. hypersomnia; dyssomnias
   d. parasomnias; dyssomnias

8. _____ type anorexics rely on diets to lose weight; _____ type anorexics use vomiting or laxatives for this purpose.
   a. Non-purging; purging
   b. Non-purging; binge-eating/purging
   c. Restricting; purging
   d. Restricting; binge-eating/purging

9. Wally, a patient at a mental hospital, has been observed eating the sheets on his bed. This behavior may be called
   a. rumination.
   b. pica.
   c. binge-eating disorder.
   d. anorexia nervosa.

10. The combination of a "toxic environment", genetics, physiology and personality constitutes the cause for
    a. binge-eating disorder (BED)
    b. anorexia nervosa
    c. starvation
    d. obesity

11. The most common sleep disorder is
    a. insomnia.
    b. hypersomnia.
    c. Nightmare Disorder.
    d. Sleepwalking Disorder.

12. _____ insomnia indicates the complaint of sleep problems is not related to other medical conditions.
    a. Primary
    b. Secondary
    c. Basic
    d. Advanced

13. The characteristics of narcolepsy include
    a. Cataplexy.
    b. sleep hallucinations.
    c. hypnagogic paralysis.
    d. all of the above

14. Males think that the most attractive body weight for females is _____ than the weight females think is ideal for their bodies.
    a. Heavier
    b. thinner
    c. the same
    d. more similar to the average weight of super models

15. Studies of the neurobiological dimensions of eating disorders have determined that
    a. dopamine is related to eating disorders.
    b. decreased levels of norepinephrine in the hypothalamus lead to the development of eating disorders.
    c. brain levels of serotonin are directly related to binge-eating.
    d. none of the above.

16. The hormone melatonin
    a. is responsible for determining skin color.
    b. can be effective in resetting circadian rhythms of blind people
    c. is produced by the hippocampus.
    d. both b and c

17. _____ has many specific types including delayed sleep phase, jet lag, and shift work types.
    a. Primary insomnia
    b. Secondary insomnia
    c. Sleeping Disorder
    d. Circadian Rhythm Sleep Disorder

18. The most effective treatment plan for obese children and adolescents is
    a. behavior modification programs
    b. self-directed weight loss programs
    c. bariatric surgery
    d. commercial self-help programs

19. Biological treatments for dyssomnia include the use of
    a. benzodiazepine medications.
    b. tricyclic antidepressants.
    c. bright light to "trick" the brain into resetting the biological clock.
    d. all of the above

20. Greta eats a candy bar for science. After eating it, she thinks that her body size has increased dramatically. Latitia also eats a candy bar for science, but does not believe her body size has increased. Prior to eating the candy bar, Greta thought that she was bigger than Latitia, although they are both the same size. Greta demonstrates a pattern consistent with individuals diagnosed as_____; Latitia demonstrates the pattern associated with individuals diagnosed as _____.
    a. anorexia, bulimia
    b. bulimia, anorexia
    c. bulimia, no eating disorder
    d. no eating disorder, anorexia

21. Research suggests that eating disorders and _____ are related, since it often occurs at a high frequency in families of individuals with eating disorders.
    a. anxiety disorders
    b. conduct disorders
    c. schizophrenia
    d. starvation

22. Cognitive-behavioral treatment for bulimia involves all but which of the following?
    a. regularly scheduled meals
    b. weight gain to within normal range
    c. development of coping strategies
    d. changing attitudes about body image

23. Following short-term treatment for bulimia, Phoebe, the woman whose case is discussed in the text,
    a. never binged or purged again.
    b. continued to binge or purge but much less frequently than before.
    c. eventually lost her desire to vomit and ceased binging and purging.
    d. became a world-class chef.

24. When treating anorexia, you should remember that
    a. initial weight gain is a good indication of responsiveness to treatment.
    b. dysfunctional thoughts must be altered, which can be a difficult process.
    c. since the family is usually the major cause of the disorder, it should be excluded in therapy.
    d. it is relatively easy to motivate those suffering from anorexia to gain weight.

25. Which type of sleep apnea involves a complete stop in breathing for brief periods of time and is often associated with central nervous system disorders?
    a. obstructive sleep apnea
    b. central sleep apnea
    c. mixed sleep apnea
    d. circadian sleep apnea

26. _____ are a form of parasomnia occurring during REM sleep that involve frightening and anxiety-provoking dreams that are often remembered, while _____ occur during NREM sleep and are not remembered.
    a. Nightmares; sleep terrors
    b. Sleep terrors; nightmares
    c. Nightmares; sleep paralysis
    d. Sleep terrors; sleep paralysis

27. Which of the following is(are) component(s) of a polysomnographic evaluation?
    a. electroencephalograph
    b. electrocardiogram
    c. electrooculograph
    d. all of the above

28. The incidence of eating disorders
    a. has decreased since the 1960s.
    b. has increased dramatically since the 1950s.
    c. has not been determined.
    d. has remained constant for the past 50 years.

29. Unlike most other disorders, the strongest contribution to the etiology of eating disorders seems to come from
    a. personality factors.
    b. psychological factors.
    c. biological factors.
    d. sociocultural factors.

30. One major difference between anorexia nervosa and bulimia nervosa is
    a. bulimics do not use exercise as a way to burn calories.
    b. anorexics actually lose too much weight.
    c. bulimics tend to be overweight.
    d. anorexics do not have psychological or medical consequences to their dieting.

31. Individuals who experience marked distress due to binge eating, but do not engage in extreme compensatory behaviors, would meet the diagnostic criteria for _____.
    a. bulimia
    b. binge-eating disorder (BED)
    c. anorexia
    d. rumination disorder

32. _____ are sleep problems that involve difficulties in getting enough sleep, problems with sleeping when you want to, and complaints about the quality of sleep such as not feeling refreshed even after a full night's sleep.
    a. Parasomnias
    b. Dyssomnias
    c. Sleep anxiety disorders
    d. Polysomnias

33. The class of sleep disorders classified as _____ is characterized by abnormal behavioral or physiological events that occur during sleep, such as nightmares and sleepwalking.
    a. narcolepsy
    b. physsomnias
    c. parasomnias
    d. kineticsomnias

34. To prevent insomnia, one should include all these sleep hygiene approaches except
    a. establish a bedtime routine.
    b. increase exposure to bright and natural light during daytime.
    c. increase exercise just before bedtime.
    d. limit fat in your diet.

35. For prevention of eating disorders, it is necessary to identify risk factors. The most significant of these for young girls is
    a. being overweight.
    b. being underweight.
    c. dieting.
    d. concern about being overweight.

True or False Questions

36. Bulimia is characterized by excessive weight loss due to binge eating and purging.
     TRUE or FALSE

37. Many of the individuals with binge-eating disorder are in weight-control programs.
     TRUE or FALSE

38. It is dangerous to wake someone during a sleepwalking episode.
    TRUE or FALSE

39. Benzodiazepine medications are commonly prescribed for obstructive sleep apnea.
    TRUE or FALSE

40. Sleep paralysis occurs when a person who is awake suddenly collapses from a loss of muscle tone.
    TRUE or FALSE

41. Anorexia nervosa is more prevalent in ethnic minorities, suggesting that sociocultural factors play a large role in the development of the disorder.
    TRUE or FALSE

42. The most successful programs for treating obesity in adults still result in patients regaining up to 50% of their weight loss back within a year.
    TRUE or FALSE

43. Young children with anorexia nervosa are at increased risk, since they tend to restrict both food and fluid intake.
    TRUE or FALSE

44. In addition to a polysomnographic (PSG) evaluation, a person's total sleep time and sleep efficiency may be used to assess sleeping problems.
    TRUE or FALSE

45. Throughout the ages, society valued thinness as an indicator of female beauty.
    TRUE or FALSE

46. If you are starving, you might be likely to begin collecting recipes.

    TRUE or FALSE

47. Biological and genetic factors may be involved in precipitating eating disorders, but are not as significant in maintaining eating disorders.

    TRUE or FALSE

48. Men report problems with insomnia at the same rate as women.

    TRUE or FALSE

49. Sleepwalking and sleep terrors occur primarily during NREM sleep.

    TRUE or FALSE

50. When a well-rested student momentarily nods off during a boring lecture she is experiencing microsleeps.

    TRUE or FALSE

51. Antidepressant drugs do not appear to be effective in the short-term reduction of bulimic symptoms.

    TRUE or FALSE

52. The mortality rate from eating disorders is the highest for any psychological disorder, including depression.

    TRUE or FALSE

Essay Questions

53. Discuss some of the dangers of bulimia nervosa.

54. Describe some of the sociocultural factors involved in the development of eating disorders.

55. Compare and contrast treatments used for bulimia. Discuss the effects of treatment.

56. Discuss the different causes of obesity.

57. What are parasomnias? Describe the different types of parasomnias presented in the text.

58. Discuss the biological, psychological, and cultural influences on the etiology of insomnia.

59. Describe five psychological treatments for insomnia and discuss the effectiveness of these treatments.

THINKING ALLOWED
Chapter 8 Activities

Monitor print advertising for cues that may encourage dysfunctional eating patterns. What could you write to the advertisers to voice your concern? How could you use statistics from the text?

Monitor and record your eating patterns for a week, correlating them with your moods and stress levels. Does this task, increasing your awareness of food, also increase the likelihood you will develop an eating disorder?

Call a friend or study partner and discuss a concept in this chapter that has been too difficult for you? Does explaining it help clarify it for you?

You could have predicted this one: Compute your own sleep efficiency over a two-week period. If possible, compare your findings with those of your study group

Chart your sleep patterns and your moods over a period of several weeks. How do your moods affect your sleep? And how does your sleep affect your mood? Can you separate the causes and effects?

Imagine you are experiencing each of the sleep disorders described. How would each affect your life, including the impact on others (e.g., family members, roommates, partners, etc.). What would you do for treatment?

HOW WELL DID YOU DO?

Evaluate your own work.

INTERNET RESOURCES

Eating Disorders:

Anorexia Nervosa

A list of resources gleaned by the University of Iowa.

http://www.lib.uiowa.edu/hardin/md/anorexia.html

Assessment and Treatment of Bulimia Nervosa

This article discusses the assessment and treatment of bulimia nervosa and considers how this disorder can best be handled in a managed care environment.

http://www.aafp.org/afp/980600ap/mcgilley.html

The Something Fishy Website on Eating Disorders

This web page is a potpourri of information devoted to eating disorders, including treatments, prevention, and issues for men with eating disorders.

http://www.something-fishy.org/

Sleep Disorders:

Chronic Insomnia: A Practical Review

Discusses the assessment and treatment of insomnia (i.e., good sleep habits, exposure to bright light, periodic limb movements during sleep in the elderly, and medication).

http://www.aafp.org/afp/991001ap/1431.html

National Sleep Foundation

The National Sleep Foundation is a nonprofit organization devoted to raising funds and awareness about the importance of sleep for health and productivity. Answers to questions regarding sleep disorders and proper sleep hygiene can be found here.

http://www.sleepfoundation.org/

SleepNet Web Page

This is a great starting place for finding sleep information on the Internet. Contains links to other sleep-related web pages.

http://www.sleepnet.com/

Solutions

KEY WORDS

1. (299)
2. (299)
3. (305)
4. (299)
5. (332)
6. (333)
7. (326)
8. (332)
9. (337)
10. (300)
11. (326)
12. (326-327)
13. (302)
14. (326)
15. (330)
16. (338)
17. (331)
18. (327)
19. (337)

SAMPLE QUESTIONS

Multiple Choice Questions

1. C, 299
2. C, 324-325
3. C, 299
4. B, 307
5. A, 332
6. C, 302
7. D, 326
8. D, 303
9. B, 326
10. D, 322
11. A, 326
12. A, 326
13. A, 332
14. A, 308
15. D, 313
16. B, 332
17. D, 332
18. A, 322
19. D, 326
20. C, 299
21. A, 304
22. B, 317-318
23. C, 317-318
24. B, 319-320
25. B, 329
26. A, 337-338
27. D, 326
28. B, 308
29. D, 308
30. D, 303
31. B, 305
32. B, 326
33. C, 326
34. C, 326
35. D, 299-300

True or False Questions

36. F, 299
37. T, 305
38. F, 338-339
39. F, 332
40. F, 333
41. F, 308
42. T, 322
43. T, 303
44. T, 330
45. F, 308
46. T, 312
47. F, 320
48. F, 326
49. T, 338
50. F, 326
51. F, 317
52. T, 308

Essay Questions

53. Be sure to discuss both the relationship between eating disorders and death rates as well as some of the medical conditions that can occur as a result of binge-eating and purging. (See textbook pages 300; 302-303.)

54. Your answer should deal with the issues of cultural standards of beauty, social pressure, and family influences, such as perfectionistic mothers. Remember that these disorders are culture-specific. (See text pages 308-312.)

55. Your discussion should include reference to drug as well as psychosocial treatments. The effectiveness of treatment should be noted based on reductions in binging and purging. Be sure to discuss long-term and short-term effects of treatments. (See textbook pages 317-318.)

56. Be sure to discuss the influences of the "toxic environment", genetics, physiology and personality. (See textbook page 322.)

57. You should state that parasomnias are disturbances in arousal and sleep state transitions that intrude upon the sleep process. The different types of parasomnias that should be described are: nightmare disorder, sleep terror disorder, and sleepwalking disorder. (See textbook pages 326-327.)

58. Topics for this discussion can include body temperature, the "biological clock," biological vulnerability, and drug use (biological), unreasonable expectations about sleep, stress, and learning of insomnia in children (psychological), and cultural values regarding sleep. (See textbook pages 229-330.)

59. You should write about five of the following: cognitive, cognitive relaxation, graduated extinction, paradoxical intention, progressive relaxation or sleep hygiene, sleep restriction, and stimulus control. Be sure to discuss the effectiveness of the treatment method if it is mentioned in the text. (See textbook pages 336-338.)

SEXUAL AND GENDER IDENTITY DISORDERS

LEARNING OBJECTIVES

1. Describe how sociocultural factors influence what are considered "normal" sexual behaviors.

2. Describe the defining clinical features, causes, and treatments of gender identity disorder, and distinguish gender identity disorder from transvestic fetishism.

3. Define sexual dysfunction.

4. Describe how sexual dysfunctions are organized around the sexual response cycle.

5. Describe the defining clinical features and known causes of sexual dysfunctions, including important gender differences.

6. Describe the psychosocial and medical treatments for sexual dysfunctions, including what is known about their relative effectiveness.

7. Identify the common clinical features of each of the major paraphilias.

8. Explain what is known about the causes of paraphilias.

9. Describe available psychosocial and drug treatments for paraphilias, including what is known about their relative effectiveness.

CHAPTER SUMMARY

By now you know what to do with chapter summaries and sample tests.

Reliable data about normal sexual practices are rare because large-sample _____ surveys are required. This information is necessary for effective planning of programs to limit _____ _____ diseases and unwanted pregnancies. A recent large-scale survey of sexual behavior showed lower/the same/higher rates of homosexual behavior in males, as compared with earlier data. This finding is/is not consistent with international data. College students and young adults engage in alarmingly high rates of _____ _____ sex. The number of partners and types of sexual activity practiced by college women has/has not remained fairly constant since 1975, although use of _____ has increased. Still, more than _____ % practice unprotected sex.

random; sexually transmitted; lower; is; high risk; has; condoms; 50

Though most men and women tend toward _____ relationships, gender differences in sexual behavior exist. For example, many more men/women report masturbating, perhaps because masturbation is more _____ _____ for them. Males/Females express a more permissive attitude toward casual sex. Females report having had more/fewer sexual partners than males and a lower frequency of intercourse.

monogamous; men; anatomically convenient; Males; fewer

Men and women are moving together/apart in their attitudes, _____, and sexual behaviors. Today the absence of sexual _____ is considered a clinical disorder. Sexual norms vary across _____, and there are variations within Western cultures. Premarital sexual behavior is culturally acceptable in approximately one-third/one-half/two-thirds of more than 100 societies surveyed worldwide.

together; standards; desire; cultures; one-half

Recent studies and media interpretations suggest that homosexuality may have a _____ or biological etiology. As with most other complex behavior patterns, it is likely that _____, as well as a hereditary_____, plays a powerful role in the development of heterosexual and homosexual orientations. Young boys who prefer traditionally "girl" activities may grow to feel more different from _____ and thus find them more _____ or attractive. Identical twins reared in the same home had the same sexual orientation _____% of the time; this is evidence for the contribution of heredity/environment/ both. In one study, researchers found that each additional _____ _____ was correlated with a 1/3 greater chance of a boy being homosexual.

genetic; environment; predisposition; boys; exotic; 50; both; older brother

_____ _____ disorders refer to psychological dissatisfaction with one's biological gender because it is inconsistent with one's sense of _____. The goal is not sexual but the desire to live life in a manner consistent with the _____ _____. Gender identity disorder, which is common/rare and more typical in males/females, differs from intersex individuals or _____ and from the homosexual arousal patterns of a male with effeminate behavior or a female with masculine behavior. In some cultures, individuals with gender identity disorders are held in esteem. Exposure to certain _____ at critical periods in utero may contribute to the etiology, though research is sparse. Between ages 18 months and _____ years may be a critical period for gender identity development, and learning of gender roles may be influenced. Sex _____ surgery is a treatment used only after a trial period of _____. It involves physically altering an individual's _____ to be consistent with gender identity. Current research suggests that the majority of individuals opting for the surgery generally have a successful/unsuccessful adjustment. Some therapists use psychosocial treatment for the disorder, teaching behaviors, _____, and even arousal stimuli to correspond with the client's identity/body. Surgery and _____ _____ therapy are the most common treatments for intersexuality but recent research suggests that _____ treatments to help the person adapt to their anatomy may be more appropriate.

Gender identity; identity; opposite gender; rare; males; hermaphrodites; hormones; three; reassignment; living as the desired gender; anatomy; successful; fantasies; body; hormonal replacement; psychological

_____ _____ are characterized by impairment in ability to become sexually aroused or achieve orgasm. The majority of sexual dysfunctions occur in both heterosexual and homosexual interactions. Sexual dysfunction may be lifelong or _____ after normal functioning, and situational or _____ to all attempts. It may be associated with psychological factors or to a combination of psychological and _____ factors. The stages of sexual response, (_____, _____, and _____) are each associated with specific dysfunctions. Individuals with _____ sexual desire disorder seem to have no interest in sexual activity. Individuals with _____ _____ disorder associate sexual thoughts and activities with fear, panic, or disgust. For some clients, it may be a form of _____ disorder.

Sexual dysfunctions; acquired; generalized; medical; desire; arousal; orgasm; hypoactive; sexual aversion; panic

The sexual arousal disorders are male _____ disorder and female sexual arousal disorder. These can occur even when _____ is strong. They involve failure to achieve or maintain erection in men and _____ in women. Erectile disorder is the most common impairment reported by men, and they are likely/not likely to seek treatment. Prevalence rates are easier/more difficult to estimate for female sexual arousal disorder because they are less likely to _____. At the orgasm end of the sequence, _____ _____ is defined as the frequent inability (never or almost never) to achieve orgasm despite desire and _____. It is the most common complaint in women seeking sex therapy. In men (although rarely reported), it is called _____ ejaculation. The more common orgasm disorder experienced by males is _____ _____. The feeling of lack of _____ may be more important than timing in defining "premature." Premature ejaculation is primarily a problem with younger men; _____ _____ is more likely among older men. Sexual pain disorders, also called _____, are characterized by _____ during sexual intercourse even if sexual desire, arousal and _____ are possible. Some women also report _____, or involuntary muscle spasms in the outer third of the vagina when intercourse is attempted.

erectile; desire; lubrication; likely; more difficult; consider it a problem; inhibited orgasm; arousal; retarded; premature ejaculation; control; erectile disorder; dyspareunia; pain; orgasm; vaginismus

Clinical _____ of sexual behavior consists of interviewing, medical evaluation, and _____ measurement. Physiological assessment may include use of a penile _____ _____ for men, or a vaginal _____ for women. Measurements of arousal are taken concurrent with exposure to erotic stimuli. Measurement of nocturnal _____ _____ may show whether erection can occur; it can/cannot rule out medical or psychological causes of erectile problems.

assessment; psychophysiological; strain gauge; photoplethysmograph; penile tumescence; cannot

Sexual problems are/are not usually associated with other presenting symptoms. Neurological diseases and chronic illness (diabetes, _____ and kidney problems) may interfere with sexual functioning. A major physical cause of sexual dysfunction is the use of _____ and antidepressant medications such as Prozac. Drug and alcohol abuse suppresses/enhances sexual arousal, and chronic abuse can cause permanent _____ damage and _____ problems. _____ disease, such as arterial insufficiency and venous leakage have been associated with erectile problems in males.

are; heart; antihypertension; suppresses; neurological; fertility; Vascular

Psychological causes of sexual dysfunctions may include _____, although recent data suggest that anxiety may increase sexual arousal in certain situations. Changing _____ or affect with music may make a difference. Current theory suggests that people with sexual dysfunctions react to sexual situations with positive/negative affect, become cognitively _____, and fail to achieve _____.

anxiety; mood; negative; distracted; arousal

Psychological theory implicates early learning of a negative _____ set called "erotophobia" in the development of sexual disorders. Negative or _____ sexual events may also contribute to sexual dysfunction. Deterioration in personal relationships and poor _____ skills may also play a role. Negative sexual _____ or myths that reflect social and cultural expectations are more common in people with dysfunctions. Most/few sexual dysfunctions include a combination of physical and psychological causes. An individual's specific biological _____, such as a tendency to develop _____ anxiety, may interact with psychological factors to produce a dysfunction.

cognitive; traumatic; sexual; scripts; Most; predispositions; performance

Because ignorance is a major contributor to sex problems, _____ is often an easy and effective treatment. _____ and Johnson revolutionized sex therapy with a brief, direct therapeutic program. The therapy includes basic education about sexuality and emphasizes increasing _____ and decreasing _____ anxiety. The methods of _____ focus and _____ pleasuring are also used in a gradual program. The success of the program was <u>less than/same as/greater than</u> more recent results, but more successful sex therapies have evolved from these pioneering methods. Premature ejaculation can be treated by the _____ technique. Female orgasmic disorder can be remedied by training in _____. Low sexual desire <u>has also/has not</u> responded to sex therapy.

education; Masters; communication; performance; sensate; non-demand; greater than; squeeze; masturbation; has also

Almost all medical treatments for sexual dysfunction are directed at _____ disorder, and many are effective. One therapy involves injection of vasodilating drugs into the _____ immediately before intercourse to facilitate erection. This method may cause discomfort or pain, and studies have reported high _____ rates. Penile _____, or prostheses, with tubes or pumps are surgical alternatives. Also, _____ _____ therapy creates a vacuum that draws <u>air/blood/semen</u> into the penis, which is then trapped by placing a ring around the _____ of the penis. New oral medications such as _____ have caused enthusiastic initial response, but most such treatments in the past eventually showed _____ effects and _____ results. While sex therapy is often effective, services and _____ _____ are not available in all areas. More attention should be focused on sexuality among _____ people.

erectile; penis; attrition or dropout; implants; vacuum device; blood; base; Viagra; side; disappointing; trained therapists; elderly

A _____ is a disorder that is characterized by sexual arousal toward unconsenting people or toward objects. It is more common in <u>males/females</u>, and it is <u>typical/unusual</u> for several to appear in the same person. Many people with paraphilias have comorbid mood, anxiety, or _____ _____ disorders. _____ are characterized by sexual attraction to an inanimate object or a source of specific _____ stimulation. _____ refers to observing unsuspecting individuals undressing or naked, in order to become sexually aroused. _____ refers to sexual arousal from exposing one's genitals to unsuspecting _____. These people usually require <u>more/less/no</u> anxiety to heighten arousal. In transvestic fetishism, arousal is associated with the act of _____-_____. It is substantially <u>different from/similar to</u> other fetishes. Sexual _____ involves inflicting pain or humiliation on a sexual partner for sexual arousal. Sexual _____ involves seeking to suffer pain or humiliation to attain sexual arousal. A closely related condition is hypoxiphilia, which involves _____-_____ to enhance the sensation of orgasm.

paraphilia; males; typical; substance abuse; Fetishes; tactile; Voyeurism; Exhibitionism; strangers; more; cross-dressing; similar to; sadism; masochism; self-strangulation

Sadistic rape, not classified as a paraphilia, is an assault frequently associated with _____ personality disorder. Some rapists may present as _____. Many rapes are opportunistic; others are _____. In one study, only _____ were aroused by depictions of both consenting and forced sex; some responded similarly to _____ alone. Pedophilia involves sexual attraction to _____. _____ occurs when a child victim is a member of the perpetrator's family; the victim here is usually <u>younger/older</u> than victims of a pedophile. Most child molesters <u>are/are not</u> physically abusive and do not believe that their actions are harmful for the child. However, they damage the child's trust and ability to share _____.

antisocial; sadists; vindictive; rapists; violence; children; Incest; older; are not; intimacy

The development of deviant sexual arousal patterns may occur in the context of sexual and social inadequacies, although not all adults with such difficulties develop deviant patterns. Early experience and the nature of an individual's sexual _____ may play a role. According to an operant conditioning paradigm, deviant sexual behavior is reinforced through association with _____. Different rates of _____ may account for why <u>males/females</u> show more paraphilias. Trying to suppress unwanted fantasies seems to <u>increase/decrease</u> their intensity.

fantasies; pleasure; masturbation; males; increase

Sometimes the presenting client does not know the actual source of arousal, so careful _____ is necessary. Appropriate social and _____ skills are also examined. Psychological treatment to decrease deviant sexual arousal often utilizes a _____ approach to modify associations from pleasurable to neutral. Covert _____ achieves this by associating arousing _____ and the behaviors that led to intervention with negative _____. In orgasmic _____, patients are instructed to masturbate to their usual fantasies but to replace them with a more desirable fantasy just before orgasm. While many treatments yield success, results are poorest for _____ and people with multiple _____. _____ _____ treatment provides patients with coping skills and teaches them to recognize early signs of temptation in order to prevent relapses. Medical treatment for paraphilics involves drugs such as anti-androgens and hormonal agents that reduce _____ levels, but only while they are being taken. Without treatment, paraphilias are _____ and recurrent. Treatment of individuals with deviant sexual behaviors appears promising, but _____ are not widely available.

assessment; relationship; behavioral; sensitization; images; consequences; reconditioning; rapists; paraphilias; Relapse prevention; testosterone; chronic; well-trained therapists

KEY WORDS

Practice defining the important concepts listed below. Follow the definition suggestions provided in the introduction to this Guide. Be precise and accurate, and check your work with the text. Add to the definition later as you encounter more information about the term. Whenever possible, include examples. Use only the space to the right of the word so that later you can cover either the word or the definition to use one to cue the other. Define additional important terms you'll find in the chapter.

1. exhibitionism

    _____

    _____

2. female sexual arousal disorder

    _____

    _____

3. fetishism

    _____

    _____

4. gender identity disorder

    _____

    _____

5. hypoactive sexual desire disorder

    _____

    _____

6. incest

    _____

    _____

7. inhibited orgasm

    _____

    _____

8. male erectile disorder

_____

_____

9. male orgasmic disorder

_____

_____

10. paraphilias .

_____

_____

11. pedophilia

_____

_____

12. sadistic rape

_____

_____

13. sexual aversion disorder

_____

_____

14. sexual dysfunction

_____

_____

15. sexual masochism

_____

_____

16. sexual pain disorders

_____

_____

17. sexual sadism

_____

_____

18. transvestic fetishism

_____

_____

19. voyeurism

_____

_____

SAMPLE QUESTIONS

As one of the later stages of your study for this chapter, you can assess your progress by taking a sample test. Don't make the mistake of studying just for these questions. They are merely a small sample of the many questions that could appear on an exam. An excellent way to help yourself is to generate your own questions and answers. This will help you focus on important concepts, make better distinctions among similar ideas, practice writing responses, and engaging the material in general. Try them on your friends in your study group.

Multiple Choice Questions

1. The difference between hypoactive sexual desire disorder and sexual aversion disorder is that
    a. hypoactive sexual desire disorder involves excessive sexual desire.
    b. sexual aversion disorder involves excessive sexual desire.
    c. hypoactive sexual desire disorder involves fear, panic, or disgust brought about by the thought of sex or a brief touch.
    d. sexual aversion disorder involves fear, panic, or disgust brought about by the thought of sex or a brief touch.

2. _____ refers to psychological dissatisfaction with one's biological gender.
    a. Paraphilia
    b. Gender identity disorder
    c. Transvestic fetishism
    d. Dyspareunia

3. _____ describes a group of disorders in which sexual arousal occurs in the context of inappropriate objects.
   a. Paraphilia
   b. Gender identity disorder
   c. Transvestic fetishism
   d. Dyspareunia
   e. My diary

4. The incidence of _____ shows the largest difference between the genders in sexual behaviors.
   a. oral sex
   b. casual sex
   c. masturbation
   d. unprotected sex

5. The major aspect(s) involved in the assessment of sexual behavior include(s):
   a. interviewing
   b. thorough medical evaluation
   c. psychophysiological assessment
   d. all of the above

6. Which of the following is not a paraphilia?
   a. sadistic rape
   b. fetishism
   c. exhibitionism
   d. sexual sadism

7. Major biological contributions to the development of sexual dysfunctions include:
   a. endocrine deficiencies
   b. neurobiological diseases
   c. anxiety
   d. both a and c

8. Research reports have suggested that homosexuality is
   a. more likely concordant among monozygotic twins than among dizygotic twins or non-twin siblings.
   b. associated with exposure to hormones before birth.
   c. dependent upon certain environmental contributions.
   d. all of the above

9. If a man can obtain a normal erectile response while asleep, but not while with a partner, the cause of his sexual dysfunction likely
   a. is psychological in nature.
   b. is physiological in nature.
   c. involves problems with his biological clock.
   d. is non-existent.
   e. is still unknown.

10. _____ is defined as recurrent, intense sexually arousing fantasies, sexual urges, or behaviors involving acts in which the psychological or physical suffering of a victim is sexually exciting to a person. Recurrent, intense sexually arousing fantasies, sexual urges, or behaviors involving acts of being humiliated, beaten, bound, or otherwise made to suffer is characteristic of _____.
    a. Sexual sadism; sadistic rape
    b. Sexual sadism; sexual masochism
    c. Sexual masochism; sadistic rape
    d. Sadistic rape; sexual masochism

11. Which of the following is NOT characteristic of sex disorders involving pain?
    a. The two types of pain disorders are dyspareunia and vaginismus.
    b. Vaginismus is more common than dyspareunia.
    c. Women report more cases of dyspareunia than do men.
    d. Prevalence of vaginismus does not vary significantly in different cultures.

12. Male orgasmic disorder is
    a. most commonly referred to as retarded ejaculation disorder.
    b. also known as premature ejaculation disorder.
    c. commonly referred to as retrograde ejaculation disorder.
    d. none of the above

13. The development of deviant patterns of sexual arousal may be associated with
    a. levels of "desired" arousal in consenting adults.
    b. deficiencies in consensual adult social skills.
    c. early sexual fantasies that are reinforced through masturbation.
    d. all of the above

14. Which of the following is true about sexual practices in the United States?
    a. There are more females than males engaged in exclusively homosexual activity.
    b. The regular use of condoms during sexual intercourse has not increased over the last 20 years.
    c. Sexual practices in the United States are very similar to those in Britain and France.
    d. Masturbation is positively correlated with better sexual functioning in older age.

15. _____ is a psychosocial treatment carried out entirely in the imagination of the patient.
    a. Orgasmic reconditioning
    b. Covert sensitization
    c. Imaginary relapse reconditioning
    d. Relapse prevention

16. Because of the high risk involved, it is disturbing that approximately _____ of men in the United States have had 20 or more sexual partners.
    a. 5%
    b. 13%
    c. 25%
    d. 50%

17. A likely explanation for the gender differences in frequency of masturbation is
    a. anatomical differences between men and women.
    b. women being socialized to associate sex with intimacy whereas men are socialized to associate sex with physical gratification.
    c. gender differences in attitudes toward sexuality.
    d. greater societal approval of masturbation in women than in men.

18. What is considered to be "normal" sexual behavior
    a. is remarkably similar across cultures.
    b. is culture-dependent.
    c. is determined by the dominant religious organizations.
    d. will vary greatly depending on gender.
    e. should be determined by the legislature or ruling group

19. Unlike most boys his age, young Tim spends most of his time with girls, playing games usually associated with girls. According to one theorist, this pattern may contribute to homosexual development in Tim because
    a. it makes girls too familiar to consider as sex partners.
    b. it makes boys more exotic.
    c. it makes boys more attractive.
    d. all of the above derive from the theory.

20. Which of the following sexual disorders are gender-specific?
    a. vaginismus and sexual arousal disorder
    b. hypoactive sexual desire disorder
    c. vaginismus and premature ejaculation
    d. dyspareunia and premature ejaculation

21. According to the text, each stage of sexual activity has disorders associated with it. These stages, in order, are
    a. desire, orgasm, arousal.
    b. arousal, desire, orgasm.
    c. desire, arousal, orgasm.
    d. arousal, orgasm, desire.
    e. lather, rinse, repeat.

22. As you prepare to open your own Sexual Disorders Clinic, you need to order some specialized equipment. All of the following devices can be used to measure the ability of individuals to become sexually aroused except
    a. penile strain gauge.
    b. vaginal photoplethysmograph.
    c. sphygmomanometer.
    d. all of the above are appropriate measures.

23. You have a friend who plans to use alcohol as part of a seduction scenario. You warn of the increased risk of unprotected sex in these conditions. You also point out the effect(s) of alcohol on sexual arousal and behavior:
    a. alcohol increases arousal and facilitates performance.
    b. alcohol suppresses central nervous system functioning, thus making it more difficult for men to achieve erection and for women to achieve lubrication.
    c. alcohol makes one socially more inhibited.
    d. alcohol increases central nervous system functioning, thus making it easier for men to achieve erection but more difficult for women to achieve lubrication.

24. A client you are treating for her sexual dysfunction relates a recent situation where a sexual encounter seemed likely. In that situation she probably
    a. had excessively high expectations.
    b. became totally focussed on sex alone, to the exclusion of any distraction.
    c. underestimated how physically aroused she was.
    d. all of the above
    e. none of the above

25. Tom thinks he shows his love and worthiness as a sex partner by working hard at the office and keeping the house in good repair. His wife Maria can't feel sexy unless he woos her with gifts and loving words. Theorist John Gagnon would say they differ in their
    a. cognitive restructuring.
    b. irrational beliefs.
    c. texts.
    d. scripts.
    e. proposals.

26. Roderick and his partner are seeking treatment for Roderick's premature ejaculation. The therapist encourages the couple to stimulate Roderick's penis to nearly full erection and then to squeeze the penis firmly to quickly reduce arousal. After repeating this process, insertion is to be attempted without thrusting and the penis removed if arousal proceeds too quickly. This treatment is called
    a. torture.
    b. erotic desensitization.
    c. stimulus removal.
    d. the squeeze technique.
    e. retarded ejaculation.

27. Core beliefs about sexual aspects of oneself are called
    a. sexual maps.
    b. sexual self-schemas.
    c. sexual identification.
    d. sexual modes.
    e. sexual paradigms.

28. About 50% of patients who seek treatment at sexuality clinics complain of
    a. sexual aversion.
    b. loss of appetite.
    c. premature ejaculation.
    d. vaginismus.
    e. hypoactive sexual desire.

29. Which of the following statements characterize men with sexual dysfunction?
    a. They show decreased arousal under "performance demand" conditions.
    b. They are distracted by nonsexual stimuli.
    c. They experience negative affect.
    d. a and c
    e. all of the above

30. Which of the following is a procedure used to strengthen more appropriate patterns of sexual arousal?
    a. the squeeze technique
    b. telephone scatologia
    c. klismaphilia
    d. orgasmic reconditioning

31. According to Dr. Csernansky in the videotape or CD-ROM "ABNORMAL PSYCHOLOGY: LIVE!", "Clark" meets the DSM-IV criteria for
    a. Sexual Addiction Disorder.
    b. Hypoactive Sexual Desire Disorder.
    c. Male Erectile Disorder.
    d. both Male Erectile Disorder and Hypoactive Sexual Desire Disorder.

True or False Questions

32. The "squeeze" technique described in the text is used by sexual sadists and sexual masochists to enhance arousal and sexual pleasure.

    TRUE or FALSE

33. Treatment success rates for paraphilia have ranged from 70% to 100% in a large number of clinics and offices.

    TRUE or FALSE

34. Only women suffer from vaginismus and only men suffer from dyspareunia.

    TRUE or FALSE

35. A study presented in the text revealed that a higher percentage of males than females report they masturbate.

    TRUE or FALSE

36. Jim is sexually attracted to Susan and he constantly fantasizes about her. Jim's fantasies would be considered fetishism.

    TRUE or (FALSE)

37. Sex reassignment surgery is a controversial treatment for gender identity disorders.

    (TRUE) or FALSE

38. Victims of incest tend to be older than victims of pedophilia.

    TRUE or FALSE

39. Some possible confounds of sexual aversion disorder are panic disorder and posttraumatic stress disorder.

    (TRUE or FALSE)

40. Gender identity disorder is often referred to as transsexualism.

    (TRUE or FALSE)

41. Sexual dysfunctions are the most prevalent of any physical or psychological disorder in the United States.

    (TRUE) or FALSE

42. It is rare for several different sexual dysfunctions to occur in the same patient.

    TRUE or (FALSE)

Essay Questions

43. You're on the Oprah panel with several people who seek sex-change surgery. Describe gender identity disorders and discuss causes and treatments. What process precedes surgery?

44. Discuss the methods of assessment and treatment used for paraphilia. What are some of the suspected causes of these disorders?

45. Discuss the factors involved in the development of sexual orientation.

46. List the four different types of sexual dysfunctions and describe one disorder from each type of dysfunction. What are the treatments for disorders involving sexual dysfunctions?

HOW WELL DID YOU DO?

Less than 60%	Restudy the chapter (don't just reread); rework your notes completely. You can improve if you increase your efforts.
60-80%	Restudy and rewrite, especially the weak areas; discuss problem areas with study partners.

Over 80%	You're on the right track; continue as you are; focus on trouble areas with study group.
Over 95%	Nice job, especially if you know the whole chapter this well. Be sure to reward your behavior, help others in your study group (they'll help you on your weak chapters), and don't forget to review.

THINKING ALLOWED

Chapter 9 Activities

Some countries are taking active measures to reduce population growth. Would it make sense to try to encourage sexual disorders? If so, which ones, and how would you do it?

Covert sensitization can decrease the attractiveness of other stimuli as well. Try it against a food that you'd like to stop eating. Does it work for you?

Some social theorists have suggested chemical or even physical castration of sex offenders as an alternative to prison time. Do you expect this would alter their drives and behaviors? Or are the behaviors learned and likely to recur? What does the data show? Is this a temporary problem for which a permanent solution is excessive? If it is effective, how does this relate to the belief that rape and abuse are expressions of power rather than sex?

Should taxpayers pay for men to be given Viagra through Medicare? If so, should they also pay for female contraception? Explain.

INTERNET RESOURCES

Annotated DSM-III-R Diagnostic Information

Contains diagnosis information on transsexualism, gender identity disorder and transvestic fetishism.

http://www.genderweb.org/medical/psych/dsm3r.html

Online Sexual Disorders Screening for Women

http://www.med.nyu.edu/Psych/screens/sdsf.html

Online Sexual Disorders Screening for Men

These are screening tests designed to indicate the presence of sexual symptoms that may need evaluation by a professional.

http://www.med.nyu.edu/Psych/screens/sdsm.html

Female Sexual Dysfunction: Evaluation and Treatment

Discusses the causes and treatments of female sexual dysfunction.

http://www.aafp.org/afp/20000701/127.html

AACE Clinical Practice Guidelines for the Evaluation and Treatment of Male Sexual Dysfunction

These guidelines present a framework for the evaluation, treatment, and follow-up of the patient who is experiencing sexual dysfunction. Click on "Male Sexual Dysfunction © 1998" link.

http://www.aace.com/clin/guidelines/

Solutions

KEY WORDS

1. (372)
2. (357)
3. (372)
4. (350)
5. (356)
6. (375)
7. (359)

8. (357)
9. (360)
10. (372)
11. (374)
12. (374)
13. (357)
14. (354-356)

15. (374)
16. (361)
17. (374)
18. (373)
19. (372)

SAMPLE QUESTIONS

Multiple Choice Questions

1. D, 357
2. B, 350
3. A, 370
4. C, 346-347
5. D, 361-362
6. A, 374
7. B, 364-365
8. D, 346
9. E, 364
10. B, 373
11. D, 361

12. A, 360
13. D, 366
14. C, 346
15. B, 378
16. C, 346-347
17. A, 346-347
18. B, 345-346
19. D, 350
20. C, 361
21. C, 354

22. C, 368-370
23. B, 364-365
24. C, 364
25. D, 367
26. D, 369
27. B, 345-346
28. E, 356
29. D, 354
30. D, 379
31. D, Video, CD-ROM

True or False Questions

32. F, 369
33. F, 378-379
34. F, 361
35. T, 346-347

36. F, 371-372
37. T, 353
38. T, 375
39. T, 357

40. T, 350
41. T, 354
42. F, 364

Essay Questions

43. Your answer should include a description of the definitional criteria. Discussion of causes should include exposure to hormones and environmental factors during young age. Treatments for gender identity disorders include sex reassignment surgery (preceded by months of living as the desired gender) and psychosocial treatments. (See textbook pages 350-354.)

44. Discussion of assessment techniques should include psychophysiological assessment procedures. Treatment methods include covert sensitization, orgasmic reconditioning, and drug treatment. Possible causes of paraphilia include early inappropriate sexual experiences, inadequate development of consensual adult arousal patterns, inadequate development of appropriate social skills for relating to adults, inappropriate sexual fantasies that are strongly reinforced by masturbation, but with repeated attempts to inhibit undesired arousal and behavior. (See textbook pages 371, 376-380.)

45. Discussion of differential exposure to hormones, biological contributions (genetic tendencies), gene-environment interactions, and experience should be included in your answer. (See textbook pages 349-350.)

46. The types of dysfunctions are: desire (hypoactive sexual desire disorder and sexual aversion disorder); arousal (male erectile disorder and female sexual arousal disorder); orgasm (inhibited female orgasm, inhibited male orgasm, and premature ejaculation); and pain (dyspareunia and vaginismus). Discussion of treatments should include the importance of education, psychosocial treatments, and medical treatments. (See textbook pages 354-361.)

SUBSTANCE-RELATED AND IMPULSE-CONTROL DISORDERS

LEARNING OBJECTIVES

1. Describe the nature of substance-related disorders.

2. Distinguish among substance use, substance intoxication, substance abuse, and substance dependence.

3. Describe the physiological and psychological effects of alcohol.

4. Identify what is known about the prevalence, course, and cultural and social factors related to alcohol use and abuse.

5. Describe the physiological and psychological effects of sedative, hypnotic, or anxiolytic substance use disorders.

6. Describe the physiological and psychological effects of stimulants.

7. Distinguish opioids from hallucinogens, and describe their psychological and physiological effects.

8. Describe the psychological and physiological processes involved in substance dependence, including the role of positive and negative reinforcement, expectancies, and social and cultural factors.

9. Identify the genetic contribution to substance-related disorders, with particular emphasis on alcoholism.

10. Describe the main features of the integrative model of substance-related disorders.

11. Describe various psychological and medical treatments for addictions.

12. Identify the role of early prevention and relapse prevention programs, including what is known about their relative effectiveness.

13. Describe what constitutes an impulse-control disorder, and identify examples of this condition.

CHAPTER SUMMARY

By now you know what to do with chapter summaries and sample tests.

Substance-related disorders involve the abuse of _____ and other substances that people use to alter the way they think, feel, and _____. They are extremely pervasive and costly in terms of human and financial loss. Drug use in the United States has declined/increased somewhat over the last two decades. Substances are _____ that are ingested to alter _____ or behavior. Common and legal drugs, such as alcohol, nicotine, and caffeine are/are not considered substances. Psychoactive substances cause one to become intoxicated or "high". _____-_____ _____ refer to the inability to resist acting on a drive or temptation.

drugs; behave; declined; chemicals; mood; are; Impulse-control disorders

Substance _____ involves the ingestion of substances in moderate amounts that do not significantly interfere with functioning. Substance _____ is the physiological reaction to ingesting substances. Intoxication is associated with impaired _____, mood changes, and lowered motor ability. Whether or not a person becomes intoxicated depends upon how much of the drug is taken and the person's individual _____ _____.

use; intoxication; judgment; biological reaction

The definition of substance abuse is problematic. The DSM-IV defines substance abuse by the degree to which substance use _____ _____ a person's life. Substance _____ is usually associated with the state of being addicted to a substance. One definition of substance dependence is the state of being _____ dependent on the drug, requiring greater and greater amounts of the drug to experience the same effect (_____), and responding physically in a negative way when the substance is no longer ingested (_____). A second view of substance dependence involves the measurement of drug-_____ behaviors. This definition relies on behaviors associated with substance use and is sometimes referred to as _____ _____.

interferes with; dependence; physiologically; tolerance; withdrawal; seeking; psychological dependence

In _____, substance-dependent people react physically in a negative way when the substance is not taken. Withdrawal from alcohol can include alcohol withdrawal _____ (or _____ _____). Symptoms of withdrawal include chills, fever, diarrhea, nausea, and body aches and pains. Different drugs have different _____ in terms of withdrawal symptoms. Dependence may be present without abuse, as in the case of medical treatments using _____ drugs.

withdrawal; delirium; delirium tremors; courses; addictive

DSM-IV classification of substance-related disorders includes several subtypes of diagnosis, including dependence, abuse, intoxication, and/or _____. The presence of symptoms of other disorders complicates the diagnosis of substance-related disorders. Reasons why they may occur _____ with other disorders include: 1) the high overall prevalence in American society of several disorders, including substance-related disorders; 2) intoxication and withdrawal can _____ symptoms of depression, psychosis, and anxiety; and 3) several other disorders have a high likelihood of a _____ problem of substance abuse. According to DSM-IV criteria, a symptom is a result of substance abuse when it occurs while intoxicated or within _____ weeks after withdrawal. Earlier versions of the DSM included alcoholism and drug abuse under the category _____ personality disturbances.

withdrawal; concurrently; cause; secondary; six; sociopathic

_____ decrease central nervous system activity, resulting in behavioral sedation. These include alcohol, and sedative, hypnotic and anxiolytic drugs including _____ and benzodiazepines. These substances are among those most likely to produce symptoms of _____, tolerance, and withdrawal.

Depressants; barbiturates; dependence

_____ is the most commonly used depressant, and its use has been prominent across cultures and generations. The initial effect of ingesting alcohol is apparent _____. However, continued drinking causes increasingly more areas of the brain to be _____.

Alcohol; stimulation; depressed

Alcohol passes to the small _____ where it is absorbed into the bloodstream and circulated throughout the body. Alcohol that goes to the lungs can be detected by a _____ test. In the brain, alcohol interacts with a number of different neuroreceptor systems, including the gamma-aminobutyric acid (GABA) system, the glutamate system, and the _____ system. Symptoms of alcohol _____ include hand tremors, nausea, anxiety, transient hallucinations, and insomnia. Individuals experiencing alcohol withdrawal _____ may have frightening hallucinations and body tremors.

Intestine; breathalyzer; serotonin; withdrawal; delirium

Alcohol has contact with almost every important organ in the body. There may be a _____ predisposition that renders some people more vulnerable to organ damage than others. Consequences of excessive long-term drinking include _____ disease, brain damage, pancreatitis, and cardiovascular disorders. The organic brain syndromes of dementia and _____ disease may also result from excessive alcohol consumption. Dementia involves a loss of general cognitive abilities, and Wernicke's disease is associated with confusion, decreased muscle _____, and unintelligible speech.

genetic; liver; Wernicke's; coordination

Because alcohol enters the bloodstream, it can harm the developing fetus of a pregnant woman. _____ _____ _____ (FAS) is seen in some children whose mothers drank excessively while pregnant. Typical symptoms include cognitive deficits, characteristic _____ features, learning disabilities, and behavior problems. The probability of having a child with FAS varies significantly across individual women and may be related to the alcohol-metabolizing enzyme called _____ _____ (ADH). African American and certain Native American women appear to be at lower/greater risk for having a child with FAS. A proposed explanation for this is that some racial groups may have more of a form of the ADH enzyme called beta3. Expression of FAS may depend on _____ vulnerability passed on by both parents.

Fetal alcohol syndrome; facial; alcohol dehydrogenase; greater; genetic

People who are dependent on alcohol may fluctuate between periods of heavy drinking, moderate drinking, and even _____. About 20 percent with severe dependence have spontaneous remission. Jellinek championed the notion of alcoholism as a _____ that will progress if not treated. The current conceptualization is that alcohol dependence may be progressive, but the course of alcohol abuse is highly.

abstinence; disease; variable

Alcohol use and violence have been linked in correlational studies. While some laboratory experimental studies have demonstrated a _____ effect of alcohol on violent behavior, these results should be interpreted with caution.

causal

Other _____ substances include sedative, hypnotic, and anxiolytic drugs. Barbiturates are addictive sedative drugs, originally prescribed to aid _____. Before their addictive quality was understood, barbiturates were widely prescribed. Benzodiazepines are used to reduce _____. While they are not appropriate for relief of everyday stress, benzodiazepines are considered less/more safe than barbiturates. The benzodiazepine, _____, recently gained popularity among teenagers because it has the same effect as alcohol without the identifiable odor. Another misuse involves men giving the drug to women without their knowledge for the purpose of _____ _____.

depressive; sleep; anxiety; more; Rohypnol ("roofies"); date rape

The DSM-IV criteria for sedative, hypnotic, and anxiolytic drug use disorders <u>are/are not</u> similar to those for alcohol use disorders. For example, both include maladaptive behavioral changes, inappropriate sexual or aggressive behavior, mood swings, and impaired _____ and functioning. These drug types affect the _____ system as alcohol does, making it particularly dangerous to mix alcohol with benzodiazapines or barbiturates. The use of benzodiazapines has <u>increased/decreased</u>, while barbiturate use has decreased. Benzodiazapines may be misused less than barbiturates because _____ _____ __ _____ _____ __ _____.

are; judgment; GABA; increased; they have an upper limit of effectiveness

_____ include amphetamines, cocaine, nicotine, and caffeine. These have the effect of <u>elevating/lowering</u> activity level, alertness, and mood. _____, a designer drug classified as an amphetamine, first gained popularity during the early 1980s. Stimulants are the <u>most/least</u> commonly consumed psychoactive drugs.

Stimulants; elevating; Ecstasy; most

_____ induce feelings of elation and vigor. After a period of time, the opposite effect occurs, and a person may feel _____. Drugs used to treat attention deficit hyperactivity disorder and to induce weight loss are amphetamines. Continued amphetamine use can cause changes in _____, anxiety, hot and cold spells, and vomiting. _____ symptoms include apathy, excessive _____, irritability, and depression. _____ builds quickly, increasing the danger of amphetamine use. Amphetamines stimulate the central nervous system by blocking <u>production/reuptake/reception</u> of norepinephrine and dopamine.

Amphetamines; depressed; sociability; Withdrawal; sleeping; Tolerance; reuptake

In the 1970s, cocaine, derived from the South American coca bush, replaced amphetamines as the most widely used _____. In <u>small/large</u> doses, cocaine improves alertness, increases blood pressure, produces euphoria, and decreases appetite. However, it also makes the heart beat more rapidly and _____, which can have fatal consequences.

stimulant; small; irregularly

Cocaine use decreased during the 1980's. Crack cocaine, used by approximately 17 percent of cocaine users, is a _____ form of cocaine that is smoked. Cocaine creates an "up" feeling by blocking _____ reuptake in the brain. As late as the 1980's, cocaine was believed to be a "wonder drug" for its inducement of euphoria with no apparent addictive qualities. Now it is known that cocaine dependence is more _____ than that of other drugs but equally dangerous. Cocaine has a unique _____ pattern that produces feelings of apathy and boredom, which frequently motivate _____.

crystallized; dopamine; gradual; withdrawal; relapse

Almost _____-_____ of Americans smoke nicotine cigarettes, although this fraction is decreasing. Smoking among teenagers has remained high and steady. _____ is an addictive substance that stimulates the central nervous system, relieving stress and elevating mood. Other effects are high blood pressure and increased risk for heart disease and _____. Nicotine affects the brain by stimulating midbrain nicotinic acetylcholine receptors and the "pleasure pathway" in the _____ system. The DSM-IV describes symptoms associated with nicotine withdrawal. That nicotine is addictive is evident from the high rate of _____. There is a high proportion of cigarette smokers who also experience severe _____.

one-quarter; Nicotine; cancer; limbic; relapse; depression

Another commonly used stimulant is caffeine, consumed regularly by ___ percent of Americans. In large doses, caffeine creates a "jittery" feeling and insomnia. Regular use can result in _____ and dependence. _____ symptoms include headaches, drowsiness, and unpleasant mood. Caffeine appears to block reuptake of the neurotransmitter.

90; tolerance; Withdrawal; adenosine

_____, also referred to as analgesics, refer to naturally occurring chemicals in the poppy that have a _____ effect. Opiates such as heroin, opium, codeine, and morphine act to reduce _____ and induce euphoria. Opioids are the family of substances that includes opiates, their synthetic variations, and the similar substances that occur naturally in the _____. Opiates create a feeling of euphoria followed by _____ and slow breathing.

Opiates; narcotic; pain; brain; drowsiness

Withdrawal from these substances is extremely _____, which may help to explain why some individuals continue to use them. Common symptoms are vomiting, chills, muscle aches, diarrhea, and insomnia. Opiate use has decreased, possibly being replaced by _____. However, use of _____, a combination of heroin and cocaine, is increasing. Because opiates are usually taken _____, opiate users are at risk for HIV infection.

unpleasant; cocaine; speedballs; intravenously

_____, such as marijuana and LSD, produce paranoia, hallucinations, and altered sensory perception. _____, the most routinely used illegal substance, consists of the dried parts of the plant, cannabis sativa. Cannabis intoxication is associated with mood swings and heightened _____ experiences. Some first-time users experience no apparent effects, and some users can "turn off" the high, if so motivated. High doses can cause paranoia, hallucinations, and dizziness. Long-term effects include impairments in _____, concentration, motivation, self-esteem, work functioning, and interpersonal relationships. Apathy or impairment in motivation is known as _____ _____.

Hallucinogens; Marijuana; sensory; memory; amotivational syndrome

Evidence for tolerance to marijuana is contradictory. Some chronic users experience tolerance, while others experience a _____ _____, characterized by a more pleasurable experience with repeated use of the drug. Major signs of _____ do not usually occur with marijuana. The psychological dependence observed with other substances has/has not been reported in marijuana use. The role of marijuana in medical treatments is controversial. Marijuana contains over 80 varieties of chemicals called _____; the primary one is called tetrahydrocannabinols (THC). The brain makes a neurochemical, called anandamide, which is similar to THC.

reverse tolerance; withdrawal; has not; cannabinoids

D-lysergic acid diethylamide (_____), a laboratory-produced drug, is the most common of the hallucinogenic drugs. Often occurring naturally in various plants, other hallucinogens include psilocybin, lysergic acid amide, dimethyltryptamine, mescaline, and phencyclidine. Users of hallucinogenic substances report a variety of sensory distortions. The _____ component of the visions can be extremely powerful. Tolerance is developed slowly/quickly to a number of the hallucinogens, and many users report no withdrawal symptoms. Some believe that users of these drugs are at high risk for dangerous behaviors, but evidence suggests that the risk is/is not greater than that incurred from use of other types of drugs. "Bad trips," involving frightening _____ episodes, may occur. The mechanism by which LSD and other hallucinogens influence the brain is not yet understood.

LSD; emotional; quickly; is not; hallucinogenic

Other drugs of abuse include _____, _____, and designer drugs. Inhalants include various substances found in volatile solvents; they are rapidly absorbed into the blood stream by the lungs. _____-_____ steroids are derived from or a synthesized form of _____. There are legitimate medical uses for steroids, but illicit use involves taking these drugs to improve physical abilities or bulk up. Users often administer the drug according to a schedule that involves breaks from the use (_____) or combine several types of steroids (_____). Designer drugs is the term used to refer to a growing body of drugs developed by _____ _____ to target specific disorders or diseases. This technology has also been applied to illicit or recreational drugs. Examples include Ecstasy and Ketamine.

inhalants; steroids; Anabolic-androgenic; testosterone; cycling; stacking; pharmaceutical companies

Drug abuse and dependence appear to involve a combination of biological and _____ factors. The availability of drugs is an obvious precursor to the use of them. Animal studies support the notion of a _____ component in substance abuse. Human twin studies also suggest that certain people may be genetically vulnerable. Most research on drug abuse comes from studies of _____, perhaps since this drug is legal. Genetics may play a smaller/larger role in alcoholism with men than with women. Alcoholism may be related to chromosomes 1, 2, 7, and 11. The field of research called _____ _____ concerns how genes influence behavior.

psychosocial; genetic; alcoholism; larger; functional genomics

Neurobiological factors may also play a large role in substance-related disorders. Substances positively reinforce users because of their initial _____ consequences. They can also _____ reinforce or remove unpleasant feelings (_____ effect). Drugs may be alike in activating a reward center in the brain. Olds' work with rats led to pioneering discoveries of brain areas that create feelings of _____. This is believed to include the dopaminergic system and _____-releasing neurons. These neurons are found in the ventral tegmental area (VTA), the nucleus accumbens (NA), and the _____ cortex.

pleasurable; negatively; anxiolytic; pleasure; opioid; frontal

Research projects have attempted to discern the factors that drive some individuals to addiction while other individuals do not become addicted. Drugs have powerful psychological effects, including positive and negative reinforcement. Other terms for variants of _____ reinforcement are tension reduction, negative affect, and self-medication. In one study, children reporting consistent negative affect were more likely to use drugs. One way to prevent drug use may be to address feelings of _____ and _____.

negative; stress; anxiety

Solomon's opponent-process theory suggests that with drug dependence, the motivation for using drugs shifts from a desire to produce a _____ to a desire to decrease the increasingly unpleasant _____. Self-medication for symptoms such as _____ is another way that individuals may become addicted to substances. It is likely that the complex interactions among stressors, negative feelings, other psychological disorders, and _____ predispositions will guide future research on substance-related disorders.

high; low; anxiety; genetic

Cognitive factors also drive decisions to use substances. The _____ effect indicates that those who expect to gain pleasure from drinking alcohol are most likely to drink it. Access or _____ to substances obviously influences their use. Also, indirect effects of substance use, such as decreased effective parenting by alcoholic parents contributes to substance use in _____.

expectancy; exposure; adolescents

Society holds two prominent views of substance abuse. The _____ _____ view sees drug users as lacking character. The _____ model of dependence assumes an underlying physiological vulnerability and does not blame individuals for their substance-related problems. These views taken independently are too _____ to account for the complex interaction of factors associated with substance abuse. Beliefs, norms, and _____ conditions across cultures affect the prevalence of substance-related disorders and how such disorders are manifest. In general, drug users may become dependent when multiple _____ are present. The pathways that lead people to drug abuse are variable and no single factor is a perfect predictor of dependency. The idea that a particular disorder may arise from multiple and different paths is called _____.

moral weakness; disease; simplistic; social; stressors; equifinality

Successful treatment of substance abuse is associated strongly with a person's _____ to change. Goals of treatment range from helping people through the withdrawal process to teaching _____. Biological treatment may include _____ _____, or providing the person with another drug that has a similar makeup to the addictive drug. For example, methadone is an _____ agonist. Methadone, combined with counseling, has shown some success in the treatment of _____ addicts, but these people may have to take methadone for the rest of their lives because heroin and methadone are _____-_____. Nicotine _____ and gum have been used for cigarette-smoking addicts.

motivation; abstinence; agonist substitution; opiate; heroin; cross-tolerant; patches

Antagonist drugs <u>augment/block/mimic</u> the effects of psychoactive drugs. Naltrexone, a common opiate-antagonist drug, produces unpleasant withdrawal symptoms and may be successful in the treatment of highly _____ addicts. _____ treatments are used to make ingestion of the abused substance extremely unpleasant. Disulfiram (Antabuse) is used for this purpose with people who are dependent upon _____. For cigarette smokers, _____ _____ is used as an aversive treatment. Medications may also be used for people undergoing withdrawal. Clonidine is used during _____ withdrawal; desipramine has been somewhat effective for cocaine abuse.

block; motivated; Aversive; alcohol; silver nitrate; opiate

It is widely believed that _____ treatment is necessary, in addition to biological interventions. Inpatient hospital treatment for substance abuse provides supportive therapy, but it can be extremely expensive. _____ _____ is the most popular model for treatment of substance abuse. This and other 12-step programs are based on the belief that alcoholism is a _____ and alcoholics must recognize their addiction and its destructive impact. Although the program is pervasive in society, and many believe that it has saved their lives, Alcoholics Anonymous has also been criticized for its emphasis on spirituality and its disease model. Although its emphasis on _____ makes systematic study difficult, Alcoholics Anonymous appears to be successful for people who maintain long-term contact with the program. However, a high _____ rate is suspected. Some researchers believe that abusers may be capable of becoming "social users." This notion of _____ drinking is extremely controversial.

psychosocial; Alcoholics Anonymous; disease; anonymity; attrition; controlled

Multiple types of psychosocial treatments exist. _____ therapy involves pairing the addictive substance with unpleasant stimuli. _____ sensitization involves imagining unpleasant scenes involving substance use. Contingency management involves _____ of behaviors aimed toward eliminating use of the addictive substance. A community reinforcement approach involves relationship therapy with a significant other, identification of _____ and _____ of drug-taking, adoption of new recreational activities, and assistance with social service needs. It is likely that no single treatment package will be effective with all substance abusers; individualizing treatment components to meet the needs of clients is essential.

Aversion; Covert; reinforcement; antecedents; consequences

The _____ prevention treatment model involves motivating the user to stop and examine beliefs about the benefits of substance abuse. Strategies for avoiding _____ _____ situations and for dealing with _____ are developed. _____ factors probably contribute to trends toward and away from substance use, so it is worthwhile to consider sociocultural treatment interventions. This type of prevention may be most effective.

relapse; high risk; cravings; Sociocultural

The DSM-IV-TR includes _____ more impulse control disorders-called impulse-control disorders not _____ classified-that are not included under the categories we have previously discussed. Intermittent _____ disorder is characterized with episodes of individuals acting on aggressive impulses that result in serious _____ or the destruction of property. Rarely diagnosed, this disorder is most treatable through _____-_____ interventions and drug treatments. The rare and not well-studied disorder of _____ involves recurrent stealing of items that are not needed. The _____ that a person with this disorder feels just before stealing can only be relieved by the theft. _____ is an impulse-control disorder in which the person has an irresistible urge to set fires. These individuals are fascinated not only by fire, but also by the equipment involved in _____ and _____ _____ fires. Affecting up to 5% of adult Americans, _____ gambling is on the rise. Problem gamblers experience increasing needs to gamble larger amounts of _____ and for longer amounts of _____ and go through _____ symptomswhen attempting to stop. Trichotillomania refers to the urge to pull out ones own _____ from anywhere on the body. More common in <u>males/females</u>, most individuals try to _____ this behavior in order to escape social consequences.

five; elsewhere; explosive; assaults; cognitive-behavioral; kleptomania; tension; Pyromania; tension; setting; putting out; pathological; money; time; withdrawal; hair; females; conceal

KEY WORDS

Practice defining the important concepts listed below and at the end of the text chapter. Follow the definition suggestions provided in the introduction to this Guide. Be precise and accurate, and check your work with the text. Add to the definition later as you encounter more information about the term. Whenever possible, include examples. Use only the space to the right of the word so that later you can cover either the word or the definition to use one to cue the other. Define additional important terms you'll find in the chapter. (page #)

1. agonist substitution

   _____

   _____

2. antagonist drugs

   _____

   _____

3. benzodiazepines

    _____

    _____

4. component treatment

    _____

    _____

5. depressants

    _____

    _____

6. expectancy effect

    _____

    _____

7. fetal alcohol syndrome

    _____

    _____

8. GABA system

    _____

    _____

9. hallucinogens

    _____

    _____

10. impulse-control disorder

    _____

    _____

11. opiates

    _____

    _____

12. stimulants

_____

_____

13. substance abuse

_____

_____

14. substance dependence

_____

_____

15. substance intoxication

_____

_____

16. tolerance

_____

_____

17. withdrawal

_____

_____

SAMPLE QUESTIONS

As one of the later stages of your study for this chapter, you can assess your progress by taking a sample test. Don't make the mistake of studying just for these questions. They are merely a small sample of the many questions that could appear on an exam. An excellent way to help yourself is to generate your own questions and answers. This will help you focus on important concepts, make better distinctions among similar ideas, practice writing responses, and engaging the material in general. Try them on your friends in your study group.

Multiple Choice Questions

1. _____ are psychoactive substances that are among the most likely to produce physical dependence, tolerance, and withdrawal. These substances include alcohol and anxiolytic drugs.
   a. Opioids
   b. Depressants
   c. Stimulants
   d. Hallucinogens

2. Two important aspects of a definition of substance dependence are _____ and _____.
   a. tolerance; withdrawal
   b. withdrawal; relapse
   c. relapse; tolerance
   d. alcohol delirium; tolerance

3. Hallucinogenic drugs
   a. include LSD.
   b. occur naturally in a variety of plants.
   c. can be produced synthetically.
   d. all of the above

4. People who abuse or are dependent upon alcohol
   a. are likely to go through periods marked by different levels of alcohol use.
   b. were aided by a methodically sound study of Alcoholics Anonymous members by Jellinick.
   c. may be at an increased risk to behave aggressively.
   d. both a and c

5. Which of the following is characteristic of nicotine?
   a. DSM-IV describes an intoxication pattern for nicotine.
   b. It takes nicotine between 30 and 45 seconds to reach the brain.
   c. Nicotine is considered to be highly addictive.
   d. none of the above

6. Caffeine is a _____ which affects the brain stem by _____.
   a. stimulant; blocking the reuptake of the neurotransmitter adenosine.
   b. depressant; blocking the reuptake of the neurotransmitter adenosine.
   c. stimulant; aiding in the reuptake of the neurotransmitter adenosine.
   d. depressant; aiding in the reuptake of the neurotransmitter adenosine.

7. A probable psychological cause of substance-related disorders is
   a. positive reinforcement.
   b. negative reinforcement.
   c. both a and b
   d. none of the above

8. _____ is a method in which a drug with a similar chemical makeup is given in place of an addictive drug, and _____ are used to block the effects of psychoactive drugs.
   a. Antagonist substitution; agonist drugs
   b. Agonist substitution; antagonist drugs
   c. Relapse prevention; agonist drugs
   d. Relapse prevention; antagonist drugs

9. Alcohol may influence which of the following systems?
   a. GABA system
   b. glutamate system
   c. serotonin system
   d. all of the above

10. The term opioids refers to _____ substances that have a narcotic effect, while opiates are _____ that have a narcotic effect.
    a. all; substances found in the poppy
    b. naturally occurring; synthetic drugs
    c. synthetic; all substances
    d. all; chemicals in the brain

11. Which of the following is not considered in the text as a cognitive factor related to causes of substance-related disorders?
    a. cravings
    b. expectancy effect
    c. opponent process theory - negative reinforcement
    d. none of the above

12. Nicotine is a _____, alcohol is a _____, and morphine is a _____.
    a. stimulant; depressant; opioid
    b. stimulant; depressant; hallucinogenic
    c. depressant; stimulant; opioid
    d. opioid; hallucinogenic; stimulant

13. Relapse prevention is a treatment method that
    a. looks at the learned aspect of dependance.
    b. sees relapse as a failure of cognitive and behavioral coping skills.
    c. looks at relapse as inevitably leading to more drug use.
    d. both a and b

14. Jim is unable to cut down or control his substance use. He has been experiencing decreased effects when taking the same amount of drugs. Jim's drug use has begun to disrupt his work and family responsibilities. According to DSM-IV, what would Jim's diagnosis be?
    a. substance intoxication
    b. substance dependence
    c. substance abuse
    d. none of the above

15. _____ refers to the physiological reaction called drunkenness or high.
   a. Substance use
   b. Substance abuse
   c. Substance dependence
   d. none of the above

16. Pulling one's own hair from anywhere on the body refers to
   a. pyromania
   b. kleptomania
   c. intermittent explosive disorder
   d. trichotillomania

17. Which of the following is true of substance-related disorders?
   a. They kill 500,000 Americans every year.
   b. They cost hundreds of billions of dollars each year.
   c. They play a role in homelessness.
   d. all of the above

18. Drug use has _____ in recent years.
   a. Declined
   b. increased dramatically
   c. remained the same
   d. increased slightly

19. Substance abuse is defined as
   a. more than three glasses of wine or four glasses of beer.
   b. daily use of a substance.
   c. weekly use of a substance.
   d. the use of substances to the point that education, job, or relationships with others are disrupted.

20. The text differentiates two types of substance dependence. The type associated with tolerance and withdrawal is referred to as _____ dependence; whereas, the type associated with drug-seeking behaviors is referred to as _____ dependence.
   a. psychological; physiological
   b. physiological; psychological
   c. alcohol; marijuana
   d. marijuana; alcohol

21. Which of the following is the most routinely used illegal substance in the United States?
   a. opioids
   b. heroin
   c. cocaine
   d. marijuana

22. A person with a genetic vulnerability to substance dependence
    a. will inevitably develop that dependence.
    b. may choose not to use the substance in order to avoid becoming dependent.
    c. will be more likely to try the substance.
    d. has no control over whether he or she initiates use of the substance.

23. Pathological gamblers display which of the following behaviors?
    a. need to gamble with increasing amounts of money
    b. restlessness without gambling
    c. jeopardizing of relationships, jobs, education, or finances to support gambling
    d. all of the above

24. The liver of an average-size person can metabolize how much alcohol per hour?
    a. 7 to 10 grams (one glass of beer)
    b. 12 to 16 grams (two glasses of beer)
    c. 3 to 4 grams (a half glass of beer)
    d. The liver does not metabolize alcohol.

25. Factors that affect whether alcohol will cause organic damage include
    a. frequency of use.
    b. whether the body has time to recover between binges.
    c. blood alcohol levels attained while drinking.
    d. all of the above

26. "Heroin chic" refers to
    a. all-night dance parties that often involve drug use.
    b. the lifestyle of an opiate addict.
    c. advertising that glamorizes the physical symptoms of opiate use.
    d. the feeling of euphoria induced by heroin use.

27. In the CD-ROM or videotape, "ABNORMAL PSYCHOLOGY: LIVE!", Dr. Csernansky claimed that "Tim" could be diagnosed with a second psychological disorder. This disorder, which often co-occurs with alcohol abuse, was
    a. an underlying anxiety disorder.
    b. an underlying stress disorder.
    c. an underlying depressive disorder.
    d. an underlying personality disorder.

28. In the CD-ROM or videotape, "ABNORMAL PSYCHOLOGY: LIVE!", "Tim" described a long period of abusing alcohol. The behaviors he described as being associated with his abuse include all of the following EXCEPT
    a. drinking while he was at work.
    b. numerous "blackouts".
    c. lack of contact with his family.
    d. limited social interactions.

True or False Questions

29. Controlled drinking has been shown to be an effective cure for alcohol abusers.

    TRUE or FALSE

30. Polysubstance abuse is characterized by the use of multiple substances.

    TRUE or FALSE

31. Even though it is classified as a depressant, the initial effect of alcohol is an apparent stimulation.

    TRUE or FALSE

32. Major signs of withdrawal seen with other drugs also occur with marijuana.

    TRUE or FALSE

33. Studies have shown that genetic factors may influence the prevalence of fetal alcohol syndrome.

    TRUE or FALSE

34. There are vast differences in prevalence of alcohol abuse and dependence in different cultures.

    TRUE or FALSE

35. According to research by John Hasting, marijuana is more addictive than caffeine.

    TRUE or FALSE

36. Positive reinforcement is considered as a cause of substance related disorders, in that people may use drugs to escape unpleasant situations.

    TRUE or FALSE

37. It is possible to use an illegal substance repeatedly without abusing it.

    TRUE or FALSE

38. If abused, all substances are physiologically addicting.

    TRUE or FALSE

39. The DSM-IV definition of substance dependence emphasizes the physiological aspects of tolerance and withdrawal.

    TRUE or FALSE

40. Early use of alcohol may predict later abuse.

    TRUE or FALSE

41. Enkaphalins and endorphins are natural stimulants in the human body.

    TRUE or FALSE

42. In recent years, strategies for preventing substance abuse have shifted from education-based approaches (e.g., DARE) to more comprehensive approaches involving skills training, stricter laws, and community-based interventions.

    TRUE or FALSE

Essay Questions

43. Discuss the relationships among the factors involved in an integrative model of substance-related disorder.

44. Describe the differences among substance use, intoxication, abuse, and dependence.

45. Describe two biological and two psychosocial treatments of substance related disorders.

46. Discuss the impact of biological, psychological, social, and cultural dimensions on the causes of substance-related disorders.

HOW WELL DID YOU DO?

Less than 60%	Restudy the chapter (don't just reread); rework your notes completely. You can improve if you increase your efforts.
60-80%	Restudy and rewrite, especially the weak areas; discuss problem areas with study partners.
Over 80%	You're on the right track; continue as you are; focus on trouble areas with study group.
Over 95%	Nice job, especially if you know the whole chapter this well. Be sure to reward your behavior, help others in your study group (they'll help you on your weak chapters), and don't forget to review.

THINKING ALLOWED
Chapter 10 Activities

As a college student, you may see a substantial amount of alcohol abuse. Do you observe any behaviors that meet the criteria for a disorder? What makes the difference?

What are the positive and negative implications of the phrase "to suffer from drug abuse?" How is this different from more traditional views of excessive drug use?

As you know, much taxpayer funding pays for treatment of dependency problems. Write to your legislators insisting that money should be spent only on programs with empirical proof of effectiveness.

Some substances of abuse are always legal, others are legal under certain circumstances, and others are always illegal. What do you think accounts for the differences, and what, if any, changes would you think appropriate?

INTERNET RESOURCES

<u>Alcoholics Anonymous</u>

The official web page for Alcoholics Anonymous; information includes the "Twelve Steps to Recovery".

http://www.alcoholics-anonymous.org/

<u>Binge Drinking among college students</u>

High-risk drinking, its causes and consequences.

http://www.edc.org/hec/pubs/factsheets/scope.html

<u>Cocaine Anonymous Home Page</u>

This group uses the Twelve Steps program to help recovering cocaine addicts. Includes phone numbers for local chapters as well as web links.

http://www.ca.org/

<u>National Clearinghouse for Alcohol and Drug Information</u>

Resource for current and comprehensive information about substance abuse prevention and treatment.

http://www.health.org/

<u>Web of Addictions</u>

This web site provides fact sheets on drugs and abuse, links to other Internet resources, and places to get help with addictions.

http://www.well.com/user/woa/

Solutions

KEY WORDS

1. (416)
2. (417)
3. (398)
4. (420)
5. (393)
6. (412)
7. (FAS) (396)

8. (395)
9. (393)
10. (387)
11. (393)
12. (393)
13. (389)
14. (389)

15. (389)
16. (390)
17. (390)

SAMPLE QUESTIONS

Multiple Choice Questions

1. B, 393
2. A, 390
3. D, 406-407
4. D, 394
5. C, 403
6. A, 404
7. C, 411-412
8. B, 416
9. D, 395
10. A, 404-405

11. C, 411-412
12. A, 393
13. D, 420
14. C, 390
15. D, 390
16. D, 424
17. D, 387-388
18. A, 387-388
19. D, 389-390

20. B, 389-390
21. D, 406-407
22. B, 410-411
23. D, 423-424
24. A, 394
25. D, 394
26. C, 405
27. C, video, CD-ROM
28. A, video, CD-ROM

True or False Questions

29. F, 418
30. T, 387
31. T, 394
32. F, 406-407
33. T, 396

34. T, 396
35. F, 406-407*
    * Figure 11.2
36. F, 411
37. T, 389-390

38. F, 392
39. F, 389-390
40. F, 394
41. T, 400
42. T, 421

Essay Questions

43. Your answer should include a discussion of equifinality. Be sure that you discuss how the factors relate to one another, not just what the factors are. (See textbook pages 414-415.)

44. Highlight the definitions provided by the textbook. (See textbook pages 387-393.)

SUBSTANCE-RELATED AND IMPULSE-CONTROL DISORDERS

45. Biological treatments that can be described include agonist substitution, antagonist treatment, aversive treatment and the use of several medical substances. Some psychological treatment methods include inpatient hospital treatment, support groups (e.g., Alcoholics Anonymous), and controlled use. (See textbook pages 416-419.)

46. Your discussion should include familial, genetic, and neurobiological influences (biological), positive and negative reinforcement, and cognitive factors (psychological). Social factors such as family influence and social values should be addressed, as well as the cross-cultural variations discussed in the textbook. (See textbook pages 409-414.)

PERSONALITY DISORDERS

LEARNING OBJECTIVES

1. Describe the essential features of personality disorders according to DSM-IV-TR and why they are listed on Axis II.

2. Describe the essential characteristics of each of the Cluster A (odd/eccentric) personality disorders, including information pertaining to etiology and treatment.

3. Describe the essential characteristics of each of the Cluster B (dramatic/erratic) personality disorders.

4. Identity the differences between psychopathy and antisocial personality disorder.

5. Describe the essential characteristics of each of the Cluster C (anxious/fearful) personality disorders, including information pertaining to etiology and treatment.

CHAPTER SUMMARY

By now you know what to do with chapter summaries and sample tests.

_____ is made up of the characteristic ways that a person thinks and behaves. Personality _____ involve pervasive and enduring ways of thinking and behaving that cause significant functional impairment or distress to oneself or significant others. They typically originate during childhood and are considered chronic. They are Axis ___ disorders in the DSM-IV.

Personality; disorders; II

Personality disorders involve problem characteristics that occur over time. Personality problems may be described in terms of dimensions versus categories. A _____ approach implies that personality disorders are extreme versions of normal personality variations. A _____ approach implies that personality disorders are qualitatively different from psychologically healthy behavior. The DSM groups personality disorders in a _____ way, without rating *how much* an individual qualifies for a given disorder. The use of a categorical model is problematic in that it allows clinicians to _____ disorders, i.e., to consider them real entities.

dimensional; categorical; categorical; reify

Research has suggested that there are "five factors" that are basic parts of personality. These factors include _____ ___ _____ (creative vs. imperceptive), _____ _____ (even-tempered vs. temperamental), _____ (organized vs. unreliable), _____ (kind vs. hostile), and _____ (active vs. passive). Studies in several different cultures have suggested the universality of these dimensions. The DSM ranks personality disorders along three clusters. Cluster A involves odd or _____ characteristics, cluster B involves emotional or _____ behaviors, and cluster C involves anxiety and _____ characteristics.

openness to experience; emotional stability; conscientiousness; agreeableness; extraversion; eccentric; erratic; fear

Personality disorders originate in _____, with maladaptive personality characteristics developing over time until they are evident to others. There has been little/much research to determine the specific developmental course of these disorders.

childhood; little

Borderline personality disorders is diagnosed less/more commonly in females than in males. Disorders that historically have been associated with women (including histrionic and _____ personality disorders) are now believed to have equivalent prevalence across genders. Diagnosis of various personality disorders may be influenced by clinician bias regarding gender. Some have argued that histrionic personality disorder is biased toward/against females with its emphasis on symptoms that are typical _____ of females. _____ gender bias refers to biases in the criteria for a disorder. _____ gender bias refers to bias in the way assessment measures are used.

more; dependent; against; stereotypes; Criterion; Assessment

In psychiatric diagnosis, _____ refers to the presence of more than one disorder in a given individual. Because roughly _____-_____ of those diagnosed with a personality disorder also meet the criteria for a second personality disorder, this category has particularly high/low comorbidity rates.

comorbidity; one-half; high

People with _____ personality disorder display excessive mistrust and suspicion of other people without any apparent justification. Other characteristics may include argumentative interactions, excessive complaining, and hostility. There is a small association between having paranoid personality disorder and having a relative with _____. Inaccurate _____ of others' actions have been proposed as causes of the disorder. Early childhood _____ may contribute to a maladaptive view of the world. Some subpopulations may be particularly susceptible to paranoid personality disorder. These include prisoners, refugees, people with hearing impairments, and the _____.

paranoid; schizophrenia; perceptions; learning; elderly

Treatment for this disorder is problematic because people with excessive suspicion are not likely to seek help or to develop _____ relationships with mental health professionals. Therapy typically involves a _____ approach, but clients often do not continue in therapy long enough to be helped.

trusting; cognitive

_____ personality disorder is marked by a pattern of detachment from social relationships and a limited range of emotions in social situations. Individuals with this disorder seem cold and _____. Bleuler coined the term schizoid to describe those who turn inward and away from the outside world. Individuals with this disorder do not seem to want social interaction and do not appear to be affected by _____ or _____. For some people, this social isolation may be extremely _____, but they are unwilling or unable to express their emotions. This disorder does/does not involve the unusual thought processes that characterize other Cluster A disorders, such as ideas of _____.

Schizoid; indifferent; praise; criticism; painful; does not; reference

No/Much significant research on the biological or psychosocial contributions to this disorder has been reported. The characteristic preference for social isolation appears similar to _____, a condition for which some biological etiology has been proposed. Research has suggested that a lower density of _____ receptors is related to subjective reports of detachment.

No; autism; dopamine

Treatment often encourages development of interest in social relationships and teaching about the _____ experienced by others (empathy). _____ _____ training is also desirable for these individuals, including the use of role-playing by the therapist. Clinicians report extreme difficulty/ease in treating these individuals effectively.

emotions; Social skills; difficulty

_____ personality disorder is characterized by social isolation combined with bizarre behaviors and beliefs about the world. Ideas of _____, _____ thinking, and illusions are common. Illusions such as feeling as if someone is in the room when the individual is really alone must be distinguished from the false belief that someone is in the room, seen in other disorders, such as _____. A small minority of people with schizotypal personality disorder develops schizophrenia. As one might imagine, _____ deficits appear in both of these diagnoses. _____ beliefs or practices can lead to a mistaken diagnosis of schizotypal personality disorder.

Schizotypal; reference; magical; schizophrenia; social; Cultural

Schizotypal personality disorder has been described as one phenotype of a _____ genotype. That is, these individuals have schizophrenia _____, but they lack the biological or environmental conditions necessary for the full expression of schizophrenia. New research has found generalized brain abnormalities in individuals with this disorder. Few treatments are available for schizotypal personality disorder, and their effectiveness is modest. Many of the people who request clinical help also require treatment for _____ _____ disorder. _____ _____ training is a common intervention, although some therapists instead choose to help clients _____ ___ their isolated lifestyle. As with schizophrenia, haloperidol medication has demonstrated some success with individuals having schizotypal personality disorder. Side effects may act as deterrents to taking the medication. In general, these individuals do/do not improve over time.

schizophrenia; genes; major depressive; Social skills; adjust to; do not

People with _____ personality disorder violate social norms, displaying irresponsible, impulsive and deceitful behaviors. They appear to have no conscience and to feel no _____, and most have long histories of lying and cheating others. About 83 percent of these individuals also display drug abuse. Once called *manie san delire* (mania without delirium), antisocial personality disorder describes those with unusual emotional responses and impulsive rages, but with _____ reasoning ability. Among many labels, the terms _____ and antisocial personality disorder figure most prominently in the literature. Hare's Revised Psychopathy Checklist is a common assessment tool that focuses on underlying _____ _____ such as being self-centered or manipulative. The DSM uses concrete and observable _____ for diagnosis.

antisocial; remorse; intact; psychopathy; personality traits; behaviors

There is both overlap and independence between Cleckley's concept of _____ and the DSM-IV concept of antisocial personality disorder. For instance, some psychopaths do not display the _____ characteristics of antisocial personality disorder. Furthermore, _____, referring to all people who get into trouble with the law, overlaps with both concepts. Identifying psychopaths in the criminal population may have important implications for predicting their future criminal behavior. _____ psychopaths are members of culturally deviant subgroups, such as a gangs. It is important to note that some psychopaths have little or no interactions with the legal system. Higher levels of ___ may explain this ability to avoid any legal redress for psychopathic behavior. However, the relationship between IQ and delinquency does not apply to African American youths, which suggests that _____ differences exist.

psychopathy; aggressiveness; criminality; Dyssocial; IQ; cultural

Many adults diagnosed with antisocial personality disorder displayed symptoms of _____ _____ when they were children. Many children with conduct disorder become juvenile offenders and may become involved with drugs. Symptoms of conduct disorder include school _____ and running away. Lack of remorse, included in the criteria for antisocial personality disorder, is/is not included in the conduct disorder diagnosis. There appears to be a genetic factor involved in both antisocial personality disorder and _____. A gene-environment _____ suggests that genes and environment are interdependent in the expression of the disorder. Genetic studies should be interpreted with care, particularly since criminality is an extremely _____ category. Environmental factors play a key role in criminality.

conduct disorder; truancy; is not; criminality; interaction; heterogeneous

The _____ hypothesis of antisocial personality and psychopathy implicates low levels of arousal in the cerebral cortex. The Yerkes-Dodson u-shaped curve predicts that people with either high or low arousal levels will experience positive/negative affect and perform well/poorly in situations. Therefore, the dangerous risk-taking behaviors of people with antisocial personality disorder may be efforts to increase/decrease an abnormally low/high arousal level. Evidence for this theory was seen in the low skin conductance activity, low heart rate, and slow-frequency brain wave activity of youths who eventually became criminals.

underarousal; negative; poorly; increase; low

According to the cortical _____ hypothesis, the cerebral cortex of psychopaths is in a more primitive state than that of other adults. This hypothesis helps to explain the sometimes _____ and impulsive behaviors exhibited by these individuals. Low frequency theta brain waves are characteristic of psychopaths, and these are not usually seen in other adults. However, these waves may also reflect simple _____ or drowsiness.

immaturity; childlike; boredom

Psychopaths may also have a higher threshold for the experience of fear than others. This is called the _____ hypothesis. The hypothesis is supported by the endorsements of psychopaths to items that most people would find _____ on the Activity Preference Questionnaire. Classical conditioning studies with the pairing of tones and electric shocks also distinguish psychopaths from other adults. Psychopaths may have difficulty learning to avoid _____. Some researchers have attempted to explain antisocial behavior by theorizing a malfunction of one or more of three major brain systems. These systems include the _____ _____ system (BIS), the _____ system (REW), and the _____/_____ system (F/F).

fearlessness; unpleasant; punishment; behavioral inhibition; reward; fight/flight

Some research suggests that psychopaths are/are not deterred from achieving a goal when presented with cues that the goal is impossible to achieve. _____ children may mediate a coercive family process, where parents do not make _____ on the child because to do so would create more aversive behavior. Environmental factors that may be involved in antisocial behaviors include _____ parenting and low family social status. _____ has also been implicated in the onset of antisocial personality disorder. Persons with histories of higher numbers of traumatic events have been found to engage in higher/lower levels of antisocial behavior.

are not; Aggressive; demands; inconsistent; Stress; higher

The course of psychopathic behaviors may be traced from childhood well into adulthood, with a "burn out" after age ___. The cause of this burn out is _____. Antisocial personality disorder may be related to some genetic predisposition and its interaction with environmental _____. Treatment for the disorder is simple/difficult, because often clients do not believe that they need treatment. The threat of _____ is used as a deterrent for antisocial behaviors. There is general pessimism about the _____ of the disorder in adults.

40; unknown; stressors; difficult; incarceration; prognosis

Efforts to prevent this outcome are evident in treatment strategies for _____, particularly in the area of parent training. Parent training has some/no documented success; various risk factors often impede the process for the families of antisocial children. Programs that combine a behavioral approach with efforts to improve family relationships may be more successful. Preschool prevention programs have included family _____ _____ in addition to parent training.

children; some; social supports

People with _____ personality disorder lead extremely unstable lives, often with intense and tumultuous relationships. Impulsive drug use, eating disorders, _____-_____, and suicide attempts are common. Borderline personality disorder appears to run in families and may be linked with _____ disorders. Environmental influences play a pervasive role. _____ factors are also being examined to determine how individuals with the disorder process information.

borderline; self-mutilation; mood; Cognitive

Early trauma, such as physical or _____ _____, is prevalent in people with borderline personality disorder. The disorder shares characteristics with _____-_____ _____ disorder (PTSD), and behaviors consistent with borderline personality disorder have been seen in persons trying to adjust to a new _____ quickly (which could be perceived as highly stressful).

sexual abuse; post-traumatic stress; culture

There are few/many controlled studies dealing with treatment outcomes of clients with borderline personality disorder. Some of these clients respond well to medical treatments, although drug abuse and _____ with treatment are frequent complications. _____ _____ therapy aims to help borderline clients cope with life stress that triggers suicidal behaviors. This relatively new method appears to hold promise.

few; noncompliance; Dialectical behavior

_____ personality disorder is characterized by excessive displays of emotion, intended to make the person the center of attention. These individuals may have an impressionistic, black-and-white _____ style. Speech is characterized by _____ (or exaggeration) and a lack of detail. Some believe that the features of the disorder, such as overconcern with physical appearance and overdramatization, are characteristic of the stereotypical Western female, which may lead to _____ among women. Histrionic personality disorder is associated more often with _____ _____ disorder than chance would predict. Some have suggested that these disorders may represent ___-_____ alternative expressions of the same underlying condition. Therapy for histrionic personality disorder involves modification of _____-_____ behaviors. Some therapists also focus on problematic _____ _____.

Histrionic; cognitive; hyperbole; overdiagnosis; antisocial personality; sex-typed; attention-getting; interpersonal relationships

Psychoanalytic theory uses the term _____ to describe people who display an exaggerated sense of self-importance and preoccupation with attention from others. Narcissistic personality disorder is characterized by this self-importance, grandiosity, and a lack of _____ for other people. This disorder has high comorbidity with _____. Some theorists purport that, as children, narcissistic clients lacked the necessary _____ involvement to grow out of the grandiose infant state of development.

narcissistic; empathy; depression; parental

Treatment for narcissistic personality disorder often focuses on the client's distorted self-perception, hypersensitivity to _____, and lack of _____. _____ therapy attempts to replace grandiose fantasies with attainable day-to-day pleasures. _____ training may aid in dealing with criticism.

evaluation; empathy; Cognitive; Relaxation

In _____ personality disorder, low self-esteem and extreme sensitivity to the opinion of others lead one to seek/avoid social relationships. One possible cause may be a predisposed "_____," which in childhood drives parental rejection. Mild support for this theory is based on _____ data. Behavioral intervention techniques for anxiety and _____ _____ deficits have been somewhat successful for these clients. Common techniques include _____ _____ and behavioral rehearsal.

avoidant; avoid; temperament; retrospective; social skills; systematic desensitization

_____ personality disorder is marked by destructive dependence on others that results in fear of abandonment. Unlike those with _____ personality disorder, people with dependent personality disorder tend to cling to social relationships in fear of _____. Research on infant attachment is associated with the hypothesis that this disorder may be caused by childhood disruptions in environment and _____. Treatment involves supporting the client to make _____ independently.

Dependent; avoidant; rejection; nurturing; choices

_____-_____ personality disorder, as distinguished from obsessive-compulsive disorder, is characterized by a rigid fixation on the way that daily living activities should be accomplished. This rigidity tends to impair _____ _____. New research indicates that obsessive-compulsive disorder may characterize many _____ _____ and gifted children. Treatment may deal with the _____ that underlie the need for orderliness.

Obsessive-compulsive; social relationships; serial killers; fears

The classification of personality disorders is continuously debated. Two disorders, _____ personality disorder and self-defeating personality disorder, were listed in the DSM-III-R for possible inclusion in the DSM-IV but these were not included. Current categories under study for possible inclusion in future versions include depressive personality disorder and _____ personality disorder.

sadistic; negativistic

KEY WORDS

Practice defining the important concepts listed below and at the end of the text chapter. Follow the definition suggestions provided in the introduction to this Guide. Be precise and accurate, and check your work with the text. Add to the definition later as you encounter more information about the term. Whenever possible, include examples. Use only the space to the right of the word so that later you can cover either the word or the definition to use one to cue the other. Define additional important terms you'll find in the chapter.

1. antisocial personality disorder

   _____

   _____

2. avoidant personality disorder

   _____

   _____

3. borderline personality disorder

   _____

   _____

4. dependent personality disorder

   _____

   _____

5. histrionic personality disorder

   _____

   _____

6. narcissistic personality disorder

_____

_____

7. obsessive-compulsive personality disorder

_____

_____

8. paranoid personality disorder

_____

_____

9. schizoid personality disorder

_____

_____

10. schizotypal personality disorder

_____

_____

SAMPLE QUESTIONS

As one of the later stages of your study for this chapter, you can assess your progress by taking a sample test. Don't make the mistake of studying just for these questions. They are merely a small sample of the many questions that could appear on an exam. An excellent way to help yourself is to generate your own questions and answers. This will help you focus on important concepts, make better distinctions among similar ideas, practice writing responses, and engaging the material in general. Try them on your friends in your study group.

Multiple Choice Questions

1. The DSM uses a categorical approach to personality disorders. This is a problem because
    a. the severity of the disorders is not given much consideration.
    b. these disorders may simply be extreme degrees of normal patterns.
    c. it may lead clinicians to view these disorders as real entities.
    d. all of the above

2. This week's first client shows a pervasive pattern of grandiosity, need for admiration, and lack of empathy. You diagnose _____ personality disorder, one of the Dramatic, Emotional, or Erratic cluster of disorders.
   a. narcissistic
   b. schizoid
   c. avoidant
   d. histrionic

3. A pervasive pattern of social inhibition, feelings of inadequacy, and hypersensitivity to negative evaluations, part of the Anxious or Fearful disorder cluster, is diagnosed as _____ personality disorder.
   a. narcissistic
   b. schizoid
   c. avoidant
   d. dependent

4. George lives every day on a strict schedule. He must have everything perfect and organized, and is excessively devoted to his work. However, he has difficulty completing projects. Which personality disorder is he likely to be diagnosed?
   a. paranoid
   b. obsessive-compulsive
   c. dependent
   d. borderline

5. According to the text, which is NOT true in the treatment of paranoid personality disorder?
   a. Clients often do not remain in therapy long enough to be helped.
   b. Clients usually seek help for problems such as anxiety or depression, rather than for their personality disorder.
   c. Paradoxical intervention is used; i.e. therapists intentionally lie to these clients to create mistrust.
   d. No therapy has been shown to greatly improve the lives of those with the disorder.

6. Dependent personality disorder and avoidant personality disorder have the following in common:
   a. feelings of inadequacy
   b. sensitivity to criticism
   c. need for reassurance from others
   d. all of the above
   e. none of the above

7. Which of the following might be considered in treating an individual with schizotypal personality disorder?
   a. anti-depressant medication
   b. social skills training
   c. encouraging acceptance of the behaviors without major changes
   d. all of the above

8. Which is true of avoidant personality disorder?
   a. Behavioral interventions for anxiety and social skills problems have had some success.
   b. As with most personality disorders, research on treatment effectiveness is lacking
   c. Treatments are similar to those used for social phobia.
   d. both a and c

9. The relationship between obsessive-compulsive personality disorder and obsessive-compulsive disorder (OCD)
   a. is a distant one; those with obsessive-compulsive personality disorder tend not to have the obsessive thoughts and compulsive behaviors of OCD.
   b. is a highly overlapping one; OCD encompasses all of obsessive-compulsive personality disorder characteristics, but no characteristics of other personality disorders.
   c. is as close as can be; the disorders are one and the same.
   d. none of the above

10. Personality disorders involve enduring patterns of perceiving, relating to, and thinking about the environment and oneself that
    a. may cause functional impairment.
    b. may cause subjective distress.
    c. cut across many times and places.
    d. all of the above

11. The DSM-IV system of diagnosis is _____, whereas, many theorists propose that personality disorders occur on a continuum, rather than an all-or-none dichotomous fashion. These theorists propose changing to a _____ system of diagnosis.
    a. dimension based; category based
    b. category based; dimension based
    c. behavior based; trait based
    d. trait based; behavior based

12. While personality disorders are fairly common in the general population, several of the individual personality disorders are relatively rare. Which three disorders are found in fewer than 1% of the general population?
    a. schizoid, narcissistic, and avoidant
    b. schizoid, schizotypal, and avoidant
    c. schizoid, narcissistic, and histrionic
    d. narcissistic, avoidant, and schizotypal

13. In a study described in the text, when a case history of antisocial personality disorder was ascribed to a male client, therapists diagnosed it correctly. When the same behavior was ascribed to a woman
    a. their different diagnosis proved the existence of gender bias.
    b. their different diagnosis probably reflects a belief by therapists, accurate or not, that males are more likely to display antisocial behavior.
    c. the client was more frequently labeled dependent personality disorder.
    d. all of the above

14. When clinicians use subjective impressions of clients based on interpersonal interactions, rather than behavioral observations outlined by DSM criteria, more _____ is likely to enter into diagnostic decisions.
    a. bias
    b. error
    c. accuracy
    d. expert opinion

15. A diagnosis of more than one personality disorder in the same client
    a. may indicate the disorders are poorly defined.
    b. is called comorbidity.
    c. may reveal substantial overlap among the disorder categories.
    d. all of the above

16. Which of the following statements is not true about borderline personality disorder?
    a. It is one of the more common personality disorders.
    b. People with the disorder tend to improve during their 30's and 40's.
    c. Women are affected by the disorder more often than men.
    d. People with the disorder usually have a high self-image.

17. A pervasive pattern of overconcern with orderliness, control, and perfectionism, at the expense of openness and flexibility
    a. is the DSM-IV category known as schizotypal personality disorder.
    b. is the DSM-IV definition of obsessive-compulsive personality disorder.
    c. is the DSM-IV definition of histrionic personality disorder.
    d. can be typical of people who grade these exams.

18. Your client displays schizotypal personality disorder. Because you are a well-trained responsible professional, you know to assess for a likely comorbid disorder, namely
    a. histrionic personality disorder.
    b. major depressive disorder.
    c. eating disorders.
    d. sexual disorders.

19. Deceitful, irresponsible, aggressive, irritable, and lacking remorse are characteristics describing
    a. bipolar disorder.
    b. antisocial personality disorder.
    c. borderline personality disorder.
    d. schizoid personality disorder.
    e. psychology study guide authors.

20. DSM-IV calls for categorical judgments about the diagnosis for Personality Disorders. Imagine that the new DSM-V appears just as you earn your professional license in a few years, and it calls for dimensional determinations, as many current psychologists suggest. This change would mean
    a. deciding whether to reject the Personality Disorder diagnosis.
    b. deciding whether another diagnosis is more appropriate.
    c. differential diagnosis.
    d. determining the severity of the personality disorder.

21. Many people have fantasies of unlimited power, brilliance or beauty, but a man who also believes himself grandly unique, entitled to special privileges, is arrogant, and expects to be admired and recognized as superior while envying others who are successful, might find himself with a psychological diagnosis. Which personality disorder would apply?
    a. the one named for the Greek word for "uterus"
    b. borderline personality disorder
    c. the one named for the mythological Greek character Narcissus
    d. schizotypal personality disorder
    e. psychology study guide author

22. A person identified as avoidant personality disorder has just lost a close friend to a rival and is now seeking other friendships as replacements. You know the person
    a. actually is desperate for nurturance.
    b. will assume the worst about other people.
    c. will conclude the original relationship person really wasn't good enough anyway.
    d. has been misdiagnosed.

23. In the CD-ROM or videotape "ABNORMAL PSYCHOLOGY: LIVE!", "George" exhibited all of the following behaviors associated with Antisocial Personality Disorder EXCEPT
    a. lying.
    b. fire-setting.
    c. destruction of property.
    d. abusing animals.

24. In the CD-ROM or videotape "ABNORMAL PSYCHOLOGY: LIVE!", before the age of 15, "George" had
    a. gotten drunk.
    b. smoked marijuana.
    c. destroyed property.
    d. all of these

Matching

1. __C__ antisocial personality
2. __J__ histrionic personality disorder
3. __f__ dependent personality disorder
4. __o__ avoidant personality disorder
5. __A__ paranoid personality disorder
6. __h__ schizoid personality disorder
7. __D__ narcissistic personality disorder
8. __i__ borderline personality disorder
9. __n__ schizotypal personality disorder
10. __l__ obsessive-compulsive personality disorder
11. __M__ Cluster A
12. __B__ Cluster B
13. __G__ Cluster C
14. __K__ psychopathy
15. __E__ criminality

a. excessively mistrustful and suspicious disorder of other people
b. dramatic, emotional, or erratic disorders
c. display noncompliance with social norms; irresponsible, impulsive, and deceitful behaviors
d. unreasonable sense of self-importance and lack of empathy for others
e. refers to people who experience trouble with the law
f. extreme reliance on others and unreasonable fear of abandonment
g. anxious or fearful disorders
h. detached from personal relationships and limited emotions in personal situations
i. instability of interpersonal relationships and marked impulsivity
j. overly dramatic as if acting
k. from criteria developed by Cleckley and Hare, focusing more on personality traits, such as manipulativeness and self-centeredness
l. fixation on doing things the right way
m. odd or eccentric disorders
n. socially isolated and having "odd" beliefs
o. hypersensitive to others' opinions, and low self-esteem

True or False Questions

25. A likely comorbid disorder of schizotypal personality disorder is paranoid personality disorder.

    TRUE or FALSE

26. One accepted approach to the treatment of schizotypal personality disorder is the use of tranquilizers.

    TRUE or FALSE

27. It is more difficult to identify and study psychopaths with high intelligence than those with low intelligence.

    TRUE or FALSE

28. Antisocial personality disorder and childhood conduct disorder are both associated with illegal drug involvement and other criminal activities.

    TRUE or FALSE

29. Lykken found a general learning deficit to account for psychopaths' impairment in learning to control their impulses.

    TRUE or FALSE

30. Individuals with paranoid personality disorder often do not remain in treatment long enough to get much help with their disorder.

    TRUE or FALSE

31. Pervasive dependency is the predominant criterion for the schizotypal personality disorder diagnosis.

    TRUE or FALSE

32. A person who has been diagnosed with borderline personality disorder is more likely to be male than female.

    TRUE or FALSE

33. Adults with avoidant personality disorder were likely avoiding relationships even in childhood and adolescence.

    TRUE or FALSE

34. Homelessness appears to be prevalent among individuals with schizoid personality disorder.

     TRUE or FALSE

Essay Questions

35. Pick any two personality disorders and compare and contrast them.

36. Choose either the categorical or the dimensional model of classifying personality disorders and defend it. Then defend the opposite position.

37. Knowing that it is difficult to research non-criminal psychopaths, devise a plan for identifying and gathering information about them.

38. You are the expert guest on today's Donahue show to discuss your best-selling book on post-traumatic stress disorder. Tell the caller and our audience how borderline personality disorder is similar to that disorder, and how treatment might be similar as well.

39. In the videotape "ABNORMAL PSYCHOLOGY: INSIDE-OUT", Dr. Csernansky stated that persons with a diagnosis of Antisocial Personality Disorder often are allowed second, and even third, chances to demonstrate socially appropriate behavior. Why is this so?

HOW WELL DID YOU DO?

Less than 60%	Restudy the chapter (don't just reread); rework your notes completely. You can improve if you increase your efforts.
60-80%	Restudy and rewrite, especially the weak areas; discuss problem areas with study partners.
Over 80%	You're on the right track; continue as you are; focus on trouble areas with study group.
Over 95%	Nice job, especially if you know the whole chapter this well. Be sure to reward your behavior, help others in your study group (they'll help you on your weak chapters), and don't forget to review.

THINKING ALLOWED

Chapter 11 Activities

Identify acquaintances and movie and TV characters with behavior patterns similar to those of the personality disorders. Consider which of their behaviors fit the definitions and which do not. Why are these not usually considered actually disordered? Is this a dimensional or categorical task?

It may be difficult at first to differentiate among the various disorders described in this chapter. Perhaps it will help to adopt a method from your childhood: Flashcards. Put the name of the disorder on one side and its definition on the other. Present either side of any card at random and practice generating the other side. But understand and explain, in your own (informed) words; don't merely memorize.

The usual role of a therapist is to help clients effect changes. This may not be true for clients with one of the personality disorders. Identify which one and explain why.

It is time to assess the acting skill of your study group. Have members choose personality disorders, perhaps by drawing your flashcards out of a box, and act out the characteristic behaviors. The rest of you have to identify which is being portrayed. Each member should act out several disorders. Who in the group is best at this?

Call a friend or a member of your study group. Describe two of the personality disorders and their treatments, to show off what you are learning. Be sure to return the favor by listening attentively when they ask the same of you. You'll learn something.

INTERNET RESOURCES

BPD Central

A web site devoted to furthering the understanding of borderline disorder, written with those who live with a BPD patient in mind.

http://www.bpdcentral.com/

Clinical Aspects of Borderline Personality Disorder

Pharmacotherapy of the borderline patient and advances in psychotherapy of patients with BPD. Click on personality disorder.

http://www.medscape.com/

Internet Mental Health

Information on the diagnosis and treatment of personality disorders.

http://www.mentalhealth.com/p20-grp.html

Johns Hopkins inteliHealth − Personality Disorders

Find the "Condition Center" box and click on mental health. This will take you to Mental Health Zones where you can select "Personality Disorders." Several pages about the signs and symptoms of a number of personality disorders.

http://www.intelihealth.com/IH/ihtIH

Schizophrenia Home Page

Provides links to other web pages devoted to schizophrenia (this is a good starting place for finding information on schizophrenia on the Internet).

http://www.schizophrenia.com/newsletter/buckets/intro.html

Solutions

KEY WORDS

1. (444)	5. (455)	9. (439)
2. (459)	6. (457)	10. (441)
3. (452)	7. (462)	
4. (461)	8. (437)	

SAMPLE QUESTIONS

Multiple Choice Questions

1. D, 432	10. D, 431	19. B, 444
2. A, 457	11. B, 432-433	20. D, 432
3. C, 459	12. A, 433-434	21. C, 457
4. B, 462-463	13. B, 434-435	22. D, 459
5. C, 438-439	14. A, 436-437	23. D, video, CD-ROM
6. E, 459	15. D, 436	24. D, video, CD-ROM
7. D, 444	16. D, 452	
8. D, 459	17. B, 462-463	
9. A, 462-463	18. B, 442-443	

Matching

1. c 444	6. h 439	11. m 437
2. j 455	7. d 457	12. b 444
3. f 461	8. i 452	13. g 459
4. o 459	9. n 441	14. k 446
5. a 437	10. l 462-463	15. e 446

True or False Questions

25. T, 442-443	29. F, 445-446	33. T, 459
26. F, 444	30. T, 438	34. T, 439
27. T, 445-447	31. F, 442-443	
28. T, 446-447	32. F, 452	

Essay Questions

35. Your answer should include similarities and differences in diagnostic criteria as well as common characteristics, etiology, and treatment. You may want to include a statement about the comorbidity of the two disorders as well as gender differences, if any.

36. For either model you will want to include the advantages as well as a rebuttal to any commonly mentioned disadvantages. Also, you may want to include disadvantages of the other model, which your model clearly does not have. (See textbook pages 432-433.)

37. You may want to use similar recruitment methods to those of Widom (1977). You may choose to study those professionals whose career requires them to be charming, but ruthless. You may also want to get some measure of intelligence, because higher intelligence may have kept them from being caught breaking the law. You may conduct a study of adult children of alcoholics to determine if a subsample of these individuals falls into the category of non-criminal psychopaths. You will probably use various questionnaires to determine where these individuals fall on empathy, socialization, and other characteristics of psychopathy. (See textbook pages 444-452.)

38. Be sure to include symptoms, which occur in both disorders, especially if childhood physical and sexual abuse is associated with borderline personality disorder. Also, your answer should include what treatment(s) are used with both disorders. (See textbook pages 452-455.)

39. Persons with antisocial personality disorder are capable of behaving in engaging and friendly ways. These persons may even be able to exhibit isolated acts of kindness (e.g., George's caring attitude for animals); however, these behaviors are usually short-lived. (See video and textbook pages 444-452.)

CHAPTER **12**

SCHIZOPHRENIA AND OTHER PSYCHOTIC DISORDERS

LEARNING OBJECTIVES

1. Define schizophrenia and describe the different symptoms included in this diagnosis.

2. Trace the history of schizophrenia research, including the contributions of Kraepelin and Bleuler.

3. Distinguish among positive, negative, and disorganized symptoms of schizophrenia and other psychotic disorders.

4. Describe the prevalence of schizophrenia in society.

5. Identify the potential genetic, neurobiological, developmental, and psychosocial contributions and risk factors for schizophrenia.

6. Describe what is known about abnormalities in neurocognitive and biological functioning and their relation to the certain types of schizophrenia.

7. Describe biological and psychosocial treatments for schizophrenia and the general goals of therapy.

CHAPTER SUMMARY

By now you know what to do with chapter summaries and sample tests.

Schizophrenia is a disorder characterized by delusions, hallucinations, _____ speech and behavior, and missing or _____ emotions. It affects about _____ out of every hundred persons and has devastating effects on patients and their _____. In the U.S. in 1991, the cost of schizophrenia was estimated to be $_____. Kraepelin included _____, which is immobility or extreme agitation, hebephrenia, which is immature emotionality, and paranoia, which involves _____ of grandeur or persecution, in his category for schizophrenia. He called it _____ _____, meaning early dementia, and believed it was the result of mental _____. Bleuler called the disorder schizophrenia, claiming it was an associative _____ of the individual's functions of personality. It <u>does/does not</u> mean multiple personality or Dissociative Identity Disorder. Schizophrenia is characterized by positive, _____, and negative symptoms, _____ or more of which must be present for at least _____ _____ to warrant a diagnosis of schizophrenia.

disorganized; inappropriate; 1; families; 65 billion; catatonia; delusions; dementia praecox; weakness; splitting; does not; disorganized; two; one month

_____ symptoms of schizophrenia are active psychotic behaviors, such as delusions and hallucinations. A delusion is a _____ that is not based on reality. A delusion of _____ is the belief that one is a famous or important person; a delusion of _____ is a belief that others are enemies seeking to do you harm. In _____ syndrome, a person believes that someone they know has been replaced by a double. Cotard's syndrome involves believing that a _____ _____ has changed in an impossible way. In one study, Roberts found that individuals with delusions had less depression and a lesser/greater sense of meaning in life than did people who had been, but no longer were, delusional. _____ involve sensations that are not real; for schizophrenics, these are usually _____ hallucinations, such as hearing voices. Neuroimaging researchers have discovered that the part of the brain responsible for _____ _____ (Broca's area) is active during hallucination, rather than the area responsible for language _____ (Wernicke's area).

Positive; belief; grandeur; persecution; Capgras; body part; greater; Hallucinations; auditory; speech production; comprehension

A new category for long-recognized symptoms is called _____. Schizophrenic individuals often do not have an awareness of their problem, referred to as a lack of _____. They tend to have disorganized speech, which may be manifested by _____, in which they do not answer questions directly but go off on a tangent, or by loose associations (also called _____), in which they shift among unrelated topics. _____ refers to motor dysfunctions, ranging from agitation to immobility, exhibited by schizophrenic individuals. Catatonic immobility can involve _____ _____, in which the individual's limbs can be moved by someone else and will remain in the new position. Inappropriate _____, which refers to showing emotionality that is not warranted by circumstances, is another positive/disorganized/negative symptom of schizophrenia.

disorganized; insight; tangentiality; derailment; Catatonia; waxy flexibility; affect; disorganized

_____ symptoms refer to a lack of normal behavior, including affect, speech, and motivation deficits. Flat or blunted _____ are terms used to indicate that an individual demonstrates no emotions. Neuroimaging research suggests that flat or blunted affect may be related to a difficulty expressing emotion, not a lack of emotion. It is characteristic of ___% of schizophrenics; their verbal reports of, and _____ reactions to, emotional stimuli are/are not appropriate. _____, also called apathy, is an inability to start or continue activities. _____, deficits in the amount or content of speech, may be in the form of brief answers to questions or in slowness of response. Anhedonia, the inability to experience _____, is another negative symptom of schizophrenia.

Negative; affect; 67; physiological; are; Avolition; Alogia; pleasure

Schizophrenia is divided into subtypes, based on symptoms and outcomes. The _____ type of the disorder is characterized by delusions or _____, which usually have a theme, and the absence of problems of affect, cognitive skills, speech, or catatonia. It generally has a better/worse prognosis than the other types. The _____ type, previously called hebephrenic, includes disorganized speech and behavior, and flat or _____ affect. Any delusions present lack a _____. The catatonic type of schizophrenia includes symptoms of catatonic motor behaviors, odd mannerisms, echolalia (repeating the _____ of others), and _____ (repeating the motions of others). Individuals with the disorder who do not fit into these categories are classified in the _____ subtype. The _____ type of schizophrenia refers to individuals who have had an episode of schizophrenia but no longer demonstrate the major symptoms, although some less severe symptoms may still be present. Research suggests that the _____ type has a stronger familial link than the other types and a better prognosis.

paranoid; hallucinations; better; disorganized; inappropriate; theme; words; echopraxia; undifferentiated; residual; paranoid

Other psychotic disorder categories that are not schizophrenia have been devised. Individuals with _____ disorder experience the symptoms of schizophrenia, but these symptoms disappear quickly, and the individual can often resume normal functioning. Schizoaffective disorder is diagnosed when an individual exhibits symptoms of both schizophrenia and _____ disorders. _____ disorder refers to the presence of strong delusions, in the absence of other symptoms of schizophrenia. The person's suspicions may result in social _____. This disorder has _____ subtypes, and differs from schizophrenia in the beliefs involved are possible/impossible. It appears early/late in life and must be differentiated from effects of _____ use and brain disease. The category _____ _____ disorder is used when symptoms of schizophrenia appear and disappear over the course of a month or less. It is usually preceded by a stressful situation. _____ psychotic disorder, also called folie a deux, occurs when an individual develops a delusion based on a close relationship with a _____ person.

schizophreniform; mood; Delusional; isolation; five; possible; late; drug; brief psychotic; Shared; delusional

Because schizophrenia is so complex, many attempts to classify it on the basis of onset type, pre-onset condition, or symptoms, have succeeded/failed. Crow suggests that schizophrenia can be two types: Type I, which is characterized by _____ symptoms, a good response to medication, and a good prognosis, and Type II, which is characterized by _____ symptoms and the obverse of the above.

failed; positive; negative

Schizophrenia, typically a chronic disorder, usually has an earlier onset in men/women. Developmental perspectives on schizophrenia may be helpful in understanding the _____ of the disorder. One theory, which is supported by _____ studies, is that early brain damage manifests itself later in life as schizophrenia. Older victims show fewer positive/negative symptoms and more _____ symptoms, indicating schizophrenia may improve with age. About 78% of schizophrenic individuals show relapse. The concept of schizophrenia appears worldwide; however, the symptoms vary depending on the culture. In Columbia, India, and Nigeria more/fewer people improve or recover than in other countries. In the US, African-Americans are diagnosed with schizophrenia more/less often than are white Americans, but this may be due to biased misdiagnosis of minorities.

men; causes; developmental; positive; negative; more; more

Again, because schizophrenia is so _____, its causes are difficult to identify. Genetic influences clearly create a _____ for schizophrenia in some individuals. Kallman's family studies indicate that the severity/form of the disorder in parents relates to the child's likelihood of developing schizophrenia, and that the particular form or subtype of the psychotic disorder does/does not appear to be inherited. A well-studied set of identical quadruplets were all reared in the same household and all developed schizophrenia. The onset, symptoms, courses, and outcomes were all identical/similar/different. Twin studies, which show that identical twins are more _____ for the disorder than are fraternal twins, and studies of the children of twins, one of whom has schizophrenia, give evidence of the _____ factors involved in the disorder. Fraternal twins of schizophrenics but without the disorder themselves, can be "_____" to their children. Adoptee studies examine the children of parents who have schizophrenia; the adoptees' relatives method examines the biological and adoptive families of individuals who have schizophrenia. Adoption studies have shown that children of schizophrenics, even if they do not live with their parents, have a lesser/greater likelihood of developing the disorder than do children of non-schizophrenics. In general, the more _____ you share with a schizophrenic person, the more likely you are to develop it. So far, no schizophrenia linkages have been found to _____ genes, whose locations are known. Other linkage studies have sought unsuccessfully the genes responsible for _____ sites, or for smooth-pursuit _____-_____ skills, thought to be related to schizophrenia. Schizophrenia most likely involves many _____ at many sites influencing its development; this phenomenon is called _____ _____ _____ (QTL).

complex; vulnerability; severity; does not; different; concordant; genetic (and environmental); carriers; greater; genes; marker; dopamine; eye-tracking; genes; quantitative trait loci

Dopamine is thought to be related to schizophrenia because, a) drugs that affect this _____ (neuroleptics) are effective treatment, b) side effects of the drugs produce symptoms similar to _____ disease, c) a drug used for Parkinson's disease produces schizophrenic symptoms in some people, and d) drugs that activate dopamine increase/decrease psychotic symptoms in some schizophrenics. That is, drugs that increase dopamine _____ schizophrenia; drugs that decrease dopamine _____ schizophrenia. However, a) not all schizophrenics are helped by dopamine _____, b) neuroleptics reduce symptoms more quickly/slowly than would be expected, c) neuroleptics have substantial/little effect on the negative symptoms of schizophrenia, and d) genetic linkage studies and other research do not establish a relationship between D2 receptors and schizophrenia. Also, e) clozapine, a medication that is/is not a good dopamine antagonist, is effective against the disorder. Several recent studies implicate _____ and its relationship with dopamine in the etiology of schizophrenia and the understanding of _____ _____ effects. To determine the dopamine and serotonin levels in the brain of a schizophrenic individual, scientists measure the amount of homovanillic acid (HVA) and 5-hydroxyindoleacetic acid (5-HIAA), metabolites of the neurotransmitter found in the _____ _____. Measuring by-products of the neurotransmitters may not indicate their true brain levels, due to many factors. However, more can be learned in _____ experiments where drug intake is manipulated. Also, new technology may help clarify how brain chemicals _____.

neurotransmitter; Parkinson's; increase; increase; decrease; antagonists; slowly; little; is not; serotonin; neuroleptic drug; cerebrospinal fluid; controlled; interact

Evidence that children and adults who develop schizophrenia demonstrate abnormal reflexes and attention problems suggests that _____ _____ may play a role in the disorder. Also, schizophrenics tend to have enlarged _____ in their brains and, thus, adjacent areas that are underdeveloped or _____, a finding more often seen in men than women. The discovery that the non-concordant identical twins of schizophrenics do not share this abnormality suggests that the enlarged ventricles are due to _____ influences. _____ refers to decreased activity in the frontal lobes, which has been suggested as indicative of schizophrenia, especially _____ symptoms. Researchers have attempted to link such knowledge about the brains of schizophrenics with theories about neurotransmitter activity. For example, perhaps an underactive dopamine pathway in the prefrontal lobe leads to _____ symptoms while causing excessive dopamine activity deeper in the brain, leading to _____ symptoms.

brain damage; ventricles; atrophied; environmental; Hypofrontality; negative; negative; positive

The idea that _____ infections may be related to schizophrenia is supported by the fact that the disorder was not noted prior to 1809 when, perhaps, a new virus emerged. In several studies, schizophrenics had more often experienced influenza _____. Also, observations of _____ of schizophrenic people and their twins suggest that the disorder may be related to a disturbance in second trimester development, again perhaps caused by virus.

viral; prenatally; fingerprints

Studies of children "at risk" for schizophrenia because their _____ have the disorder found that _____ of the early family rearing environment was a predictor of which children later developed schizophrenia. Other studies have found that stressors may be related to the onset of the disorder, although the _____ nature of these studies forces them to rely on potentially biased reports. One prospective study of predictors of _____ found no stressor was involved in more than half of relapse cases. Early theories of schizophrenia focused on the role of parent-child relationships. For example, a "_____" mother was one whose rejecting and domineering nature was thought to have fostered the development of the disorder in her child. Parental communication filled with conflicting messages, called_____ _____, was also thought to cause schizophrenia. These theories have/have not been supported, but they continue to cause _____ in parents. More recent research showed that families of schizophrenics tend to exhibit more criticism, hostility, and emotional _____. High _____ _____ in a family is linked to the probability of relapse for schizophrenic individuals. Although the level of expressed emotion differs across cultures, schizophrenia prevalence rates do not. Thus, it is likely/unlikely to be a cause of schizophrenia.

parents; instability; retrospective; relapse; schizophrenogenic; double binds; have not; guilt; overinvolvement; expressed emotion; unlikely

Past medical treatment for schizophrenia has involved insulin coma therapy, electroconvulsive therapy, and _____, in which connections in the brain's frontal lobe were severed (prefrontal _____). The introduction of _____ in the 1950's changed treatment for schizophrenia, since these drugs decrease hallucinations and delusions in many schizophrenic individuals. Newer medications are even more effective, with fewer _____ effects. However, patients may sometimes fail or refuse to take these medications (_____), due to negative patient-doctor relationships, high cost, poor social support, negative side effects, or other factors. Side effects may include drowsiness, _____ mouth and/or extrapyramidal symptoms, which are similar to the _____ difficulties of Parkinson's disease. These include _____, which involves an expressionless face and slowed speech and movement, and _____ _____, which involves involuntary motions of the tongue and mouth. Less frequent, injectable medications have/have not solved the problem of noncompliance.

psychosurgery; lobotomies; neuroleptics; side; noncompliance; dry; motor; akinesia; tardive dyskinesia; have not

Psychosocial intervention for schizophrenia has included the _____ therapy of the 19th century, which focused on supportive inpatient care. Traditional psychoanalysis has/has not been found effective. Paul and Lentz's use of a _____ _____ was effective in improving the social, self-care, and vocational skills of patients in the hospital. Currently, most care for schizophrenia occurs outside the hospital. While medication is the principal form of treatment, _____ have much to offer. They develop programs to increase drug _____. They may teach schizophrenic individuals _____ skills, although the effects of this treatment do not appear to last unless community _____ services help maintain them. Family therapy, by teaching family members to reduce negative _____ _____, may be a helpful ongoing addition to treatment for schizophrenia. Some programs provide _____ to help patients get and keep jobs in supported employment. Multilevel programs, along with medications, can help delay or minimize relapses. Participation in self-help and self-_____ groups is correlated with improvement, but no _____ conclusion can be drawn because the members might not be _____ of the average schizophrenic. Treatment of schizophrenia differs across cultures.

moral; has not; token economy; psychologists; management; social; support; expressed emotion; coaches; advocacy; causal; representative

KEY WORDS

Practice defining the important concepts listed below and at the end of the text chapter. Follow the definition suggestions provided in the introduction to this Guide. Be precise and accurate, and check your work with the text. Add to the definition later as you encounter more information about the term. Whenever possible, include examples. Use only the space to the right of the word so that later you can cover either the word or the definition to use one to cue the other. Define additional important terms you'll find in the chapter. (page #)

1. agonistic effects

   _____

   _____

2. alogia

   _____

   _____

3. anhedonia

   _____

   _____

4. antagonistic effects

   _____

   _____

5. associative splitting

   _____

   _____

6. avolition

_____

_____

7. brief psychotic disorder

_____

_____

8. catatonic type of schizophrenia

_____

_____

9. delusional disorder

_____

_____

10. disorganized type of schizophrenia

_____

_____

11. expressed emotion

_____

_____

12. flat affect

_____

_____

13. hallucinations

_____

_____

14. psychotic

_____

_____

15. negative symptoms

_____

_____

16. paranoid type of schizophrenia

_____

_____

17. positive symptoms

_____

_____

18. residual type of schizophrenia

_____

_____

19. schizophreniform disorder

_____

_____

20. schizoaffective disorder

_____

_____

21. shared psychotic disorder

_____

_____

22. token economy

_____

_____

23. undifferentiated type of schizophrenia

_____

_____

SAMPLE QUESTIONS

As one of the later stages of your study for this chapter, you can assess your progress by taking a sample test. Don't make the mistake of studying just for these questions. They are merely a small sample of the many questions that could appear on an exam. An excellent way to help yourself is to generate your own questions and answers. This will help you focus on important concepts, make better distinctions among similar ideas, practice writing responses, and engaging the material in general. Try them on your friends in your study group.

Multiple Choice Questions

1. Neuroleptic medications are less effective against negative symptoms of schizophrenia. Which of the following is a negative symptom?
   a. delusions
   b. hallucinations
   c. loose associations
   d. flat affect
   e. all of the above are positive symptoms

2. Which of the following is NOT a negative symptom of schizophrenia?
   a. flat affect
   b. alogia
   c. tangentiality
   d. anhedonia
   e. all of the above are negative symptoms

3. The subtype of schizophrenia in which delusions and hallucinations have themes is
   a. catatonic type.
   b. disorganized type.
   c. paranoid type.
   d. undifferentiated type.

4. The behaviors displayed in _____ of schizophrenia primarily involve motor behavior disruptions.
   a. catatonic type
   b. disorganized type
   c. paranoid type
   d. undifferentiated type

5. Individuals with _____ tend not to have flat affect or anhedonia, but may become socially isolated because of their suspicions of others.
   a. brief psychotic disorder
   b. schizophreniform disorder
   c. schizophrenia, disorganized type
   d. delusional disorder

6. Delusions experienced by those with delusional disorder tend to be _____; delusions experienced by those with schizophrenia tend to be _____.
   a. impossible; at least possible
   b. at least possible; impossible
   c. vivid; vague
   d. vague; vivid

7. Grandpa has us all worried and, frankly, scared. He has suddenly become suspicious of everyone and has some wild ideas about needing to protect himself from his loving family. His doctor has ruled out drugs and brain disease and suggests a psychological diagnosis:
   a. delusional disorder.
   b. schizophrenia.
   c. schizoaffective disorder.
   d. brief psychotic disorder.
   e. none of the above

8. In an obsolete category system, Type I form of schizophrenia was associated with a(n) _____ prognosis and _____ _____.
   a. pessimistic; no intellectual impairment
   b. optimistic; no intellectual impairment
   c. optimistic; intellectual impairments
   d. pessimistic; intellectual impairments

9. According to one study on the relapse rates of schizophrenia, approximately _____ of people who have one episode of schizophrenia will have no lasting impairments or further episodes.
   a. 100%
   b. 75%
   c. 50%
   d. 25%

10. The 48% concordance rate of schizophrenia in identical (monozygotic) twins, who share 100% of their genetic information, tells us that
    a. schizophrenia is not a purely genetic disorder.
    b. schizophrenia is not a purely environmentally-controlled disorder.
    c. environmental influences play some role in schizophrenia.
    d. genetic influences play some role in schizophrenia.
    e. all of the above

11. We need to use caution when drawing conclusions from family and twin studies of schizophrenia, because
    a. researchers study only their own families.
    b. individuals with schizophrenia are often taken away from their families.
    c. when people share environments as well as genes, it is difficult to separate out the influences of each
    d. none of the above

12. The most common type of hallucination that individuals with schizophrenia experience is
    a. visual.
    b. auditory.
    c. olfactory.
    d. somatic.
    e. none of the above

13. Which of the following has the highest chance of developing schizophrenia?
    a. the child of two parents with schizophrenia
    b. someone in the general population
    c. the nephew of someone with schizophrenia
    d. the sister of a male with schizophrenia
    e. all of the above have an equal chance of developing the disorder

14. The likelihood that schizophrenia is a polygenic abnormality explains
    a. why researchers cannot seem to find one site for a schizophrenic gene.
    b. why there are differences in severity among those with the disorder.
    c. why risk of having the disorder increases with the number of affected relatives in the family.
    d. all of the above

15. The effectiveness of antipsychotic medications in those with schizophrenia
    a. suggests an overactive dopamine system in persons with schizophrenia.
    b. suggests an underactive dopamine system in persons with schizophrenia.
    c. does not completely explain the role of dopamine in schizophrenia.
    d. both a and c

16. One characteristic of schizophrenia that differentiates it from other disorders described in DSM-IV is that the concept of schizophrenia
    a. is made up of a number of behaviors or symptoms that aren't necessarily shared by all the people with the disorder.
    b. has been recognized as a serious problem since the early 1800's.
    c. was first identified in the United States.
    d. has a single biological cause that has been identified through the use of PET scan technology.

17. Guido believes that his computer comes to life at night and transmits messages about humans to Pluto. Assuming this is not true, it is an example of
    a. affective flattening.
    b. frequent derailment.
    c. a delusion.
    d. alogia.
    e. tangentiality.

18. After Steve was asked how his summer break was he offers the following reply "My summer was great. Yes, great as the great wall of China. China is one place I have never been. I sure do like to travel. My brother used to work for a travel agent a long time ago. It sure has been a long time since I've seen my sister." His reply is an example of
    a. loose associations.
    b. silly affect.
    c. catatonia.
    d. a negative symptom.
    e. waxy flexibility.

19. Almost every day you see a middle-aged man walking the streets with two large garbage bags slung over his shoulder. He seems to be homeless, and he spends a great deal of time apparently talking to and answering people you can't see. His muttering seems incoherent and he will often suddenly laugh or giggle for no obvious reason. IF he is displaying schizophrenia (and he may not be) what type is it?
    a. paranoid
    b. disorganized
    c. Type II – neg.
    d. catatonic
    e. residual

20. Elaine grimaces throughout the day and often imitates the words and movements of others. She is most likely displaying the _____ type of schizophrenia.
    a. Catatonic
    b. hebephrenic
    c. affective
    d. paranoid
    e. disorganized

21. Roberto has experienced disorganized speech and hallucinations for the past six years. He has also experienced several major depressive episodes during this time period. Roberto would most likely receive
    a. a diagnosis of comorbid schizophrenia and bipolar disorder.
    b. a diagnosis of schizoaffective disorder.
    c. a diagnosis of schizophreniform disorder. occa. less less than 6 months
    d. a diagnosis of delusional disorder.
    e. a diagnosis of major depression.

22. After Olga's last final examination she began experiencing auditory hallucinations and told her friends about her plans to reunite all missing children from around the world with their parents. Olga's friends were relieved two weeks later when Olga reported that she was not hearing any voices and did not have any plans for reuniting missing children. Olga most likely experienced
    a. an undiagnosable event.
    b. a shizophreniform disorder.
    c. a brief psychotic disorder.
    d. a shared psychotic disorder.

23. Researchers have found that _____ may be related to both the onset of schizophrenia, and to relapse.
    a. stressful life events
    b. alcohol intoxication
    c. excessive studying for psych exams
    d. poor sleeping habits
    e. none of the above

24. You are very hopeful when your sister with schizophrenia is prescribed a powerful neuroleptic drug. At the same time, you know it is likely to affect her _____ more than her _____.
    a. anhedonia; delusions
    b. alogia; hallucinations
    c. delusions; flat affect
    d. hallucinations; delusions
    e. alogia; flat affect

25. Tardive dyskinesia is
    a. a side effect of some anti-psychotic drugs.
    b. a neuroleptic drug.
    c. a brain site affected by schizophrenia.
    d. a reference to enlarged cerebral ventricles.
    e. a side effect of schizophrenia.

26. Which of the following statements is/are true?
    a. The lifetime prevalence rate of schizophrenia is nearly equal for men and women.
    b. Schizophrenia affects about 10% of the population.
    c. People with schizophrenia have a higher rate of suicide and accidents.
    d. a and c
    e. all of the above

27. Alexander told his dormitory counselor that the entire freshman class was trying to get him to leave school, and explained to her how other students were breaking into his professors' offices and changing his answers on homework and exams. Alexander is experiencing
    a. hallucinations.
    b. tangentiality.
    c. delusions of grandeur.
    d. disorganized thinking.
    e. none of the above

28. Treatment with magnets has a long history in medical quackery. However, transcranial magnetic stimulation shows some promise as a real treatment of
    a. hallucinations.
    b. tangentiality.
    c. delusions of grandeur.
    d. disorganized thinking.
    e. flat affect.

29. In which of the following situations would an individual with schizophrenia be most likely to experience hallucinations?
    a. sitting on a busy subway train
    b. sitting in a classroom full of students when the professor is eliciting class participation
    c. sitting in an empty waiting room
    d. sitting on a swing in the middle of a crowded playground

30. Research on methods to prevent schizophrenia involve
    a. identification of high-risk children.
    b. prospective studies.
    c. longitudinal studies.
    d. all of the above

31. During your volunteer work at a group home for people with schizophrenia, you have a series of conversations with one young man. He seems lucid, coherent, and reasonable on every occasion. You begin to think he has been misdiagnosed and wonder why he is there. Suddenly, he tells you he is the queen of England, working closely with God to rid the world of evil spirits. You realize his schizophrenia subtype is
    a. catatonic.
    b. disorganized.
    c. paranoid.
    d. residual.
    e. undifferentiated.

32. The higher rates of schizophrenia among African-Americans as compared to whites in the United States appears to be due to
    a. specific biological influences that are more prevalent among African-Americans than whites.
    b. improved immunizations for white children.
    c. cultural conceptualizations of bizarre behavior.
    d. misdiagnosis of schizophrenia.

33. When pregnant mothers suffer diseases or are exposed to harmful toxins, their children sometimes develop problems later in life. One of these risks, whose reduction may help prevent schizophrenia, is
    a. a virus.
    b. cigarette smoke.
    c. automobile exhaust.
    d. alcohol.
    e. measles.

34. According to the CD-ROM or videotape "DEFICITS OF MIND AND BRAIN", recent research using PET scans on schizophrenic patients who had never been administered neuroleptic medications indicated unusual activity in the
    a. Basal Ganglia.
    b. Reticular Activating System.
    c. Left Globus Pallidus.
    d. Right Septum.

35. In the CD-ROM or videotape "DEFICITS OF MIND AND BRAIN", one of the patients described as exhibiting symptoms of Schizophrenia was "Marsha". According to Dr. Early, Marsha displayed all of the following symptoms EXCEPT
    a. paranoia.
    b. auditory hallucinations.
    c. persecutory delusions.
    d. anxiety attacks.

36. In the CD-ROM or videotape "ABNORMAL PSYCHOLOGY: LIVE!", "Etta" has experienced long periods of psychosis. During the video, which of the following made it most difficult for the clinician to conduct his interview?
    a. her extremely disorganized thought processes
    b. her active delusions
    c. her engagement in hallucinatory experiences
    d. her catatonic state

37. In the CD-ROM or videotape "ABNORMAL PSYCHOLOGY: LIVE!", "Etta" displayed involuntary, "tic-like" hand movements that were described as being related to a condition known as Tardive Dyskinesia. These movements are most likely caused by
    a. her schizophrenia.
    b. her long history of taking antipsychotic medications.
    c. the degradation of her Peripheral Nervous System.
    d. her being nervous in front of the camera.

True or False Questions

38. The term schizophrenia was first introduced by Emil Kraepelin.

    TRUE or FALSE

39. Schizophrenia can disrupt a person's emotional functioning.

    TRUE or FALSE

40. According to researchers, the most active area of the brain during auditory hallucinations is normally involved with language comprehension.

    TRUE or FALSE

41. A positive symptom of schizophrenia is flat affect, but alogia is a negative symptom.

    TRUE or FALSE

42. The rarest type of schizophrenia is the paranoid type.

    TRUE or FALSE

43. Paranoid is a subtype of delusional disorder in DSM-IV.

    TRUE or FALSE

44. As adults with schizophrenia enter later adulthood, they tend to display more negative symptoms.

    TRUE or FALSE

45. Studies have found abnormally small lateral ventricles in the brains of schizophrenic people.

    TRUE or FALSE

46. Thorazine is a type of neuroleptic drug.

    TRUE or FALSE

47. Symptoms of schizophrenia are classified as positive, negative, and neutral.

    TRUE or FALSE

Essay Questions

48. Many people believe that only medical interventions are useful with schizophrenia. We know, however, there is still a substantial role to be played by psychologists and other nonmedical professionals. Discuss two of the psychosocial interventions that have been used in the treatment of schizophrenia.

49. Compare and contrast schizophrenia with any of the other psychotic disorders.

50. Discuss the research that has been conducted on auditory hallucinations in individuals with schizophrenia.

51. Choose two of the types of studies on the genetic influence in schizophrenia. Discuss some of the major findings and how they support a genetic link, as well as the limits on these studies.

52. Discuss the evidence for the view that schizophrenia is caused by a viral infection.

HOW WELL DID YOU DO?

Less than 60%	Restudy the chapter (don't just reread); rework your notes completely. You can improve if you increase your efforts.
60-80%	Restudy and rewrite, especially the weak areas; discuss problem areas with study partners.
Over 80%	You're on the right track; continue as you are; focus on trouble areas with study group.
Over 95%	Nice job, especially if you know the whole chapter this well. Be sure to reward your behavior, help others in your study group (they'll help you on your weak chapters), and don't forget to review.

THINKING ALLOWED

Chapter 12 Activities

From a personal ad: "Sophisticated schizophrenic male seeks good-looking schizophrenic female for romantic foursome." A well-known poem: "Roses are red; Violets are blue; I'm schizophrenic; And so am I." *Me, Myself, and I: The Autobiography of a Schizophrenic.* What is wrong with these? In a recent survey, nearly 62% of respondents believed that "schizophrenia" means "multiple personality" (i.e., dissociative identity disorder). Find other examples of this error. Why do you think it is so common in the media and in stand-up comedy routines?

Several books provide detailed and compassionate case studies of schizophrenic patients. Read one for a better understanding of the experience of the disorder. Suggestions: Eden Express by Mark Vonnegut (son of novelist Kurt Vonnegut, Jr.), *Is There No Place on Earth for Me?* by Susan Sheehan, or the books excerpted in the chapter. By the way, after reading his book, do you think schizophrenia is the correct diagnosis for Vonnegut?

Volunteer or apply for a job to work with mental patients in a state institution, a community mental health center, a group home, or the local Mental Health Association. It is important work, and a great experience. How do your observations correspond with the text descriptions?

INTERNET RESOURCES

<u>Schizophrenia Home Page</u>

Provides links to other web pages devoted to schizophrenia (this is a good starting place for finding information on schizophrenia on the internet)

http://www.schizophrenia.com/newsletter/buckets/intro.html

<u>Schizophrenia: Questions and Answers</u>

Questions and answers regarding schizophrenia provided by the National Institutes of Health.

http://www.nimh.nih.gov/publicat/schizo.html

Solutions

KEY WORDS

1. (488)
2. (477)
3. (477)
4. (488)
5. (472)
6. (477)
7. (482)
8. (480)
9. (481)
10. (479)
11. (493)
12. (477)
13. (475)
14. (474)
15. (483)
16. (479)
17. (483)
18. (480)
19. (480)
20. (480)
21. (482)
22. (497)
23. (480)

SAMPLE QUESTIONS

Multiple Choice Questions

1. D, 477
2. C, 478
3. C, 479
4. A, 480
5. D, 481
6. B, 481
7. A, 481
8. B, 483
9. D, 483
10. E, 486
11. C, 486
12. B, 475
13. A, 487*
14. D, 488
15. D, 489-490
16. A, 471-472
17. C, 474
18. A, 478
19. B, 479
20. A, 480
21. B, 480
22. C, 482
23. A, 492-493
24. C, 488
25. A, 489-490
26. D, 483
27. E, 472
28. A, 475
29. C, 475
30. D, 492-494
31. C, 479
32. D, 483
33. A, 492
34. C, video, CD-ROM
35. D, video, CD-ROM
36. A, video, CD-ROM
37. B, video, CD-ROM

True or False Questions

38. F, 471
39. T, 474
40. F, 475
41. F, 474
42. F, 479
43. F, 479
44. T, 477
45. F, 490-492
46. T, 489-490
47. F, 472

Essay Questions

48. You should include detail about each type of intervention, how it has been used with schizophrenia, which problems this intervention hopes to alleviate or correct, as well as how successful the technique has been with this particular patient problem. (See textbook pages 492-493.)

49. Your answer should include similarities and differences in symptoms, etiology (if known), and treatment (if specified).

You may also want to mention similarities or differences in prevalence, onset, and prognosis. (See textbook pages 471-482.)

50. Your answer should include when these hallucinations most frequently occur, according to research, as well as the information on the brain activity during hallucinations. Finally, you should include a statement about the researchers' theory on the source of the "voices". (See textbook page 475.)

51. Be aware of the role of shared experiences and social learning in some of the results, and do not forget that genetics is not the sole determinant in schizophrenia. (See textbook pages 485-488.)

52. Point out evidence that schizophrenia may be a new disorder, that it has been associated with prenatal exposure to influenza. Be sure to include autopsy findings and the role of fingerprints. (See textbook page 492.)

DEVELOPMENTAL AND COGNITIVE DISORDERS

LEARNING OBJECTIVES

1. Describe the central defining features of ADHD.

2. Identify the main features and types of learning disorders, and explain how they are typically treated.

3. Define pervasive developmental disorders, and describe the three main symptoms clusters of autistic disorder.

4. Define mental retardation, including the main DSM-IV-TR categories used to classify people with mental retardation.

5. Describe what is known about the incidence and prevalence of mental retardation.

6. Describe the symptoms of delirium and demential, including what is known about their prevalence, causes, and treatment.

7. Identify the principal causes of and treatments for amnestic disorders.

CHAPTER SUMMARY

By now you know what to do with chapter summaries and sample tests.

Early disruptions in the pattern of normal development can cause later problems and may be related to developmental disorders. Understanding _____ development may shed light on the causes of developmental disorders and suggest possible treatment or _____ of these disorders. Both psychological and biological factors interact to cause developmental disorders. Also, understanding normal development will prevent the error of assuming that normal behavior, such as _____ (the repetition of other's speech), is a symptom of a disorder.

normal; prevention; echolalia

The primary characteristics of attention deficit/hyperactivity disorder (ADHD) are _____ and _____-_____. These symptoms may contribute to secondary problems such as poor academic performance, poor peer relationships, and low self esteem. ADHD is diagnosed in boys four times more often than girls; the reason for this gender difference is _____. About 30/50/70 percent of children with ADHD continue to have symptoms of the disorder as adults. _____ factors have been linked to ADHD, with relatives of a child with the disorder also being likely to exhibit ADHD or other psychopathology such as mood disorders and substance abuse. Genetic research suggests that there may be _____ of ADHD related to particular chromosomes or _____ receptors. A lack of activity in the _____ cortex and basal ganglia has been associated with ADHD, as has malfunctioning in the right hemisphere. Other theories, that have not been supported by evidence, suggest that _____, such as food additives, cause the disorder. One response to this theory was the Feingold diet; although evidence shows it to be effective/ineffective. Psychological and _____ factors, such as negative responses from parents and teachers, may contribute to ADHD. Treatment for ADHD typically includes biological and psychological dimensions, focused on both short and long term issues. _____ medications such as Ritalin are useful for reducing impulsivity and increasing attention, but they do not appear to improve social skills or academic performance, and their effects do/do not last when the drugs are discontinued. _____ interventions usually target specific behaviors for systematic reinforcement or extinction. Some programs incorporate _____ training. Not all children respond to these treatments.

inattention; hyperactivity-impulsivity; unknown; 70; Genetic; subtypes; dopamine; frontal; toxins; ineffective; social; Stimulant; do not; Behavioral; parent

_____ disorders involve difficulties in one or more areas such as reading, mathematics, or writing. A DSM-IV diagnosis of a reading or mathematics disorder or a disorder of written expression indicates that an individual's achievement in that area is significantly below that expected for his/her _____, cognitive ability, and education level. These disorders are associated with school dropout and low employment. Definitions of learning disorders vary considerably from state to state; consequently, it is difficult to know the prevalence of the disorders. Among school age children, the estimates range from ___% to ___%. Difficulties with _____ are the most common of the learning disorders. Learning disorders may have a _____ basis, since the parents and siblings of individuals with these disorders have a higher rate of the disorders than do non-relatives. _____ studies also support a genetic influence. Abnormalities in neurological structure and functioning may contribute to learning disorders. Psychosocial factors also play a role. People with learning disorders have different types of cognitive problems and probably represent several _____ subgroups. _____ for these disorders focuses on teaching individuals skills to deal with the problem, and occurs mainly in _____ settings.

Learning; age; 10; 15; reading; genetic; Twin; etiological; Treatment; educational

_____ disorders include expressive language disorder, stuttering, tic disorders, and selective mutism. _____ _____ refers to a refusal to speak in certain situations in spite of the ability to speak, and usually occurs between the ages of 5 and 7. Some clinicians believe this disorder is caused by _____. Treatment usually focuses on _____ management, which involves praise and reinforcers for _____ and ignoring other attempts to communicate.

Communication; Selective mutism; anxiety; contingency; speaking

Tourette's syndrome is characterized by _____, which are sudden, repeated, involuntary motor movements, or the involuntary repetition of obscenities. Tourette's is believed to be inherited through a _____ gene or genes. The drug haloperidol is used to reduce the tics. Behavioral treatment includes _____-_____ (teaching people to be aware of their tics), _____ training (teaching people to relax the muscles involved in the tic), and _____ _____ (teaching people to substitute another response for the tic).

tics; dominant; self-monitoring; relaxation; habit reversal

Stuttering refers to a disturbance in speech fluency, including _____ of syllables, _____ of sounds, and other speech problems. About ____% of children who stutter stop doing so after a year of school. Genetic factors may play a role in etiology. In the _____ breathing method of treatment, a stutterer takes a deep breath when a stuttering episode begins.

repetition; prolongation; 80; regulated

_____ language disorder occurs when a child has less expressive language (ability to use language) than receptive language (ability to understand language). One psychological theory of this disorder suggests that it may be caused by a lack of verbal interactions with parents. A biological theory of the disorder implicates _____ _____ _____ during critical periods in language development. Studies indicate that this disorder tends to _____ _____ and thus treatment may be unnecessary.

Expressive; middle ear infections; correct itself

_____ disorder is a pervasive developmental disorder characterized by communication and socialization impairment, and restricted patterns of behavior and interests. Autistic children do not develop normal peer relationships; although they may have the same amount of contact with others, these contacts are qualitatively different from that of normal children. About 25/50/75 percent of autistic children never develop useful speech, and many demonstrate echolalia. Autistic children also tend to prefer that their environment not be changed, a condition referred to as _____ ___ _____. They also engage in stereotyped and ritualistic behavior, _____ patterns of activity. Sex differences in the prevalence of autism are related to IQ, with males/females being more prevalent in the higher IQ ranges and males/females being more prevalent in the lower IQ ranges. This disorder is universal, and autistic behaviors are usually noted prior to 36 months of age. Three fourths of autistic children show evidence of _____ _____, and those with higher IQs require less support from family and professionals. The prognosis is best for autistic children with better _____ skills.

Autistic; 50; maintenance of sameness; repetitive; males; females; mental retardation; language

Early research that examined the causes of autism characterized the parents of autistic children as cold and unfeeling. Bettelheim suggested that autism was caused by children's inability to interact with their environment. Ferster believed that autism was the result of parents failing to reinforce children's attempts to socialize and communicate. These early theories of autism suggested that parents somehow "caused" the disorder, but later research supports/fails to support this concept. Another early theory about the cause of autism suggested that autistic children are not aware that they exist, as evidenced by their use of "he" and "she" when referring to themselves. However, research has shown that some autistic children do demonstrate _____-_____. Autism has a genetic component, but the exact genes are unknown. The prevalence of mental retardation in autistic people suggests that the disorder involves _____ _____. Abnormalities of the _____, including increased/reduced size, have been found. It is now believed that _____ factors, not environmental factors, are the main cause of autism.

fails to support; self-awareness; brain damage; cerebellum; reduced; biological

Other biological factors proposed to be involved in the etiology of autism include congenital diseases such as rubella. Family studies support/do not support the theory that genetic components contribute to the disorder. Evidence that autism has a _____ basis includes the prevalence of abnormal postures, clumsiness, and other neurological abnormalities in autistic individuals. As of yet, no theory of autism adequately integrates biological findings and psychological understanding.

support; neurobiological

At present, there is no completely effective treatment for autism. Psychodynamic treatments for autism encourage ego development. Behavioral approaches, which have been less/more effective, use reinforcement to teach autistic children specific skills, such as communication. Lovaas taught autistic children to speak by using discrimination training, which involved reinforcing sounds in response to cues, and _____, which involved selective reinforcement of approximations of the sound desired. Although it can be effective for some, not all autistic children respond well to this training. Treatment can also increase the rate of social behavior, but does not appear to affect the _____ of social interactions of autistic children. In one study, Lovaas found that intensive, _____ treatment of autism was effective in the long term for many autistic children. Also, children with autism seemed to do better/worse when integrated into regular classrooms than when placed in special education classes. Medical treatment for autism had little success. It is unlikely that any single treatment will effectively treat this complex disorder. _____ of treatment through a combination of techniques such as _____ _____, drug treatment, and school and home based interventions, may be the best way to address all facets of autism.

more; shaping; quality; early; better; Integration; behavioral intervention

The other three types of pervasive developmental disorders are Rett's disorder, Asperger's disorder, and childhood _____ disorder. These involve problems with _____, socialization, and cognition, and do/do not affect the later life of the child. It is debatable whether Rett's disorder, Asperger's disorder, and childhood disintegrative disorder are clearly _____ categories.

disintegrative; communication; do; separate

_____ disorder involves impairment in social relationships, restricted and unusual behaviors, but not the language and cognitive delays seen in autism. It is sometimes referred to as the _____ _____ _____ due to the tendency to obsess about arcane facts and utilize a formal and pedantic speaking style. A higher prevalence in families suggests a genetic contribution to the disorder. Treatment for Asperger's disorder has not been researched much, but individuals with this disorder may benefit from school, home, and work supports similar to those developed for _____ individuals; however, less of a focus on communication skills is necessary. _____ disorder, found primarily in girls, is characterized by _____-_____, mental retardation, and motor impairment. These deficits occur after a period of normal development during early childhood. This disorder does not seem to be influenced by psychological factors, suggesting a _____ cause. Treatment usually focuses on teaching communication and _____-_____ skills to reduce problematic behavior. _____ _____ disorder involves a decline in language, adaptive behavior, and motor skills after 2-4 years of normal development. The disorder appears to have a _____ origin, and abnormal brain activity is evident in many cases of childhood disintegrative disorder. Treatment involves _____ interventions designed to teach skills and drug treatment to reduce behavioral problems.

Asperger's; Little Professor Syndrome; autistic; Rett's; hand-wringing; biological; self-help; Childhood disintegrative; neurological; behavioral

Mental retardation, an Axis ___ disorder in DSM-IV, involves deficits in _____ and _____ abilities, and is present from childhood. Individuals with mental retardation may be able to carry out normal day-to-day activities, or may not be able to speak or take care of themselves. DSM-IV criteria for mental retardation include subaverage intellectual functioning, usually indicated by an IQ score below about ___; concurrent deficits in adaptive functioning, which involves significant difficulty in at least two areas such as communication, self-care, home living, and social/interpersonal skills; and age of onset during the developmental period. The four classifications of mental retardation, according to DSM-IV, are

_____ (IQ of 50-55 to 70), _____ (IQ of 35-40 to 50-55), _____ (IQ of 20-25 to 35-40), and _____ (IQ below 20-25). The AAMR classification for mental retardation is based on the level of needed supports, and includes intermittent, limited, extensive, or _____. The classification system of mental retardation used in educational settings includes the following three categories: the _____ mentally retarded, who can learn some academic skill; the _____ mentally retarded, who can learn vocational (but not academic) skills; and the severely mentally retarded, who cannot learn vocational or academic skills. _____ to _____ percent of the population is mentally retarded, and about 90% of persons with mental retardation are _____ retarded. Although mental retardation is chronic, _____ and support can reduce impairment.

II; intellectual; adaptive; 70; mild; moderate; severe; profound; pervasive; educable; trainable; One; three; mildly; training

Mental retardation is caused by a variety of factors, including genetic, prenatal, perinatal, postnatal, and environmental influences. For example, _____ _____ syndrome, caused by heavy use of alcohol by pregnant mothers, can lead to severe learning disabilities, as can malnutrition, lack of oxygen at birth, and head injuries. Mental retardation may be passed on by a dominant gene, as in tuberous sclerosis. Phenylketonuria (PKU) is a genetic disorder that can cause mental retardation if a special _____ is not followed. Some X-linked disorders, such as Lesch-Nyhan syndrome, occur in <u>males/females</u> only. _____ syndrome, a form of mental retardation with recognizable facial characteristics, is caused by trisomy 21, which refers to an extra chromosome on the 21st pair due to _____ during cell division. The rate of Down syndrome is related to maternal age. Amniocentesis is a testing procedure that can be used to detect Down syndrome prenatally, but it cannot determine the degree of impairment the child will have. _____ ___ syndrome, a second chromosomal cause of mental retardation, is an X-linked disorder, predominant in males. Individuals with cultural-familial retardation, presumed to be a result of _____ as well as biological causes, tend to score in the <u>mild/severe</u> mental retardation range, and show reasonably good adaptive skills. Cultural familial retardation accounts for up to 75% of all cases of mental retardation. Individuals with organic mental retardation, which can be traced to genetic or chromosomal causes, often exhibit more <u>mild/severe</u> forms of mental retardation. The _____ view of cultural-familial retardation suggests that individuals with mental retardation suffer from specific deficits that make them different from non-retarded individuals. The _____ view sees mental retardation as a slowed development, with the ultimate level of functioning attained being lower than that of normal individuals.

fetal alcohol; diet; males; Down; nondisjunction; Fragile X; environmental; mild; severe; difference; developmental

Treatment of mental retardation usually focuses on teaching skills needed to become _____ and productive. Early interventions, such as Head Start, target children who may be at risk for mental retardation due to _____ factors. Self-care and other skills are taught using _____ analysis, which involves breaking down an activity into separate parts, and behavioral techniques such as _____.

Communication skills may also need to be taught, possibly through _____ communication strategies which use picture books or _____ to allow an individual to communicate. Aggression in mentally retarded individual may also require intervention. _____ employment, which helps mentally retarded individuals find jobs, gives these people the opportunity to work and to contribute to the community. An issue in treatment of mental retardation includes whether these individuals should be taught in regular or special classes.

independent; environmental; task; reinforcement; augmentative; computers; Supported

_____ efforts for developmental disorders include early intervention programs and psychosocial interventions that address risk factors such as _____ and exposure to toxins. Eventually, it may be possible to detect and correct genetic abnormalities. _____ _____ _____ involves screening a developing fetus for a genetic disorder, but the technology is not yet reliable.

Prevention; malnutrition; Prenatal gene therapy

_____ disorders, formerly called organic mental disorders, involve a deficit in cognition or memory that usually occurs in adulthood. Individuals suffering from _____, which develops over hours or days and usually dissipates quickly, appear confused and disoriented, have trouble focusing, and exhibit language and memory deficits. Dementia is usually associated with a _____ _____ in cognitive functioning. _____ disorder is a diagnosis given to persons with memory dysfunctions. Although one might argue that the organic etiology of these disorders would dictate _____ treatment, the consequences of these disorders on personality and behavior are profound and psychosocial interventions are often helpful.

Cognitive; delirium; gradual decline; Amnestic; medical

Delirium is most prevalent among the _____ and certain other persons with medical difficulties. Full recovery is expected in most cases within several _____; although, some individuals will continue to have intermittent problems. The etiology of delirium has been linked to many possible factors. The DSM-IV accounts for these factors with different subtypes, including delirium due to a _____ _____ _____ (medical causes) and _____-_____ delirium (substance use/abuse). Medical treatment may be necessary to address the cause of the delirium, while _____ interventions help the person deal with the accompanying psychological and social problems. _____ efforts such as counseling patients on prescription drug use can assist people who are susceptible to delirium.

elderly; weeks; general medical condition; substance-induced; psychosocial; Preventive

_____, which develops gradually, is characterized by progressive difficulties with memory, judgment, and reasoning. The disorder includes problems with visuospatial skills and agnosia, which is an inability to _____ and recognize objects. Facial _____ is the inability to recognize faces. Victims of dementia are aware of their mental deterioration, which may contribute to _____ changes such as depression and aggression. Eventually, the individual suffering from dementia loses the cognitive abilities necessary to maintain daily functioning, and requires total care until death occurs. Although dementia can occur at any age, it is more prevalent in the _____ .

Dementia; name; agnosia; emotional; elderly

Dementia of the _____ type is characterized by, among other things, memory impairment, aphasia (_____ difficulties), coordination problems, and agnosia. The phenomenon known as _____ _____ refers to the tendency for these difficulties to become more pronounced late in the day. _____ determine the presence of this disorder based on characteristic brain damage, although clinicians correctly diagnose Alzheimer's about ____ percent of the time. The disorder progresses _____, and accounts for about 50% of the cases of dementia. Alzheimer's appears to be related to educational level, with those with a higher/lower level of education more likely to develop the disorder. The _____ _____ hypothesis suggests that the more synapses a person develops throughout life, the more neuronal death must occur before the signs of dementia are obvious. Recent research suggests that Alzheimer's disease may be more prevalent among _____, possibly due to the loss of _____, as they grow older. _____ dementia is due to blockage or damage to the blood vessels that supply the brain, which leads to brain damage. This form of dementia varies from individual to individual, depending on the nature of the brain damage. The onset of vascular dementia is less/more sudden than the onset of Alzheimer's type, although the prognosis is similar.

Alzheimer's; language; sundowner syndrome; Autopsies; 85; gradually; lower; cerebral reserve; women; estrogen; Vascular; more

Dementia Due to Other General _____ Conditions may be due to HIV disease, head trauma, Parkinson's disease, Huntington's disease, Pick's disease, Creutzfeldt-Jacob disease, or other conditions. Dementia due to HIV disease is characterized by cognitive slowness, impaired attention, and forgetfulness. Dementia due to HIV disease, as well as to some other diseases, is referred to as _____ dementia because it affects the inner areas of the brain. Language is not affected in subcortical dementia, but _____ skills are. Parkinson's disease involves motor problems, including a stooped posture, bradykinesia (_____ movement), tremors, and changes in voice. The disease is related to damage to neurons that use _____, the neurotransmitter responsible for complex movement. Huntington's disease, a _____ disorder that affects motor movement, may involve _____, which are involuntary limb movements. Dementia is also prevalent in those with Huntington's disease. Wexler and her colleagues identified the single gene that causes this disease. Pick's disease and Creutzfeldt-Jacob disease are rare conditions that involve dementia. _____-Induced Persisting Dementia is caused by prolonged use of drugs that lead to _____ brain damage.

Medical; subcortical; motor; slowed; dopamine; genetic; chorea; Substance; irreversible

Research in dementia can be fast-paced; however, care should be taken in evaluating results, and reconfirmation (_____) of results is desirable. The brain damage found in all people with Alzheimer's disease is neurofibrillary _____ and amyloid or neuritic _____. However, these can be observed only after death by _____. The neuritic plaques found in the brains of people with Alzheimer's disease seem to be caused by a buildup of _____ _____ protein, which has been linked to the 21st chromosome. Loo and his colleagues suggest that amyloid protein may induce neural cells to self-destruct (called apoptosis) or may weaken cells, causing them to be more susceptible to other stressors.

replication; tangles; plaques; autopsy; amyloid precursor

The onset and course of dementia can be influenced by social and psychological factors. For example, a person's _____ _____ _____ (e.g., substance use/abuse, exercise) may indirectly impact the disorder. Treatment for dementia can effectively reduce the suffering of individuals with the disorder. Although damage to some neurons can be compensated for by others (called _____), extensive neural damage <u>can/cannot</u> be reversed, which makes a cure for dementia improbable. Thus, treatment focuses on _____ of dementia and help in dealing with the disorder. Biological treatments for dementia include drugs, such as tacrine hydrochloride, used to enhance _____ abilities. This drug helps individuals with Alzheimer's disease regain about 6 months of lost skills; however, the cognitive decline continues even with the use of the drug. Psychosocial treatment focuses on teaching strategies to deal with symptoms of the disorder, such as memory aids. Also, psychological treatment is used to provide _____ to prevent individuals with dementia from wandering into dangerous areas. _____ training may be provided to caregivers to help them deal effectively with the individual with dementia. In general, families can benefit from _____ counseling to help them deal with the _____ stressors associated with dementia. Researchers are also exploring ways to prevent dementia, such as _____ replacement therapy for women and proper treatment of hypertension.

life style choices; plasticity; cannot; prevention; cognitive; cues; Assertiveness; supportive; emotional; estrogen

Amnestic disorder is characterized by _____ impairment without the loss of other cognitive functions. One type is Wernicke-Korsakoff syndrome, involving damage to the thalamus, which is often caused by _____.

memory; alcoholism

KEY WORDS

Practice defining the important concepts listed below and at the end of the text chapter. Follow the definition suggestions provided in the introduction to this Guide. Be precise and accurate, and check your work with the text. Add to the definition later as you encounter more information about the term. Whenever possible, include examples. Use only the space to the right of the word so that later you can cover either the word or the definition to use one to cue the other. Define additional important terms you'll find in the chapter.

1. agnosia

    _____

    _____

2. Alzheimer's disease

    _____

    _____

3. amnestic disorder

    _____

    _____

4. amyloid plaques

    _____

    _____

5. amyloid precursor protein

    _____

    _____

6. aphasia

    _____

    _____

7. apraxia

    _____

    _____

8. Asperger's disorder

_____

_____

9. attention deficit/hyperactivity disorder

_____

_____

10. autistic disorder

_____

_____

11. childhood disintegrative disorder

_____

_____

12. cultural/familial retardation

_____

_____

13. delirium

_____

_____

14. dementia

_____

_____

15. Down syndrome

_____

_____

16. Expressive language disorder

_____

_____

17. Fragile X syndrome

_____

_____

18. Huntington's disease

_____

_____

19. learning disorders

_____

_____

20. mental retardation

_____

_____

21. neurofibrillary tangles

_____

_____

22. Parkinson's disease

_____

_____

23. pervasive developmental disorders

_____

_____

24. Rett's disorder

_____

_____

25. selective mutism

_____

_____

26. stuttering

_____

_____

27. tics

_____

_____

28. Tourette's disorder

_____

_____

SAMPLE QUESTIONS

As one of the later stages of your study for this chapter, you can assess your progress by taking a sample test. Don't make the mistake of studying just for these questions. They are merely a small sample of the many questions that could appear on an exam. An excellent way to help yourself is to generate your own questions and answers. This will help you focus on important concepts, make better distinctions among similar ideas, practice writing responses, and engaging the material in general. Try them on your friends in your study group.

Multiple Choice Questions

1. Psychosocial treatments of autism
   a. were initially psychodynamic
   b. have clinical importance that was shown by Lovaas' research
   c. initially focused on the notion that autism was caused by faulty parenting
   d. all of the above

2. Approximately what percentage of people with autism have some form of mental retardation?
   a. 10%
   b. 55%
   c. 75%
   d. 85%

=Asperger's
=Verbal

3. Asperger's disorder shares characteristics similar to autistic disorder except for
   a. the language delay present in autistic disorder
   b. the language delay present in Asperger's disorder
   c. impairments in social relationships seen in autistic disorder
   d. impairments in social relationships seen in Asperger's disorder

4. _____ is found almost exclusively in females, and is characterized by constant hand-wringing, mental retardation, and impaired motor skills
   a. Asperger's disorder
   b. Rett's disorder
   c. Childhood disintegrative disorder
   d. Autistic disorder

5. Research on the treatment of autism by Lovaas showed that
   a. intensive behavioral treatment was more beneficial than less intensive treatment
   b. children were more likely to improve when placed in regular classrooms
   c. both a and b
   d. none of the above

6. Autism is more prevalent among *Women* _____ with IQ's under 35 but more prevalent among *Males* _____ in the higher IQ range
   a. males; females
   b. females; males
   c. neither males nor females; females
   d. males; neither males nor females

7. Tics are involuntary movements that often occur in rapid succession, come about suddenly, and happen in very idiosyncratic or stereotyped ways. _____ is a disorder with these characteristics
   a. Autistic disorder
   b. Selective mutism
   c. Tourette's disorder
   d. Coprolalia

8. Which of the following is not a communication disorder?
   a. expressive language disorder
   b. selective mutism
   c. Asperger's disorder
   d. stuttering

9. Characteristics of autistic disorder include which of the following?
   a. significant impact on social interactions and communication
   b. restricted patterns of behavior, interest, and activity
   c. repetitive and stereotyped patterns of behavior
   d. all of the above

10. In the DSM-IV, there are _____ groups of criteria for mental retardation, which is included on Axis _____.
    a. 2; III
    b. 3; II
    c. 4; II
    d. 5; I

11. Amniocentesis is
    a. an x-linked disorder.
    b. used to determine the degree of disability in a child.
    c. a method of testing for the presence of Down syndrome before birth.
    d. a cognitive mental disorder.

12. The four levels of mental retardation identified in DSM-IV are
    a. mild, moderate, severe, profound
    b. educable, trainable, severe, profound
    c. slight, moderate, profound, intensive
    d. borderline, custodial care, intermittent care, pervasive care

13. The educational system has developed an additional method of classification for mental retardation which
    a. is used to identify the ability of students.
    b. is split into three categories: trainable, educable, and severe mental retardation.
    c. assumes that certain individuals will not benefit from academic or vocational training.
    d. all of the above

14. Mary was 18 years old when she was involved in a serious car accident. Before the car accident her IQ was 95 and she was living independently. Now, her IQ is 50 and she has impairment in many of her adaptive functions. Under DSM-IV, what would Mary's diagnosis be?
    a. Mild Mental Retardation
    b. Moderate Mental Retardation
    c. Mental Retardation, Severity Unspecified
    d. none of the above

15. Which of the following statements is true?
    a. People with Down syndrome are at an increased risk for dementia of the Alzheimer's type.
    b. As the age of the mother increases, the chance of having a child with Down syndrome also increases.
    c. Down syndrome is also known as fragile-X syndrome.
    d. both a and b

16. _____ is presumed to be the cause of approximately 75% of cases of mental retardation.
    a. Chromosome-related retardation
    b. Cultural/familial retardation
    c. Neurobiological retardation
    d. none of the above

17. Which of the following disorders is the most common?
    a. Attention Deficit/Hyperactivity Disorder
    b. Childhood Disintegrative Disorder
    c. Rett's Disorder
    d. Autism

18. Which of the following is an example of a primary characteristic of Attention Deficit/Hyperactivity Disorder?
    a. poor academic achievement
    b. unpopularity with peers
    c. hyperactivity
    d. low self-esteem

19. All of the following are types of learning disorders in DSM-IV except
    a. reading disorder.
    b. mathematics disorder.
    c. school performance disorder.
    d. disorder of written expression.

20. Learning disabilities are characterized by performance that is substantially
    a. above what would be expected given the person's age, IQ, and education.
    b. below what would be expected given the person's age, IQ, and education.
    c. diminished from one year to the next.
    d. lower than 50% of the person's peer group.

21. The three major characteristics of autism include all but which of the following?
    a. impairment in social interactions
    b. restricted behavior, interests, and activities
    c. impairment in communication
    d. significant loss of previously acquired skills

22. Gender differences in the rates of mental retardation _____ generally found among people with mild mental retardation and _____ generally found among people with more severe forms of this disorder.
    a. are; are
    b. are not; are
    c. are; are not
    d. are not; are not

23. Which of the following statements is true about ADHD?
    a. Children in the United States are more likely to receive a diagnosis of ADHD than children in other places.
    b. Research consistently finds that maternal smoking is related to an increases the likelihood of having a child with ADHD.
    c. It is clear that a combination of behavioral and medical treatments is superior to medication alone.
    d. a and b only
    e. all of the above

24. Which of the following is characteristic of delirium?
    a. Delirium is characterized by reduced clarity of consciousness and cognition.
    b. Delirium develops over a course of several hours or days.
    c. Delirium was one of the first disorders to be recounted in history.
    d. all of the above

25. _____ is a gradual deterioration of brain functioning that affects judgment, memory, language, and other advanced cognitive processes.
    a. Delirium
    b. Dementia
    c. Amnestic disorder
    d. none of the above

26. Alzheimer's disease progresses _____ and eventually accounts for approximately _____ percent of all cases of dementia.
    a. rapidly; 40
    b. gradually; 50
    c. rapidly; 60
    d. gradually; 70

27. _____ is characterized by the development of memory impairment, without a loss of high-level cognitive skills.
    a. Dementia
    b. Delirium
    c. Amnestic disorder
    d. all of the above

28. Which of the following is not a cognitive disorder?
    a. Amnestic disorder
    b. Mental Retardation
    c. Delirium
    d. Dementia

29. Substance-induced delirium is often treated with
    a. cold-turkey withdrawal.
    b. psychostimulants.
    c. antidepressants.
    d. benzodiazepines.

30. Which of the following has not been implicated as a possible cause of dementia?
    a. Alzheimer's disease
    b. lack of blood flow to the brain due to stroke
    c. axon-depleting cytosis
    d. head trauma

31. The average survival time for someone with Alzheimer's disease is estimated to be approximately
    a. 8 years.
    b. 10 years.
    c. 12 years.
    d. 20 years.

32. Women may have a higher prevalence rate for Alzheimer's disease because
    a. they lack amyloid proteins.
    b. they lack testosterone.
    c. they lack estrogen.
    d. they do not seek treatment.

33. Which of the following is not an early symptom of HIV-induced dementia?
    a. language deficits
    b. social withdrawal
    c. clumsiness
    d. forgetfulness

34. Which of the following statements about the caregivers of people with dementia is false?
    a. More than 50% eventually become clinically depressed.
    b. They use more psychotropic medications than the general public.
    c. Some will engage in some form of elder abuse.
    d. None. All of the above are true.

35. A type of amnestic disorder that results from prolonged and excessive alcohol use is
    a. Broca-Mandling syndrome.++++
    b. Wernicke-Korsakoff syndrome.
    c. McGowin-Swenson syndrome.
    d. Monger-Rolland syndrome.

36. Supportive counseling for caregivers of people with dementia
    a. seems to be more necessary for African-American families than for white families.
    b. may involve assertiveness training, though little evidence for its effectiveness exists.
    c. includes information about the causes and treatments of the disorder, and even about financial and legal issues.
    d. all of these are true except a

37. Biological treatments for dementia are usually ineffective because
    a. there is no effective treatment for the primary disorder.
    b. no medications exist that provide even temporary symptom relief.
    c. vitamin E treatments have proven ineffective.
    d. persons with dementia rarely participate in treatment.

38. Which of the following chromosomes has not been linked to the onset of Alzheimer's disease?
    a. 21
    b. 19
    c. 2
    d. 14

39. The disorders grouped under the category of cognitive disorders share the common impairment of
    a. memory.
    b. thinking.
    c. perception.
    d. all of the above

40. An episode of delirium often indicates
    a. the presence of a medical condition that is causing the brain to dysfunction.
    b. that the individual is about to experience a progressive decline in cognitive functioning.
    c. that the individual is suffering from another psychological disorder.
    d. none of the above

41. After Mr. Khalil's 85th birthday he began to experience difficulties that appeared to be characteristic of delirium. His psychologist is careful about making a diagnosis, as she realizes that a diagnosis of delirium in the elderly is difficult
    a. since the majority of assessment techniques that are used to make such a diagnosis were designed primarily for use with children.
    b. since the DSM-IV criteria are so rigid that many people with the disorder do not get properly diagnosed.
    c. due to the combination of medical illnesses and medications used to treat illnesses within the elderly population.
    d. all of the above

42. The predominant cognitive deficit displayed by individuals with Alzheimer's disease is
    a. facial agnosia.
    b. impairment of their memory.
    c. aphasia.
    d. apraxia.

43. Which of the following factors can trigger delirium?
    a. sleep deprivation
    b. excessive stress
    c. head injury
    d. all of the above

44. What does glial cell-derived neurotrophic factor (GDNF) do?
    a. Preserve and possibly restore neurons.
    b. Break down amyloid plaques.
    c. Regulate dopamine production.
    d. Cure hypothyroidism.

45. Even though the origins of cognitive disorders are clearly based in brain dysfunction causes, these disorders are still included in a textbook on abnormal psychology because
    a. they are easily treated with behavioral interventions.
    b. the consequences of the disorders often include profound changes in a person's behavior and personality.
    c. they are almost always seen in people who have other DSM-IV disorders.
    d. all of the above

46. The most plausible explanation for the negative correlation between cigarette smoking and Alzheimer's disease is that
    a. nonsmokers are likely to eat a healthier diet, and diet has been implicated in the development of Alzheimer's disease.
    b. smokers are likely to eat a healthier diet, and diet has been implicated in the development of Alzheimer's disease.
    c. nicotine combats the Alzheimer's disease process.
    d. nonsmokers live longer, and are thus more likely to develop Alzheimer's disease, which appears in later life.

47. Genes identified as _____ give a person a nearly 100% chance of developing Alzheimer's disease.
    a. degenerative
    b. susceptible
    c. deterministic
    d. influential

True or False Questions

48. Selective mutism is a common disorder that is more prevalent among girls than boys.
    TRUE or FALSE

49. The impairment in social relationships and restricted or unusual behavior or activities found in autism are also characteristic of Asperger's disorder.
    TRUE or FALSE

50. Attention deficit/hyperactivity disorder is one of the most common reasons for referral of children to mental health services in the United States.
    TRUE or FALSE

51. The problems associated with Rett's disorder appear before any normal development is apparent.
    TRUE or FALSE

52. In the DSM-IV, autistic disorder, Rett's disorder, Asperger's disorder, and childhood disintegrative disorder are formally recognized as being different from each other.

    TRUE or FALSE

53. Children diagnosed with childhood disintegrative disorder follow normal patterns of development until they reach two to four years of age.

    TRUE or FALSE

54. Children who have expressive language disorder have very limited speech only in certain situations.

    TRUE or FALSE

55. Echolalia is a phenomenon unique to autism.

    TRUE or FALSE

56. Researchers have found that anxiety produces stuttering.

    TRUE or FALSE

57. Being diagnosed as severely mentally retarded means the person has lower levels of cognitive functioning than if diagnosed as profoundly mentally retarded.

    TRUE or FALSE

58. Seventy-five percent of persons with mental retardation have no known biological cause for the disorder.

    TRUE or FALSE

59. ADHD is not considered a serious problem because most children eventually stop displaying the symptoms as adults.

    TRUE or FALSE

60. The relative complexity of the written word in English may explain cultural differences in the diagnosis of reading disorders.

    TRUE or FALSE

61. Dementia of the Alzheimer's type is a subcortical dementia, and Huntington's disease is a cortical dementia.

    TRUE or FALSE

62. Delirium is more prevalent among cancer patients, people with AIDS, and older adults.

    TRUE or FALSE

63. Wernicke-Korsakoff syndrome is a reversible type of amnestic disorder caused by heavy alcohol consumption.

    TRUE or FALSE

64. Multiple infarctions are damaged areas of the brain characteristic of vascular dementia.

    TRUE or FALSE

65. A definite diagnosis of Alzheimer's disease can be made only after specific types of damage to the brain are found in autopsy.

~~TRUE~~ or FALSE

66. Delirium brought on by withdrawal from drug use is usually treated with benzodiazepines.

~~TRUE~~ or FALSE

67. Families of persons with dementia obtain little benefit from psychosocial interventions.

TRUE or ~~FALSE~~

68. Delirium, dementia, and amnestic disorder are all types of cognitive disorders.

~~TRUE~~ or FALSE

69. Caregivers of people with dementia tend to use more psychotropic medications, and report more stress symptoms, than the general public.

~~TRUE~~ or FALSE

70. Neurons in the brain often regenerate after they are damaged and die.

TRUE or ~~FALSE~~

71. Dementia pugilistica is named after boxers who suffer trauma due to repeated blows to the head.

~~TRUE~~ or FALSE

Essay Questions

72. You are deciding how to intervene with your autistic client. Discuss four different dimensions of treatment for autistic disorders and their effectiveness.

73. Some workers in the mental health field suggest that the pervasive childhood disorders are different names for the same single disorder that lies on a continuum. Describe the pervasive developmental disorders and highlight any potential support for or against this view.

74. Describe the communication disorders outlined in the textbook. What are some of the suggested causes and potential treatments for these disorders?

75. Discuss the probable social, psychological, and biological causes of autistic disorder. How are these causes integrated?

76. Describe the biological, psychological, and social causes of mental retardation discussed in the text.

77. Describe some of the treatment methods for mental retardation.

78. Delirium and dementia share many of the same characteristics. Describe the similarities between the two disorders, as well as how you might differentiate between them.

79. List and describe at least four disease processes that often result in dementia.

80. Identify the name previously given to cognitive disorders, and the reason for changing the name.

HOW WELL DID YOU DO?

Less than 60%	Restudy the chapter (don't just reread); rework your notes completely. You can improve if you increase your efforts.
60-80%	Restudy and rewrite, especially the weak areas; discuss problem areas with study partners.
Over 80%	You're on the right track; continue as you are; focus on trouble areas with study group.
Over 95%	Nice job, especially if you know the whole chapter this well. Be sure to reward your behavior, help others in your study group (they'll help you on your weak chapters), and don't forget to review.

THINKING ALLOWED

Chapter 13 Activities

As a psychological professional, you will sometimes be required to inform parents that their child has a psychological or developmental disorder. Imagine yourself in that situation. What approach and information would you employ?

Call a friend and describe the various kinds of disorders outlined in this chapter, just for your own rehearsal.

Some people have suggested that children with Down Syndrome would be treated more normally if their appearance were more "normal". What is your opinion of plastic surgery for them?

What are some societal changes that could prevent developmental disorders?

Buy and play with an Aerobie®. These rings, invented by a Stanford professor, hold the record as the object that can be thrown by hand the farthest distances. And they're fun. From the first day of production, they have been inspected, trimmed, packaged, and shipped around the world by developmentally disabled adults working in a sheltered workshop.

The move of disabled persons from large institutions to small group homes (transinstitutionalization) was triggered in part by a television expose. A young investigative reporter took a TV camera into a large institution and revealed the shocking lack of care offered there. What are some of the issues involved in moving group homes into residential neighborhoods? What are the advantages for the residents? By the way, that enterprising young reporter was Geraldo Rivera, still a controversial national TV commentator.

Volunteer or apply for a job to work in a group home, a sheltered workshop, or a developmental disabilities center. It's a great experience and an opportunity to make a real difference. How does the text material inform your work?

INTERNET RESOURCES

Alzheimer's Association

The Alzheimer's Association web site contains information on local chapters, coping strategies for caregivers, and scientific progress towards effective treatment and understanding of this disorder.

http://www.alz.org/

Autistic Spectrum Disorders

Many of the listed sites are actively engaged in basic research to identify causation, remedies, and prevention strategies.

http://www.coping.org/links/12autism.htm

CH.A.D.D. (Children and Adults with Attention Deficit Disorders)

Includes information on the symptoms of ADHD, treatments, and as well as CH.A.D.D. chapters throughout the country.

http://www.chadd.org/

Dementia

A web page fact sheet describing the symptoms of dementia.

http://www.mentalhealth.com/p20-grp.html

Diagnosis and Evaluation of the Child with ADHD

Recommendations for the assessment and diagnosis of school-aged children with ADHD.

http://www.aap.org/policy/ac0002.html

Down Syndrome WWW Page

This WWW page was established in 1995 and provides information on healthcare guidelines for patients, education resources, events & conferences, and Down Syndrome organizations worldwide.

http://www.nas.com/downsyn/

Dyslexia Online

Devoted to "resolving misconceptions of dyslexia and related attention deficit and anxiety disorders.

http://www.dyslexiaonline.com/

Parenting a Child with Special Needs: A Guide to Readings and Resources

Developed to respond to the information needs of parents who have recently learned that their child has a disability.

http://www.nichcy.org/pubs/newsdig/nd20.htm

Sexual Differences in Pervasive Developmental Disorders

Characteristics of children with PDD, how girls differ from boys, and diagnosis, assessment, and treatment issues. (To access the article, you will need to register with Medscape. Registration is free. Type PDD into the search box and click on the Expand to All Dates link.)

http://www.medscape.com/

Solutions

KEY WORDS

1. (539)
2. (541)
3. (552)
4. (547)
5. (547)
6. (541)
7. (541)
8. (518)
9. (508)
10. (518)
11. (518)
12. (532)
13. (536)
14. (538)
15. (530)
16. (515)
17. (531)
18. (545)
19. (513)
20. (525)
21. (547)
22. (544)
23. (517)
24. (518)
25. (515)
26. (515)
27. (515)
28. (515)

SAMPLE QUESTIONS

Multiple Choice Questions

1. D, 523-524
2. C, 520-521
3. A, 518
4. B, 518
5. C, 523-525
6. B, 518
7. C, 515
8. C, 518
9. D, 518-520
10. B, 527
11. C, 531
12. A, 527-528
13. D, 527-528
14. D, 527-528
15. D, 530
16. B, 532
17. A, 508
18. C, 508-509
19. C, 513
20. B, 513
21. D, 518-520
22. C, 530
23. D, 508-512
24. D, 536
25. B, 538
26. B, 541-542
27. C, 552
28. B, 536
29. D, 538
30. C, 546-548
31. A, 541
32. C, 541
33. A, 544
34. D, 548-551
35. B, 552
36. D, 548-551
37. A, 549-550
38. C, 547
39. D, 536
40. A, 536
41. C, 536
42. B, 541
43. D, 536
44. A, 549
45. B, 536
46. D, 546
47. C, 547

True or False Questions

48. F, 515
49. T, 518
50. T, 508-509
51. F, 518
52. T, 507
53. T, 518

54. F, 515
55. F, 519
56. F, 515
57. F, 527-528
58. T, 530
59. F, 508

60. T, 513
61. F, 541
62. T, 536-537
63. F, 552
64. T, 543
65. T, 541

66. T, 538
67. F, 548
68. T, 536
69. T, 548
70. F, 536
71. T, 547

Essay Questions

72. Your answer should include four of the following: psychological treatments, communication, socialization, timing and setting, biological treatments, and integrating treatments. Critically analyze the treatments you choose to discuss. (See textbook pages 523-525.)

73. Make use of the DSM-IV diagnostic criteria to supplement your descriptions. Look at the similarities (e.g., problems in development) and differences (e.g., time at onset) between the disorders. (See textbook pages 517-525.)

74. The communication disorders you should describe are stuttering, selective mutism, tic disorders, and expressive language disorder. Discussion of potential causes may include anxiety, parental influences, and biological factors. Treatments include reinforcement, regulated breathing, psychological treatments, and "self-correcting." (See textbook page 515.)

75. Discussion of this topic can include child-rearing practices, early reinforcement history, medical conditions, and genetic and neurobiological influences. Include discussion about the integration of these different dimensions. (See textbook pages 520-522.)

76. Your answer should include genetic and chromosomal influences. Cultural/familial retardation should be discussed. Be sure to differentiate between the difference view and the developmental view. (See textbook pages to 529-532.)

77. Treatment methods to be included in your discussion involve the Head Start program, task analysis, communication training, and "supported employment". (See textbook pages 532-534.)

78. Your answer should reflect the common characteristics shared by both disorders (e.g., impairments in memory, language, etc.). Differentiation between the disorders is based on speed of onset and the ability of delirium characteristics to remit with appropriate treatment (see textbook pages 536-546).

79. An answer reflecting any four of the following (with a description of each) would be appropriate: Alzheimer's disease, vascular disease, HIV, Huntington's disease, Parkinson's disease, Pick's disease, Creutzfeldt-Jacob disease (see textbook pages 541-546.

80. The previous name was organic mental disorders. The reason for the change is that it is now believed that many of the recognized psychological disorders have some type of related Central Nervous System dysfunction. The prior name is no longer distinctive (see textbook page 536).

MENTAL HEALTH SERVICES: LEGAL AND ETHICAL ISSUES

LEARNING OBJECTIVES

1. Differentiate the legal concept of mental illness from a clinically diagnosed psychological disorder.

2. Discuss the relation between dangerousness and mental illness.

3. Describe the relation among mental illness, deinstitutionalization, and homelessness.

4. Describe the specific legal standards for invoking the insanity defense and the issue of competency to stand trial.

5. Define the concept of patient rights in the mental health system, including the right to treatment and the right to refuse treatment.

CHAPTER SUMMARY

By now you know what to do with chapter summaries and sample tests.

When making laws concerning mental illness, the state must balance the rights and protection of mentally disordered individuals with the rights of _____ to be protected from harm by the mentally disordered. The balance between these two rights changes as the focus of society and _____ shifts from individual rights to societal rights. La Fond and Durham noted two trends in the way that the legal system deals with mental health issues: the liberal era (1960-1980) focused on _____ rights, and the _____ era (1980-present) focused on the rights of the majority. While some people assume the state is eager to hospitalize people, the actual mandate is to keep people _____ unless very serious problems exist.

society; politics; individual; neoconservative; free or at liberty

_____ commitment laws deal with placing individuals in mental institutions, even against their will. _____ commitment laws refer to placing individuals accused of criminal activity in mental institutions for _____ or because they have been determined not guilty by reason of _____. Historically, states have allowed involuntary commitment when several conditions have been met: need for treatment, _____, or inability to care for oneself, also called having a "_____ _____." The two types of authority a state can use to commit someone are _____ _____, used when individuals are judged to be hazardous to public welfare, and _____ _____, used when individuals are not likely to act in their own best interest. If the friends or family of an individual wish to have that person involuntarily committed to a mental institution, they must go through _____ proceedings which respect the rights of the individual. However, in an emergency situation when an individual or others are in immediate _____, authorities can certify this status and commit the individual against his or her will.

Civil; Criminal; assessment; insanity; dangerousness; grave disability; police power; parens patriae; legal; danger

The legal definition of mental illness is not simply based on the presence of a diagnosable DSM-IV disorder, but may include impairment in functioning or need for _____. Many states exclude mental retardation or _____-_____ disorder from their definition. The vague definition allows flexibility, but also subjectivity and possible _____. While public and individual rights often clash, they can be addressed in _____. Research assessing whether mentally ill individuals are any more violent or dangerous than other people has had _____ results. Relative risk of dangerousness of mentally ill groups, but not individuals, can be reliably assessed, based on specific histories, and in the short/long term only. The Supreme Court has decreed that people who can survive in the community should not be detained unless _____. These restrictions have caused mentally ill people to spend more time in ____. This trend is referred to as the _____ of the mentally ill.

treatment; substance-related; bias; court; mixed; short; dangerous; jail; criminalization

The movement of the mentally ill out of large mental hospitals, or _____, contributes to homelessness, although other factors are unemployment and the shortage of affordable _____. The two goals of deinstitutionalization were to remove the mentally ill from large hospitals and to provide _____ _____ for them. However, adequate community care has not been provided, leading to _____, or the movement of the mentally ill from large hospitals to other institutions, such as nursing homes. Many of these are/are not equipped to care for the needs of mentally ill patients. Due to the related problems of the homeless and the mentally ill who may not be _____ but still need care, groups such as the National Alliance for the Mentally Ill have asked for laws making involuntary commitment easier with some success. Changes in laws have/have not increased the number of people in mental institutions, but they have changed the number of people committed _____. In the special case of _____ offenders, commitment is often used not so much for treatment, which is often effective/ineffective, but to protect the public and _____ the offender.

deinstitutionalization; housing; community centers; transinstitutionalization; are not; dangerous; have not; involuntarily; sexual; ineffective; punish

The earliest modern precursor to the insanity defense was the _____ rule, which established that individuals who are not aware of their behavior or of its wrongfulness are not responsible for their criminal activity. A revision to this rule, the Durham rule, added the presence of a _____ _____ to these requirements. Psychology professionals were/were not able to assess reliably whether a disorder caused the criminal behavior. The American Law Institute (ALI) concluded that the insanity defense should be based on a lack of _____ ability to understand the wrongfulness of behavior or an inability to _____ behavior. These suggestions include the notion of _____ _____, indicating that the mental illness affected the individual's understanding and, thus, criminal intent. According to the ALI, individuals who successfully use the insanity defense should be given _____ in place of punishment. To be convicted of a crime, mens rea, or _____ _____, and actus rea, or proof of the crime, must be established.

M'Naghten; mental disorder; were not; cognitive; control; diminished capacity; treatment; criminal intent or "guilty mind."

The public was outraged about the use of the _____ defense in the case of John W. Hinckley, who successfully/unsuccessfully used it after attempting to assassinate President Reagan. Research shows that the general public underestimates/overestimates the frequency of the successful use of this defense, and does not realize that hospitalization for mental illness is often shorter than/the same length as/longer than jail sentences. Regardless, a Reform Act was passed in 19____ to make success with NGRI pleas easier/more difficult. The not guilty by reason of insanity (_____) defense has been replaced by _____ _____ _____ _____ (GBMI) in some states. Under the GBMI plea or verdict, offenders are/are not released if they recover from their mental illness and may be _____ for their crimes. In a few states, no _____ at all is provided. In practice, those using this plea do/do not receive treatment for mental illness more than those who do not use this plea. Problems with the insanity defense include determining the state of mind of an individual at the time of the _____ and deciding whether to provide _____ for mental illness or punishment for crime.

insanity; successfully; overestimates; longer than; 84; more difficult; NGRI; guilty but mentally ill; are not; imprisoned; treatment; do not; crime; treatment

_____ _____ _____ _____ refers to individuals' ability to understand the charges against them and to help _____ themselves, and is necessary to go to trial. Thus, individuals with severe impairments are assessed and may be detained without ever going to trial, though for only a "_____" time. This finding is much more/somewhat more/somewhat less/much less common than the NGRI verdict. The burden of proof, or evidence showing that one is NOT competent to stand trial, rests on the prosecution/defense/judge/jury.

Competence to stand trial; defend; reasonable; much more; defense

If a client threatens harm to a specific person, a therapist is obligated to _____ (or _____) that person of the danger. In most states the threat must be _____ before the therapist is required to act, but the therapist must take reasonable care to discover threats. If in doubt about this, clinicians should consult with _____ (though this spreads the _____, and potential liability, to them as well).

inform; warn; specific; colleagues; duty

Psychologists often serve as _____ witnesses, helping judges and juries make decisions by providing information about the defendant's competence or _____. The assessment of the latter is reliable only in the long/short term. Research indicates psych experts can reliably diagnose disorders (which are/are not the same as legal mental illness), judge the _____ of a person to stand trial, and detect _____, which refers to feigning impairment to avoid blame for a crime. Bias in expert witnesses can be related to their personal _____.

expert; dangerousness; short; are not; competence; malingering; beliefs

Courts have established rights for patients in mental institutions, including minimum staff:patient _____ and the right to treatment. Furthermore, this treatment must take place in the _____ _____ environment, or the least confined context possible. Decisions about the type of treatment provided were left to _____, but Congress has established agencies to protect against abuses and to act as legal _____ for people with psychological disorders. In some instances, such individuals also have the right to _____ treatment, as in the case of Joyce Brown. Also, defendants can/cannot be forced to be treated or _____, even if such treatments make them competent to stand trial.

ratios; least restrictive; professionals; advocates; refuse; cannot; medicated

Research participants also have _____, including the rights to information about the _____ of the study, privacy, respect, protection from _____, the choice whether to participate, anonymity, and confidentiality of records. _____ _____, which involves the participant understanding the study and any risks as well as benefits, must be obtained for research studies. Problems with these rights can occur if researchers minimize their description of _____ to entice participation.

rights; purpose; harm; Informed consent; risk

The government established the Agency for Health Care Policy and Research (AHCPR) in 1989 to promote uniformity in the health care fields, both by _____ with practitioners about effective treatments and by _____ ways to improve the delivery of services. The AHCPR has also developed clinical _____ guidelines, which suggest effective _____ (or treatments) for specific disorders. This reduces _____ by eliminating unnecessary treatment and leading to quicker and more effective treatment. A Task Force of the American Psychological Association has also developed guidelines for evaluating treatment of psychological problems. These should help both practitioners and _____ make treatment decisions, and prevent _____ _____ _____ from skimping on treatment. These guidelines have two _____. Clinical _____ has to do with whether the treatment is effective when compared to _____ treatments or no treatment, in controlled experiments or in _____ clinical observations. Clinical _____ relates to whether the treatment is effective in different applied settings. Here, treatment _____, or whether it is easy and acceptable for clients to implement the treatment, must be considered. Cost and _____, or the degree to which an intervention is effective across a variety of patients, are also issues of clinical _____.

communicating; researching; practice; interventions; costs; clients; health care plans; axes; efficacy; alternative; quantified; utility; feasibility; generalizability; utility

In the _____-practitioner role, mental health professionals are ethically bound to provide the treatments with the most scientifically proven _____. As the mental health system changes, the scientist-practitioner will be most able to provide valuable information about the effectiveness, feasibility, and _____ of various interventions. Understanding the legal, ethical, and professional issues in mental health services helps one understand the role of _____ in society and politics.

scientist; effectiveness; generalizability; psychologists

KEY WORDS

Practice defining the important concepts listed below and at the end of the text chapter. Follow the definition suggestions provided in the introduction to this Guide. Be precise and accurate, and check your work with the text. Add to the definition later as you encounter more information about the term. Whenever possible, include examples. Use only the space to the right of the word so that later you can cover either the word or the definition to use one to cue the other. Define additional important terms you'll find in the chapter. (page #)

1. civil commitment

_____

_____

2. clinical efficacy

    _____

    _____

3. clinical utility

    _____

    _____

4. competence

    _____

    _____

5. criminal commitment

    _____

    _____

6. deinstitutionalization

    _____

    _____

7. diminished capacity

    _____

    _____

8. duty to warn

    _____

    _____

9. expert witness

    _____

    _____

10. informed consent

    _____

    _____

11. insanity defense

_____

_____

12. malingering

_____

_____

13. mental illness

_____

_____

14. transinstitutionalization

_____

_____

SAMPLE QUESTIONS

As one of the later stages of your study for this chapter, you can assess your progress by taking a sample test. Don't make the mistake of studying just for these questions. They are merely a small sample of the many questions that could appear on an exam. An excellent way to help yourself is to generate your own questions and answers. This will help you focus on important concepts, make better distinctions among similar ideas, practice writing responses, and engaging the material in general. Try them on your friends in your study group.

Multiple Choice Questions

1. Movement of patients with disorders out of institutions or mental hospitals
   a. was one goal of deinstitutionalization.
   b. and into group homes is called transinstitutionalization.
   c. has been successful for most clients and for society.
   d. both a and b
   e. neither a or b

2. A person would not be held responsible for criminal behavior if s/he is not aware of what s/he is doing or that it is wrong under the
    a. M'Naghten rule.
    b. Durham rule.
    c. American Law Institute rule.
    d. diminished capacity rule.
    e. none of the above

3. Because a mental disorder may lessen a person's ability to understand his/her behavior and criminal intent, it is difficult to prove
    a. actus rea.
    b. mens rea.
    c. diminished capacity.
    d. involvement in the crime.
    e. none of the above

4. When a person receives the verdict "guilty but mentally ill" (GBMI), s/he
    a. is not given the option of treatment.
    b. is released on his/her own recognizance.
    c. may receive treatment and punishment.
    d. will receive treatment until recovered and then be released.
    e. all of the above

5. A person who is deemed severely mentally ill before trial for a crime probably
    a. cannot assist in his/her own defense.
    b. cannot be expected to understand the charges against him/her.
    c. is not competent to stand trial.
    d. will be hospitalized instead of tried.
    e. all of the above

6. Malingering refers to
    a. warning the potential victims of the mentally ill.
    b. hanging around on street corners.
    c. feigning symptoms, possibly to avoid criminal prosecution.
    d. reporting child abuse.
    e. a and c

7. The public is often suspicious that
    a. expert witnesses are sought who will provide impartial information to the court.
    b. expert witnesses won't become involved in court cases when they have their own strong opinions about the issues.
    c. the side that pays the expert witness determines the expert's opinion.
    d. none of the above

8. The right to treatment
   a. includes minimum staff-patient ratios.
   b. requires the least restrictive treatment option possible.
   c. promotes patient movement from smaller to larger living units.
   d. promotes patient movement from dependent to independent living units.
   e. all but c

9. The issue of the right to refuse treatment
   a. is a controversial one.
   b. seems to contradict the belief that mentally ill people may not be capable of making decisions in their best interest.
   c. appears to be supported by Riggins v. Nevada.
   d. all of the above

10. Which of the following is(are) the right(s) of research participants?
    a. the right to be protected from physical and mental harm
    b. the right to be included as an author on published research
    c. the right to be treated with respect and dignity
    d. the right to privacy
    e. all but b

11. The laws that state the conditions under which people not accused of a crime can be legally committed to a mental hospital, even against their will, are
    a. criminal commitment laws.
    b. hospitalization laws.
    c. civil laws.
    d. civil commitment laws.

12. In Congress, the laws were changed so that individuals could be committed to mental hospitals more easily if they were in need of treatment. This led to
    a. an increase in the number of patients admitted to mental hospitals.
    b. more patients admitted voluntarily.
    c. more patients admitted involuntarily.
    d. decrease in the number of patients admitted to mental hospitals.
    e. deinstitutionalization.

13. The criteria developed by the American Law Institute suggested that individuals were not responsible for their criminal behavior if
    a. they suffered from a mental disorder.
    b. due to mental illness, they could not control or recognize the inappropriateness of criminal behavior.
    c. they did not recognize that their behavior was wrong and could not control it.
    d. they could not remember it.

14. After John Hinckley tried to kill President Reagan in 1981, he was hospitalized rather than imprisoned because the jury ruled he was not responsible because
    a. a defect of reason made him unable to know what he was doing, or that it was wrong.
    b. his behavior was the result of a mental disease or defect.
    c. a mental disease or defect made him lack capacity to appreciate the wrongfulness of his act, or to conform to the law.
    d. a mental disease made him unable to appreciate the wrongfulness of his act at the time of the shooting.

15. The beliefs of the general public about the insanity defense fail to reflect reality in that
    a. the insanity defense is no longer legal in most states.
    b. the insanity defense is used successfully far less often than the public believes.
    c. the insanity defense is rarely abused, except in highly publicized cases.
    d. the insanity defense does not mean that the person does not go to jail.

16. Competence to stand trial involves _____ at the time of the trial.
    a. understanding the charges
    b. mental health
    c. ability to assist in one's own defense
    d. the absence of a diagnosed psychological disorder
    e. a and c

17. As an attorney, you are trying to decide whether your client is competent to stand trial. Which of these is NOT an issue for this decision?
    a. Can the client assist in preparing the defense?
    b. Does the client appreciate that the act was wrong?
    c. Does the client understand the charges?
    d. Does the client understand the possible trial outcomes?

18. A court case has established that psychologically disordered individuals who are incompetent to stand trial
    a. have a right to treatment.
    b. cannot be responsible for the burden of proof.
    c. cannot be forced to take psychotropic medications to make them competent to stand trial.
    d. must do as much as possible that might make them competent to stand trial.
    e. do not have a guaranteed right to treatment to make them competent.

19. Joe is being treated in a closed psychiatric ward for his panic disorder with agoraphobia. What patient rights issue arises here?
    a. The staff: patient ratio is insufficient.
    b. Less restrictive treatments are available.
    c. The patient has a right to treatment.
    d. The patient has a right to refuse treatment.

20. One reason that the APA is developing guidelines for clinical intervention is to
    a. reduce the pay rate for therapists.
    b. increase the use of expensive treatment.
    c. ensure that individuals receive effective and personalized treatment.
    d. reduce the level of skill needed by therapists.

21. Which Supreme Court decision substantially limited the governments ability to commit individuals unless they were dangerous?
    a. O'Donnell v. California
    b. Durham v. Carpenter
    c. Montgomery v. Virginia
    d. Addington v. Texas

22. Tarasoff v. Regents of the University of California is a landmark case related to what issue?
    a. Criminalization of the mentally ill
    b. Duty to warn
    c. Right to refuse treatment
    d. Informed consent

Matching

1. _____ civil commitment
2. _____ criminal commitment
3. _____ M'Naghten Rule
4. _____ Durham Rule
5. _____ American Law Institute (ALI) Rule
6. _____ diminished capacity
7. _____ not guilty by reason of insanity
8. _____ guilty but mentally ill
9. _____ competency
10. _____ mens rea
11. _____ actus rea
12. _____ duty to warn

a. physical proof of a crime
b. People are not responsible for criminal behavior if they do not know that what they are doing is wrong.
c. An abnormal mental condition can affect the degree of criminal intent.
d. offering testimony which is impartial
e. detaining a person who is deemed a danger to him/herself
f. After this defense, a person is treated for his disorder and can then be held to complete his prison sentence.
g. offering testimony to support an opinion provided by the lawyer
h. proof of criminal intent
i. A person is not responsible for criminal behavior if the act was caused by a mental disease.
j. After this defense, a person is treated for the disorder and then must be released.
k. offering testimony to make the best case for a strong personal opinion
l. A person is not responsible for criminal behavior if they are lacking in cognitive ability to appreciate the criminality of the act.
m. ability to understand charges and assist in one's own defense
n. detainment until fitness for trial can be determined or detainment after a verdict of not guilty by reason of insanity has been reached
o. apprising potential victims of danger from a therapist's client

True or False Questions

23. The insanity defense is used in over 50% of all felony cases.

TRUE or FALSE

24. Criminal commitment refers to placing individuals in prison because they are mentally disordered.

TRUE or FALSE

25. Approximately 30% of all homeless people are believed to be severely mentally ill.

TRUE or FALSE

26. The American Law Institute suggested that a mentally ill person found to be not responsible for his/her crime should be treated until recovered and released.

TRUE or FALSE

27. Diminished capacity refers to the state a student is in after taking a psychology exam.

TRUE or FALSE

28. It may be difficult to prove mens rea for a mentally ill person accused of a crime.

TRUE or FALSE

29. The outcomes, or sentences, for the verdicts "not guilty by reason of insanity" and "guilty but mentally ill" are the same.

TRUE or FALSE

30. A person must be able to understand the charges against him/her and to assist in his/her own defense in order to be judged competent to stand trial.

TRUE or FALSE

31. In legal trials, the judge and jury determine whether an individual has a "mental illness".

TRUE or FALSE

32. African-Americans are overrepresented among those who are involuntarily committed to state psychiatric institutions.

TRUE or FALSE

33. The U.S. Supreme Court decided that civil commitment for sexual predators following their prison sentences is permitted only if it involves effective treatment.

TRUE or FALSE

34. Individuals with mental illness found guilty of nonviolent crimes can be committed for periods up to 8 times as long as people without mental illness may spend in prison.

TRUE or FALSE

Essay Questions

35. Define informed consent and discuss the implications surrounding this issue with individuals who have psychological disorders.

36. Choose one of the rules that have been used in the insanity defense; describe it, and defend it as the best rule.

37. Describe malingering, how individuals with this condition might become involved in the legal system, and how mental health professionals get involved in legal cases with these individuals.

38. Discuss the goals and outcomes of deinstitutionalization.

39. Outline the major rights of mental patients.

40. Currently, people who are hospitalized with psychological disorders tend to experience more frequent hospitalizations, and each one for briefer periods, than in the past. Explain the causes of this change.

HOW WELL DID YOU DO?

Evaluate your progress, and reinforce success.

THINKING ALLOWED

Chapter 14 Activities

Only expert witnesses are allowed to offer opinions in court testimony. Did you know you can be considered an expert witness even now? In trials, your testimony would normally be limited to what you objectively saw or heard. If you tried to offer an opinion, you would be stopped and urged to give only the facts. However, you can comment about the defendant's state of mind in questions of insanity, and the opinions of several lay persons can outweigh the opinions of psychology experts in the eyes of a jury. Why do you think this exception is allowed, and do you approve?

The fascinating award-winning documentary video "The Thin Blue Line," portrays the "expert" testimony of a psychiatry professional called "Doctor Death." (He had this title before Dr. Kevorkian became known for a different reason.) See it and, after your anger dies down, discuss it with your study group. What are the value and validity of his assessments?

Stay informed about the developments in health care reform. How will it affect the delivery and cost of psychological services? And how will it change the number and types of jobs available in the field of psychology. It is likely that opportunities for people without advanced degrees in the field will increase. Why?

If the rationale for Not Guilty by Reason of Insanity statutes is to protect and help rather than punish people who are not responsible for their illegal actions, it seems that the Guilty but Mentally Ill alternative defies that notion. How? And what do you think about it?

Most therapists now tell their clients they have a duty to warn. What is this, and what effects do you think this has on the therapy process?

INTERNET RESOURCES

APA Ethics Office: Ethics Information

Information from the APA regarding ethics.

http://www.apa.org/ethics/homepage.html

APA: Ethical Principles of Psychologists and Code of Conduct

This Ethics Code provides a common set of values upon which psychologists build their professional and scientific work.

http://www.apa.org/ethics/code.html

APA: Professional, Ethical, and Legal Issues Concerning Interpersonal Violence, Maltreatment, and Related Trauma

An online report of the ad hoc Committee on Legal and Ethical Issues in the Treatment of Interpersonal Violence.

http://www.apa.org/pi/pii/professional.html

Bazelon Center for Mental Health Law

Legal advocacy site for the civil rights and human dignity of people with mental disability.

http://www.bazelon.org/

Mental Health Patient's Bill of Rights

Developed and supported by fifteen professional organizations, it sets forth fundamental principles necessary to ensure quality mental health care and protect rights of those seeking treatment.

http://www.apa.org/pubinfo/rights/rights.html

Research Ethics and Animal Research

Online brochures and information on research ethics and animal research
http://www.apa.org/science/research.html

Solutions

KEY WORDS

1. (564)
2. (579)
3. (579)
4. (574)
5. (570)
6. (567)

7. (571)
8. (574)
9. (574)
10. (577)
11. (571)
12. (575)

13. (565)
14. (567)

SAMPLE QUESTIONS

Multiple Choice Questions

1. D, 567
2. A, 570
3. B, 571
4. C, 570-573
5. D, 564-565
6. C, 575
7. C, 579
8. E, 576

9. D, 577
10. E, 577
11. D, 564
12. C, 566-569
13. B, 571
14. C, 571
15. B, 571
16. E, 574

17. B, 574
18. C, 577
19. B, 576-577
20. C, 577
21. D, 566
22. B, 574

Matching

1. e 564
2. n 570
3. b 570
4. i 570

5. l 571
6. c 571
7. j 571
8. f 572

9. m 574
10. h 571
11. a 571
12. o 574

True or False Questions

23. F, 570
24. F, 570
25. T, 567
26. T, 571

27. F, 571
28. T, 571
29. F, 574
30. T, 574

31. T, 575
32. T, 566-568
33. F, 570
34. T, 570-571

Essay Questions

35. After defining the concept, you may want to consider the extent to which these individuals can give informed consent as well as any dangers in not ensuring that these individuals are informed. (See textbook page 577.)

36. You may want to include disadvantages of the other rules that are eliminated or reduced by the one you choose. You will also want to identify what makes this particular rule different from the others. (See textbook pages 570-573.)

37. Based on the definition of the concept, malingerers may have been involved in the legal system prior to developing this "disorder". You may want to include research on how mental health professionals identify malingering as well as their success at doing so. (See textbook page 575.)

38. In addition to the specifics requested, you will want to include the concept of transinstitutionalization in your answer. (See textbook page 567.)

39. Include descriptions of the right to treatment, especially in least-restrictive environments, and the right to refuse treatment. (See textbook pages 567-579)

40. Mention the effects of the deinstitutionalization, legal rights to least restriction, newer more effective treatments and medications. (See textbook pages 567, 578-579)